THE ETHICS AND POLITICS OF SPEECH

THE ETHICS AND POLITICS OF SPEECH

Communication and Rhetoric
in the Twentieth Century

Pat J. Gehrke

Southern Illinois University Press/Carbondale

12 11 10 09   4 3 2 1

Library of Congress Cataloging-in-Publication Data
Gehrke, Pat J., 1970–
The ethics and politics of speech : communication
and rhetoric in the twentieth century / Pat J. Gehrke.
    p. cm.
Includes bibliographical references and index.
ISBN-13: 978-0-8093-2948-9 (pbk. : alk. paper)
ISBN-10: 0-8093-2948-4 (pbk. : alk. paper)
1. Oral communication—United States—History—
20th century. 2. Oral communication—Moral and
ethic aspects. 3. Rhetoric—Social aspects—United
States—History—20th century. I. Title.
P95.4.U6G35 2009
808.5—dc22   2009004496

Printed on recycled paper. ♻
The paper used in this publication meets the minimum requirements of American National Standard
for Information Sciences—Permanence of Paper for
Printed Library Materials, ANSI Z39.48-1992.∞

For Amil and Sharon,
who always supported and encouraged
the elf who wanted to be a dentist

Contents

Acknowledgments

This book would not have been possible without significant contributions from a number of colleagues and mentors who provided advice, encouragement, and necessary corrections. First and foremost is Christopher Johnstone, who oversaw the earliest years of this project and spent countless hours and boxes of red pens working over chapters many times. He has been an invaluable advisor and good friend. I also owe thanks to many of the other faculty of Pennsylvania State University who provided input into the early versions of the manuscript, most especially Thomas Benson, Stephen Browne, and Charles Scott. The years I spent in State College provided an incomparable education.

Sections of this book were greatly enhanced by the support of the Department of English and the College of Arts and Sciences at the University of South Carolina. My colleagues in the speech communication program David Berube, Erik Doxtader, Mindy Fenske, and Kristan Poirot were a constant source of both support and advice. Likewise, my colleagues in the Department of English and especially in our program in rhetoric and composition have been enormously helpful in continuing to push my thinking about contemporary rhetorical theory and historical methods. In this regard, I owe special thanks to John Muckelbauer and Daniel Smith. The College of Arts and Sciences at South Carolina also provided funding for travel to the University of Utah, where the archives of the national and regional speech associations are primarily located. That archival material can be found throughout this work and added significant depth to the study.

In the broader discipline of communication studies, I owe immense gratitude to a number of people who have moved this project forward in significant ways. First, my colleagues in the Communication Ethics Division welcomed me into the organization as a young graduate student and have been key contributors to my maturation as a scholar and as a person.

Of these, I must particularly take note of Ronald Arnett, whose countless hours of counsel and criticism I cherish and keep close in my thoughts. In addition, special thanks are owed to Ken Chase, Clifford Christians, Janie Harden Fritz, Michael Hyde, Spoma Jovanovic, Lisbeth Lipari, Christopher Poulos, and Roy Wood. The community of scholars found in the Communication Ethics Division and the quality of that community are profoundly inspiring, and I always leave our conferences reinvigorated. Likewise, a number of scholars working on the history of the discipline have made contributions to this work. Of great importance has been the work of William Keith, but thanks are also owed to David Frank, Darrin Hicks, Gerry Phillipsen, and J. Michael Sproule, who may be unaware of how our brief interactions provided noticeable improvements in this project.

Karl Kageff and the staff at Southern Illinois University Press also are due significant gratitude. From first submission to final proofs, they have provided many needed editorial changes, patiently initiating me into the peculiarities of book publishing and answering my queries. The anonymous reviewers at the Press put an enormous amount of work into tightening up the manuscript and making it more readable; this book owes a great deal to those readers. Their belief in the book and their detailed suggestions for improvement are likely the major force that brought it to publication. I was also fortunate to have Ken Rufo work on the index, for which I am thankful.

Finally, and most important of all, I must thank the one person who has offered more thought, intellect, time, and criticism than any other, my partner and frequent collaborator, Gina Ercolini. Her rigorous attention to detail tightened up this work in many places, while her personal support was, at many times, the difference between hope and surrender. She is not only the love of my life but a colleague of unmatched rigor and unrivaled intellect. I have never met a better editor, collaborator, thinker, or human being. I am profoundly grateful that we are able to share our personal and professional trials and triumphs.

THE ETHICS AND POLITICS OF SPEECH

Introduction: Communication, Speech, and History

What relationship does communication have to our ethical and political obligations and commitments? What responsibilities are bound to the practice of rhetoric? These questions have pervaded the study of communication for well over two millennia. Richard Lanham called it the "Q" question, referring to the ancient Roman orator and rhetorical theorist Quintilian.[1] Quoting Cato the Elder's *vir bonus dicendi peritus*, Quintilian held that a truly great orator must be a person who possesses both outstanding gifts of speech and excellence of character.[2] The problem, of course, is that we always seem deep in examples of rhetorical skill void of such excellence. Indeed, from its very inception, Quintilian's formula has been considered dubious. The difficulty of his proposition is easily articulated by its inverse, which we might call the Hitler problem: What does it mean for communication and rhetoric if those skilled in its arts can put them to the purposes of extraordinary evil? Lanham argued that this dilemma "has underwritten and plagued Western humanism from first to last" and has called into question not only rhetoric but also the purposes of humanities education in general.[3] This enduring struggle confronts the creature described by Kenneth Burke as "the symbol-using (symbol-making, symbol-misusing) animal."[4] It is, perhaps, the single most persistent and important question in the history of the study of communication and rhetoric.

Over the past hundred years, a scholarly discipline dedicated to the study of communication has taken root in American colleges and universities. Academic departments formed, national and regional associations arose, conferences were held, and journals and books were published, all with issues of communication at their core. That discipline has been no less plagued by the "Q" question than have been the countless thinkers who came before. This book investigates the discourses within communication studies in the twentieth century, using this historical period to explore not only how thinkers have grappled with the relationship between ethics, politics, and speech but also what modes of ethics and politics might be available for communication today. Through a variety of texts in communication, including journal articles, books, and archival documents, this study maps out linkages and breaks between communication ethics and other subgenres of communication in order to demarcate limits established by common assumptions about speech and, simultaneously, to question the necessity or naturalness of those same limits.

While many current scholars of communication have put forward new orientations toward the ethics and politics of speech, this historical study seeks to find possibilities not in what is new but instead in what has been forgotten. It takes as its aim something similar to Robert L. Scott's early writings on existentialism: "to clarify through a fresh analysis a way which has always been open and sometimes chosen, but seldom in a clear, incisive manner."[5] Doing so through historical study, rather than through philosophical analysis or political treatise, allows this clarification to come from texts familiar to scholars and students of communication. It permits us to respond to Irene Harvey's call that "perhaps it is time to consider what has been presupposed, unthematized, but nonetheless active and constitutive within this field."[6] Thus, the goals of this project are twofold: to examine those modes of ethics and politics that pervade the history of the speech communication discipline, and to produce an account based on speech communication's own history from which one might undertake the study and practice of communication with an attentiveness not only to the historical nature of knowledge but also to the productive operation of difference, otherness, and incommensurability.

While we frequently speak about such themes today, they are often taken as relatively recent changes in the study of communication that break with previous decades. Yet, like the diminution of the privileged position of the orator and the rise of politics in everyday discourse, one can find these sentiments not only in the past score of years but since at least the beginning of the twentieth century. While we often refer today to a "linguistic turn" and a perception of a rising interest in ethics, both of these movements in speech communication can also be seen as inseparable from the history of the discipline. Indeed, much of what we may sometimes say comes from the outside or threatens the traditional core of communication scholarship can also be understood as already present within the history of the discipline over the past hundred years. Inversely, what we often take for granted as central to the discipline may not be uniformly endorsed by its history. History has a tendency to complicate matters.

The uncertainties and difficulties that communication scholars face when discussing issues of agency, ethics, and politics magnify when we seek to discuss these issues alongside historical studies. As Ronald C. Arnett writes, communication ethicists who are confronted with current trends often respond with the question, "How do we affirm standards with our contemporary understanding of [the] historicality of knowledge and insight?"[7] Yet it is not only what the history of speech communication can say about the status of knowledge that troubles our ethical inquiries but perhaps even more what it might say about subjectivity and agency. As Kenneth E. Andersen noted, "Responses to the question of what it is or means to be human often profoundly affect the implicit or explicit ethical stance of communication theorists."[8] Communication and rhetoric scholars have often grounded their work on a tradition of liberal humanism and liberal democracy. From neo-Aristotelian to dialogical perspectives, the notion of the good person skilled in speech has often meant a skilled person speaking in accordance with what is best about human nature, as derived from a particular view of what it means to be human. The dominance of humanism in speech communication oriented much of twentieth-century communication ethics toward a particular set of doctrines while marginalizing or obfuscating alternative ways of thinking about agency and ethics, though never extinguishing them.

This book aims to be an intervention into the ethics and politics of speech. It proposes the possibility of an approach to ethics and a style of politics that has long been present in communication but that has only rarely received the attention of communication ethicists or political communication scholars. It opens for communication a thought from within the discipline's own literature that can connect our discipline to other fields without requiring that communication scholars simply import ways of thinking. Similarly, it fosters for communication an understanding of the position of ethics and politics as they are implicated in every act of communication scholarship, a recognition that in each act of theorizing or studying, we engage in ethical and political practices. In so doing, this study intervenes not primarily into arguments about the history or the proper definition of the discipline but far more so into the current controversies over community and incommensurability, agency and the agent, subjectivity and objectivity, and the ethics and politics of speech.

Tracing a Disciplinary Vocabulary

Of course, one does not find terms like "incommensurability" or "alterity" in early speech studies. A significant change in vocabulary has occurred in communication and rhetoric over the past two decades. When a new vocabulary emerges in a field of thought or an academic discipline, it may be part of a new way of thinking or a new set of questions and challenges, or it may be another approach to challenges and questions that have long been present but were previously articulated differently or largely left unspoken. Thus, it is quite understandable that when the vocabularies of postmodernism and post-structuralism found their way into the study of communication and rhetoric in the last decades of the twentieth century, they were taken up by some as transgressive, as a violation or surpassing of the previous age, or even as revolutionary, as offering an entirely new way out of the old debates and quagmires.

As with most transgressions or revolutions, this attitude operated primarily in relation to real or imagined policing and conservation. Just as those seeking to conserve or return to a prior age often overstate its uniformity and consistency, so too do revolutionaries and transgressors often present a past that is too one-dimensional, too solid and seamless in its operation. Neither position does justice to the opportunities for transformation that can be found in decades or centuries past. As both sides stake their claim of being for or against the retreating age, they make that age into a premise for a prescription for the future. The transgressives and the revolutionaries, in their resentment of the prior age, define themselves by being against it, still relying upon that which they reject to define what they will become.

This book seeks not so much to pick a side in the revolutions or battles of the past decades but to take a third way, a way that can embrace and even celebrate the history of thought in communication and rhetoric precisely because that history is itself a site of diverse possibilities for our future. This way undertakes to write one history of the study and teaching of communication and rhetoric in order to open up the present to the complexity and richness of its past. As such, this book is not a history of how the American scholars of speech communication built a discipline in the twentieth century but instead about how they struggled with the incessant questions of ethics and politics that were pervasive in their writings and teachings. This is not just a story or history of a discipline (though it is certainly that) but an invitation for communication, as a field of study and as a practice, to open itself to its own possibilities. This book makes use of historical study to develop a way of articulating how we can engage in ethics and politics that are neither conservative nor revolutionary but are responsive to contemporary questions with a richer and more nuanced understanding of what our history has to offer.

History as Ethical and Political Inquiry

Such purposes set this book apart from those few existing studies that have examined the history of speech communication in the past hundred years. Such histories largely take as their aims either the cataloging of events or the narrating of a cohesive or progressive development of the discipline. Their stated goals are to make sense of the history or to explain the influential factors that formed the discipline in a movement of progression.[9] For example, in the introduction to their collection of essays on "the founders and the builders" of the discipline, Jim A. Kuypers and Andrew King lay out as their goals the dispelling of myths, the reclamation of the past, and setting the record straight, but most important, they seek to build a story in which the core of the scholarly community of rhetoric finds its roots and identity in eleven men and women who wrote primarily before 1960.[10] Alternatively, Herman Cohen's impressive catalog of the discipline avoids the problems created by focusing on specific figures but attempts comprehensiveness in building an integrated understanding of the discipline. To accomplish such a solid picture of speech communication, Cohen's project required a certain anachronism, as he certainly recognized when he selected particular elements of the field to leave out of the early history because they were no longer an integrated part of the disciplinary structure at the end of the twentieth century. While each of these engages its particular historical task well, their hopes of providing coherent or progressive narratives of the discipline that might build a core community or integrated understanding of speech communication require that they turn their focus away from many of the opportunities within the discipline's history that complicate synopsis or synthesis.

History can have a more creative and practical use. It can be put to the task of tracing out problems and questions so that we can find in the past opportunities for engaging issues of today. One example of such a history in speech communication might be found in William M. Keith's study of the discussion movement and public forums of the early twentieth century.[11] Keith presents a detailed study of the meaning and practice of democracy and citizenship through historical study that can be brought to bear upon our current projects in civic engagement and deliberative democracy. Keith's study builds important connections between schools of thought and political practices and offers lessons for contemporary pursuers of old paths through the tales of explorers long forgotten. As such, it functions as a counterhistory of pertinent ideas and also as a demonstration of the ways in which the discipline has in the past engaged (and could again engage) politics and political action.

What is common among the works of Keith, Cohen, and Kuypers and King, as well as this book, is a recognition that historical studies are inevitably embroiled in discussions of the definition of the discipline. When historians speak or write about the past of a community, they not only provide descriptive accounts of what was but also generate grounds that may be mistakenly used as criteria for policing the boundaries of that community. What is most troubling is that no matter how many caveats historians might attach to their work, some readers might mistake their studies for objective descriptions of what has always been true. Edward Schiappa noted that an academic discipline, like any discourse community, is constantly changing and "can be described as similar or different depending on the interests of the person doing the describing."[12] Historians are not conspiring to deceive fellow scholars in speech communication or elsewhere, but the process of telling a history of the discipline is itself a rhetorical and political act in which some views may be privileged while others are marginalized. As James R. Andrews pointed out, historians often simply reflect the milieu from which they come.[13]

After all, our histories are stories that we tell to ourselves. If we take the generalizations that we have induced from histories as restrictive definitions, then we risk forgetting much of our past and excluding many of the opportunities for study that our past presents. If we take history as uniform, coherent, or even progressive, we likely lose what Scott noted as one of the strengths of history: its plurality and our opportunities to make diverse uses of it.[14] Even when they are marginal, infrequent, or condemned by the majority of scholars, even when they are excised by later movements in the discipline, ways of speaking and forms of study that occupied the history of the discipline do not disappear. As John M. Murphy wrote of marginalized and forgotten discourses in broader contexts, "They adapt, they go underground, they return, they inflect other ways of speaking, but they do not depart at the announcement of a new age."[15] An attentiveness to these marginalized and forgotten discourses can provide an understanding of how what may seem to have been left in the past or to be arising new in the present has a genealogy that connects it to thoughts and discourses that cut across genres or across decades.

Communication ethics scholarship in the first half of the twentieth century provides a good example. Cohen's claim that the study of ethics and the interest in politics were not prominent elements of the discipline in the first half of the twentieth century is quite accurate if one takes a narrow view of what texts might be relevant to communication ethics and to the politics of communication studies.[16] Likewise, attempting to isolate a single date as the first instance of ethics in the new discipline can work if one imposes much later disciplinary definitions and boundaries anachronistically. However, as the following chapters document, though commonly isolated from our current discussions of communication ethics and politics, a large number of essays on issues of personality development, effective persuasion, and the role of speech training in the war effort were published in speech communication journals from 1912 through the late 1940s. Likewise, while the vocabulary and orientation of ethical questions shifted significantly over the first few decades of the century, even the textbooks of the earliest years of the 1900s contain clear statements of ethics. This literature yields fruitful insights into how the discipline's ethical and political attitudes helped shape pedagogy and scholarship and into what openings might already be present in the history of the discipline for thinking about ethics.

Even in the founding year of what is now the National Communication Association, Charles H. Woolbert wrote of the ethics of public address in the *Public Speaking Review*.[17] In the first volume of the *Quarterly Journal of Speech*, we find articles on the proper relation that a speaker should have with himself or herself.[18] The connections between speech education, communication behavior, and selfhood are likewise explored in such essays as Virginia Claire MacGregor's 1934 article on personality development and Vierling Kersey's brief 1937 discussion of the importance of speech to life and in essays from the period on speech and mental hygiene.[19] Relations between the self and others can be read about in discussions of speaker-audience interaction, such as H. B. Gislason's 1916 *Quarterly Journal of Public Speaking* essay.[20] Angelo M. Pellegrini took a broader perspective when connecting public speaking to social obligations in his 1934 article.[21] While we should be careful about overstating how representative of the broader discipline such articles may have been, if we look to the models of agency, communication, and ethics at play in these studies—rather than merely to their overt political claims—we come to understand that ethics were articulated throughout much of the earliest speech communication literature.

Problems of scope and organization likewise impose enormous difficulties for writing an intellectual history. Dividing the discipline into subgenres and then studying these as relatively independent elements can aid the author and reader significantly, but as a result we may lose sight of some of the regularities that cut across these subgenres. As is illustrated by Cohen's discounting of communication ethics, the treatment of fields such as communication pedagogy independent of communication ethics can diminish our ability to study the ethics and politics of communication. Shifting vocabularies make such problems even more significant. For example, the label "science" changed dramatically in its scope and usage over the twentieth century. Thus, when Kuypers and King excised speech sciences from rhetoric in their volume, they imposed a split on thinkers from a period in which such distinctions not only were unclear but were made through terms and meanings significantly different from those found in later vocabularies of communication. As chapters 1 and 2 in this volume document, the scholars and teachers of speech in the first decades of the discipline had no trouble discussing Quintilian and mental hygiene in the same sentence or referring to public address studies as a scientific field.

Creative History

Such moves are not only completely understandable but may be almost essential to making some sense of the past. After all, no one alive today can think of the world in exactly the same way people did in 1910. The concern should not so much be with whether Cohen or Kuypers and King got history "right." In some senses, they most certainly did. Instead, these criticisms, if one can even call them criticisms, only point out the necessity of understanding that all our histories are creative acts. They require acts of rhetorical invention, organization, and style and will never make the past present but instead can help us understand what the past may be able to offer us today. As Carole Blair put it, "Histories of rhetoric are themselves rhetorical."[22]

Taking up the rhetorical task of historical study, this book seeks to use history as a creative field upon which we can unleash certain questions, certain problems of our contemporary age, and quandaries that have persisted in communication, ethics, and politics for far longer than the mere hundred years studied here. It lays no claim to being comprehensive or complete. Indeed, it shares those qualities that Blair noted as common not only to history but to any discourse, being "saturated with impure representations, intrinsic interestedness, and general obstreperousness."[23] This study could not attempt to be either a synoptic gathering or a panoptic cataloging of past scholarship. Instead, it embraces Schiappa's proposition that the discipline may have a history, but this does not mean that it has an essence, not even an essence arrived at through agreement or deliberation.[24] In short, whatever history is written here, it is not the authoritative documenting of the discipline. Instead, the approach of this study is to use historical evidence as a route by which we can explore a cluster of concepts and problems. In examining how the history of the discipline offers opportunities for thinking about ethics and politics with attention to difference, otherness, and incommensurability, this study charts a path that has long been open but has been taken only infrequently.

Selecting Historical Objects

The first body of communication studies literature for this historical study was chosen from the journals in the field. Articles were selected by surveying the table of contents for each issue of *Public Speaking Review*, the *Quarterly Journal of Speech, Communication Monographs, Philosophy and Rhetoric, Communication Quarterly*, the *Southern Communication Journal, Communication Studies*, and the *Western Journal of Communication* from their inceptions through 1999. This review was conducted with an eye toward articles that might identify the discourses through which the discipline defined itself and its methods of inquiry. In selecting articles for this study, I looked for (1) articles related to issues of ethics and morals; (2) articles having as their main focus the relationship between speech and agency, such as the role of speech courses in citizen-building or political empowerment; and (3) articles on the relationship between the study or teaching of speech and specific political or ideological positions, such as Philip Wander's ideological criticism, critical rhetoric, and the role of speech communication in wartime. In many cases, entries in the table of contents required examination of the first and last page of the article to see if it met at least one of these criteria.

This search of the literature yielded hundreds of essays that could be studied in writing a history of the ethics and politics of the discipline. That list was reduced by eliminating similar articles by the same author during the same period that did not vary radically in thesis or perspective. The smaller collection served as the body of literature studied for the first draft of this book, though by no means was every essay referenced in this work. Rather, only those most salient to the analysis, and especially those that highlight the linkages and breaks in studies of communication, were put into play. The first criterion for selection was the presence of implicit or explicit descriptions of what constitutes a good speaker, a good act, or a good person. Additionally, the analysis relied heavily upon articles that evidence particular views of agency, ethics, or politics within and between subdisciplines.

This body of literature was then supplemented by archival research at the J. Willard Marriott Library at the University of Utah, including the archives of the Eastern Communication Association, the National Communication Association, the Southern States Communication Association, and the Western Speech Communication Association. These archives yielded not only personal correspondences, organizational records, and newsletters but, more important, the program booklets and in some cases full papers and proceedings from conferences in the first half of the twentieth century. These detailed records from the conferences provided some significant information about trends and perceptions of the times. Unfortunately, many of the archives are incomplete and not yet fully catalogued, limiting their contribution to this study.

Those familiar with speech communication and its history likely have already recognized two specific choices that were made in this study of the discipline. The first is that whenever referring to the formal discipline across the twentieth century, I have chosen to use the term "speech communication." This name for our discipline, which gained prominence in the late 1950s and early 1960s, then lost favor in the late 1980s and early 1990s, reflects a particular tension and anxiety of identity that persistently appears in the twentieth century. It does not refer to a single entity or discrete object of study, such as spoken communication, but really to two dispositions struggling to find a relationship: speech and communication. The first of the two terms, "speech," is a part of the tradition of not only public speaking but the pedagogical and practical focus of speech training across the genres of oratory, radio, theater, and the like. The latter term, "communication," is indicative of the accelerating drive toward theory-building and analysis but also toward an attitude of study rather than a discipline focused on an object of study. While today the term "communication studies" is far more widely used in the discipline and personally preferred, "speech communication" far better reflects the odd and conflicted relationship that this discipline had with itself throughout the twentieth century. Thus, for the purposes of this historical study, the most appropriate term for reference to the discipline is "speech communication," even though it is anachronistic to apply it to the earliest decades of the twentieth century and archaic by our current standards. Other terms are used at times when referring to specific periods, such as "speech" and "speech sciences" in the first decades of the century and "communication studies" in the latter decades.

The second key decision made for this study was to focus on the rhetorical, philosophical, artistic, historical, and humanities-driven literature at the expense of the more specifically quantitative mode of science that emerged later in the discipline's history. As such, this is rightly a study of the side of our now two-headed discipline that includes not only rhetorical studies but also much of communication ethics, public address, cultural studies, and similarly related fields. This focus is particularly evident in the latter chapters as this study moves into the more contemporary era, when the quantitative and behavioral scientists are especially separated from the humanities. In the earliest decades, such a split had not fully developed, and hence the earlier chapters make use of a broader scope of literature. It is my sincere hope that my friends and colleagues working in the other half of the current discipline may find much of interest in the first few chapters, but there is no pretense to having written a history of the practices of quantitative communication studies.

In any study such as this, one can easily point to an essay, a book, or a figure and ask why it was not referenced or featured more prominently in the analysis. Such questions largely miss the point of the approach when they concern only the matter of what today is taken as a canonical work or what would be an additional citation to an already recognized thought. It is entirely likely that an omission of a form of thinking about speech communication in the twentieth century has occurred in this analysis and, most certainly, not every figure who might be referenced or discussed in relation to different terms and concepts has been afforded a citation or even an honorable mention. In some cases, even scholars who today are considered major figures in the discipline have been subordinated to less important roles or placed slightly out of the timeline in which they are now taught and understood.

In part, this is because the reliance upon the personal, institutional, and disciplinary memories that today guide the choice of canonical thinkers and texts would undermine the central goal of exploring the possibility of remembering our histories differently. Reminiscences of the past, such as those found in oral history projects, tell us more about the moment of recollection than about the moment being recalled. To write a history based on our current citations and references would be merely to write the present into the past, largely negating the possibility of using historical study to find opportunities or to expand our thinking. In mining the journals, archives, and dusty shelves of the annexes, one finds names long unspoken, thoughts long forgotten, and chronologies wholly different from what our biographies and anthologies present. The documents within the discipline often indicate that a particular thinker entered the discipline out of sync with his or her own timeline. For example, as early as 1931 Kenneth Burke was writing materials that are relevant to much of what is discussed in our history, but the scholarship in speech communication places him as not prominently entering the disciplinary discourse until the late 1940s and early 1950s. To locate Burke as a part of the disciplinary conversation in the 1930s would be to write backward from his canonization, skewing the field toward a reproduction of the present rather than opening it to possibilities long past.

The point is not whether this work is a comprehensive or synoptic account of the history of a field of thought—it is not—but rather whether it carefully documents the possibility of conceiving of that field of thought or the particular questions within that field in a compelling and viable way. If the goal is to explore the possibility of interrogating the artifacts of our past for a different way of putting together, of assembling, of re-membering our present possibilities, then one cannot begin by organizing such an exploration around the present as it might currently be understood. Instead, this study has used the questions of ethics and political problems as the topography upon which to map out another way of telling the story of speech communication in the twentieth century.

Mapping the Rhetorical Trajectory

This historical study of the discipline is laid out in six major chapters organized as three pairs, each pair covering a certain period of the twentieth century. The first two chapters cover the emergence of American speech communication and communication ethics as humanistic sciences from the first decade of the century through the late 1940s. In this period, one finds a strong tension between views of communication as the transfer of meaning and the psychological theories that were popular in the discipline. This tension carries over into differences between the models of persuasion often advanced by pedagogues and the views of mental health that became increasingly popular through the 1930s. Efficacy of communication and the ethics implicit in mental health literature maintained a tense relationship throughout the period, as speech communication was embroiled in both world wars and the politics of the era.

Of particular note during this period are the movements in speech communication toward a view that grounded speech and ethics in open discussion rather than in compliance-gaining. Inconsistencies in the politics of platform oratory were brought to the fore by questions about the relationship between democracy and rhetoric and in debates over the concept of discussion. As with the tensions over the incompatibility between traditional platform oratory and proper mental health, these arguments were not resolved into neat conclusions or dialectical syntheses but persisted as problems for communication scholars, changing in terminology or shifting in focus but never wholly disappearing into the past.

Chapters 3 and 4 span roughly the 1950s through the mid-1970s and mark a shift in the major metaphors for thinking about communication and ethics. Without replacing the scientific paradigm that was prevalent in earlier speech communication, the middle of the century saw a swing toward philosophical and especially existential accounts of communication. This period saw contentious arguments over the nature and status of reason, the distinction between persuasion and force, and the role of science in studying communication and ethics. In each of these arguments, we see communication scholars struggling to provide some grounds on which to base moral judgment.

The role of moral judgment in speech communication was perhaps most clearly articulated during this period, though it certainly is not unique to it. Rhetorical critics were often expected to assess the morality of a speaker's rhetorical choices. In so doing, they needed standards that could be applied in testing the morality of a rhetorical act. Truth, reason, human dignity, and additional themes were offered and criticized during the 1960s and 1970s, none of them being able to withstand critique, yet none of them being eliminated as potentially acceptable methods. Communication ethics scholars sought out stable and absolute grounds on which to base moral judgments but eventually found instead a diversity of contradictory and irreconcilable ethical positions that could neither be synthesized nor ignored.

Chapters 5 and 6 work from the late 1970s through the 1990s, emphasizing how the ethics and politics of communication were directed back onto the practices of scholarship within the discipline. The continuation of humanism as a guiding principle in most communication and ethical theories during this period was married to a continuation of the existential critiques of the previous decades. These existential critiques also developed into positions that were informed by postmodern and post-structural writings. In the process, speech communication scholars became embroiled in fundamental philosophical debates about the status of knowledge and the nature of being. What might be most interesting about these arguments is not their relationship to any particular philosophy but how they were already connected to the arguments over reason, science, mental health, and ethics that had occurred during the previous seventy years.

This historical study leads into a discussion in the conclusion of this volume of what specific opportunities might be identified from the history. In part, these opportunities include the looseness of disciplinary boundaries, the multiplicity of political methods that have always been present in the discipline, and the heterogeneity of the critical methods and objects of study. However, perhaps more important than these openings are the types of ethics and politics that are often hinted at but only rarely stated within speech communication. These are ethics that cannot privilege oneself or what is common between oneself and others but must privilege something that comes before anything that might be shared or common. These are politics that do not seek to achieve an end state or to realize an ideal vision but that operate as small moves within the gaps and ruptures in existing political sensibilities. By listening closely to the history of speech communication, we can understand these modes of ethics and politics, not as threats from the outside but as possibilities that are already present within our own past.

1 Preparing the Speaker to Stand Tall

In most histories of communication, it is common to read that ethics were not a central concern for communication scholars in the first half of the twentieth century. To support such a position, one can easily marshal evidence from the early half of the century touting the importance of efficiency and efficacy in oratory and the requisite skills-based education in public speaking. Subsequently, one might come to believe that the ethical questions of which many twenty-first century communication scholars write are largely the result of a change in times and a new awareness of the relationship between communication and every aspect of life.

There is, however, another way to tell this story. One can read the emergence of American speech communication as a moment deeply infused with concerns and questions about how one ought to live one's life. As the study of speech emerged as a discipline and the first speech journals were published, we find studies of psychology and mental hygiene, explorations of speech in everyday life, praise for the role of speech in the American political system, and discussions of the relationship between speech and war. In each of these conversations, we find models of what it might mean to be a "good person" and how this might be connected to skill in speaking or speaking well. These are not ethics that blend together softly; they pull upon one another and pose challenges to the structure of speech training and to our inherited histories of speech communication.

Such a reading unsettles our belief that to study speech is primarily to study the means by which a speaker might best achieve his or her goal. It likewise calls into question the proposition that the study of speech in the twentieth century was ever separated from ethical issues and concerns. Yet, it also identifies linkages between the social psychology of speech, American politics, and communication ethics.

This chapter focuses on the development of a social psychology of speech and its ethical commitments in the first decades of the twentieth century.

Starting in the first years of the century, it maps out how a concern with efficacy and efficiency in oral persuasion led scholars and teachers of speech to the social sciences and particularly psychology as sources for theories of the nature of the human mind. Along the way, a concern with mental health and hygiene opened opportunities for speech that moved the budding discipline away from a focus on the extraordinary events of platform oratory and toward a concern with personality development in everyday discussion and conversation. At the same time, the discipline developed ethics grounded in scientific principles and reasoning, which focused on the capacity of a speaker to master his or her self.

Speech as the Efficient Conqueror

Early-twentieth-century teachers and scholars certainly described communication, and especially speech, in terms of efficiency and efficacy. J. Berg Esenwein, twelve years before the National Association of Academic Teachers of Public Speaking was established, wrote that "all speech seeks to convey to the hearer a mental picture of that which is in the mind of the speaker—thought is alike its foundation and its completed result."[1] For Esenwein, speech was goal-oriented, and its fundamental goal was the sharing of thoughts between minds, a sort of transfer of meaning or understanding. Charles H. Woolbert said something very similar in 1916 in the second volume of the first national journal for the study of speech when he argued that it was not the place of speech teachers to train students in content or subject matter. Rather, that responsibility fell upon economists, historians, and teachers of literature, each of whom would "load" the mind of the student with knowledge. Woolbert wrote that speech was "a machine for unloading" information or knowledge into other minds.[2] Loading and unloading minds, sharing information and ideas, and transferring mental content between individual brains were for Esenwein and Woolbert the purposes of speech. In his 1938 text, *Speech Making*, James A. Winans put it plainly that the first reason to study speech is "practical efficiency."[3]

In order to ensure such a transfer, the material to be unloaded and loaded had to be made suitable for the transfer. One had to be able to do substantially more than simply state one's mental content for it to be communicated. Hence—and this is where the function of speech training became critical—knowledge to be loaded into a mind must be made, as H. B. Gislason put it in 1916, "palatable" to the audience that will receive it.[4] Thus conceived, speech was not a means of inquiry, nor was it used for any purpose other than outward expression of inward thought—the transmission of meaning to another mind. Esenwein, Woolbert, and Gislason considered the primary task of speech education to be the development of skills essential to effecting this communication—this transmission—with maximum efficiency and efficacy. The same thing may be said of the aims of teaching speech in the first two decades of the century as Joseph A. Mosher argued were the aims of debate in 1924: "not to encourage shifting of ground nor to settle problems, but rather to cultivate the student's ability to bring together and express in a complete, well-organized, sound address what may be said in support of a definite attitude toward a question of the day."[5] Speech, in these statements, was neither a problem-solving method nor a tool of inquiry. It was simply a mechanism of transmission.

In the simplicity and directness of such an explanation of speech, there was also a very palpable problem: if one needed to make knowledge palatable to the mind that was to receive it, there had to be a potential for resistance on the part of the audience. The audience, as the receptacle of the knowledge or the target of the transfer, had to have some potential to resist the orator's attempt to "load" their minds. Hence, it became a prerequisite to effective speech that a speaker be able to overcome an audience's resistances. Thus did Esenwein argue that a speaker had to master the audience: "For the audience to master the speaker is failure. For the speaker to master the audience is success."[6]

The audience, as a receptacle for the speaker's knowledge, became an object for the speaker to conquer, a target for the sharp words of a great orator. Gislason compared the speaker to a hunter who is "taking aim" at the audience, stalking the "big game" that "every wise hunter wishes to bag."[7] In the dyad of speaker and audience, giver and receiver, hunter and prey, a simple relationship of one over the other was easily articulated. However, such a simple dyad can exist only theoretically, since audiences, like the "big game" the hunter so desperately seeks, are in practice contested over by others who also seek them as a prize. Speakers compete for audiences, seeking to "load" them with contrary information and to steer them toward incompatible ends.

In the first issue of the *Southern Speech Bulletin* in 1935, William Norwood Brigance described this competition as the selling of personalities, goods, or ideas in which speech became the medium of exchange—the currency of each transaction.[8] Brigance argued that the livelihood of almost every individual depended upon his or her proficiency in handling these verbal transactions. For Brigance, it was "almost literally true that good speech has replaced the gun and the axe as an instrument of survival on the fittest terms."[9] In describing the value of "good speech" and of formal education in speech, Esenwein, Gislason, and Brigance praised the possibility of dominating others through the use of these verbal weapons. In 1934, while criticizing this trend in speech education, Angelo Pellegrini wrote that to regard public speaking "as an instrument of power over others for personal ends" was quite common.[10] That the capacity to speak in public could always be used for individual economic gain, he wrote, was the only argument he had ever heard on behalf of formal education in public speaking. Speech was for making things happen that one wished to have happen. Speech was a currency to purchase an audience's compliance, a weapon with which to take an audience against its will, a tool for overcoming an audience's resistances.

As such, speech training enhanced the utility of one's speech; it made one's words more valuable, increased the caliber of one's oratory, and strengthened the degree to which one's speech could get a job done. The cultural value of speech education, wrote W. H. MacKellar in 1937, was that it might provide the student with greater power and effectiveness so that the student could live a life of abundance and usefulness.[11] If audiences had concerns about their rights in relationship to a speaker, these were merely an impediment to the speaker's purpose or a factor to be accounted for by the speaker. The speaker was concerned only with the question of efficacy.

Psychology and the Emergence of Speech Sciences

This reading of the emergence of American speech education depicts a discipline concerned primarily with how to master an audience. Thus, just as one might study one's enemies in order to conquer them, so too did the careful study of the audience become a critical concern for the would-be orator. Esenwein required that his students study audiences in order "to know their hearts, how the strongholds of their approval may best be taken—in short, how to attract and hold them."[12] Thus, one of the first foundational questions for speech studies became the structure and function of the audience's mind, which meant more specifically the essential structure of human psychology.

In order to uncover this structure, speech scholars needed a method by which they could seek reliable knowledge about their objects of study. When the national association was formed in 1914 and the national journal began publication, speech scholars widely expressed a desire for uniformity of method. Woolbert wrote that in order to create a meaningful academic discipline, speech teachers and scholars needed to unify under a scientific methodology.[13] The ability of an academic discipline to gain institutional acceptance, according to Woolbert, depended on its possession of a "large body of observed facts, which are related to one another, and are arranged by general laws"—which is precisely the definition Woolbert gave for science.[14] As Karl F. Robinson noted, the importance of establishing speech as a discipline of scientific inquiry was underscored by statements such as the California State Department of Education's claim that the social sciences were the integrating center of the core courses.[15] Thus, pressures both within the emerging discipline and from the general climate of early-twentieth-century pedagogy moved early speech scholars such as A. B. Williamson to credit the establishment of speech as an academic discipline to "leaders in the field, men of broad experience, professors of public speaking in colleges and universities of high standing, [who] stimulated interest in scholarly research and in the scientific study of speech."[16]

Even in rhetorical studies and the study of classical rhetorical figures, appeals to scientific method and social scientific theories often dominated the early speech communication scholarship. It is, of course, possible to build a story of this period that pits the sciences against the humanities in a contest over the discipline by focusing on particular personalities that reflect such a schism, as Herman Cohen did,[17] but in the broader literature, the loose notion of science that pervaded the first decades of the twentieth century was widely accepted as the standard for good research in speech. In 1923, Giles Wilkeson Gray celebrated the American revival of speech studies but praised even more the idea that "we are just coming to realize for the first time in history that speech can be made the subject of a science."[18] For Gray, the study of the ancient Greek or Roman texts was secondary to the scientific study of speech as it functioned in his own time and place. If Plato or Aristotle were to have any validity, it was only because the scientific research of his time might bear out the theories to which these ancients had held. Communication scholars were to sift through the whole body of communication theory scientifically, discarding all that could not be proven by scientific methods. When he was criticized for being only "pseudo-scientific," Gray responded that this was largely irrelevant, as the scientific study of speech was achieving results that were more useful to the modern needs of orators than were the "outworn methods" of the Greeks and Romans.[19]

This is not to say that science replaced all other methodologies and perspectives, but it did clearly hold the dominant position in the budding discipline. In the 1935 statement of the principles for the Western Communication Association convention, the authors gave a lengthy list of subject areas intimately connected with speech studies: "mental hygiene and psychiatry, medical sciences, social psychology, sociology and the social sciences, ethics, physics, English, aesthetics, and other subjects."[20] Note that the authors, in setting the tone and theme for the annual convention, chose seven scientific terms to connect to speech: mental hygiene, psychiatry, medical sciences, social psychology, sociology, social sciences, and physics. Three terms more closely associated with liberal arts are then also attached to these scientific terms: ethics, English, and aesthetics. The positioning of these terms also reflects the prioritization of scientific thought over liberal arts, as the scientific terms take the forefront, while ethics, English, and aesthetics are the addenda. Of those terms, ethics occupies the most primary position, actually inserted between social sciences and physics, positioning it within the tail end of the scientific cluster of terms and separated from English and aesthetics.

Notably absent from this list of related subjects is history, a field that would later be ascribed to the early origins of rhetorical studies in American speech. There are significant examples of the importance of history to early speech scholars, but not as a primary or central method of scholarship. H. A. Wichelns, who was later regarded as a progenitor of rhetorical criticism and a key figure in the Cornell tradition of humanistic rhetoric,[21] wrote in 1937 that there are two types of research in any academic profession: historical and scientific. Historical methods reveal a common tradition, while science provides an academic profession with a common method.[22] Taken in this configuration, history had little role in the production of knowledge for pedagogy or application but instead served primarily a disciplinary role in the establishment of the common origins of speech studies while leaving the judgment of utility or truth to science.

For speech studies, this science was primarily found in psychology, yielding the question of proper speech to the study of the mind. The focus on science as the organizing principle of the discipline and the concern with how a speaker might master the minds of an audience set the stage for speech studies to take the shape of an applied psychology or, as Gray called it, a "psychology of speech."[23] The idea that speech ought primarily to concern itself with the structure of human thought was nothing new. Esenwein had argued in 1902 that since speech has as its purpose the transfer of thought, "it must always be viewed in light of the laws of thought."[24] In seeking to conquer the audience, Gislason wrote that a speaker was, at base, "grappling with human minds."[25] As Earl S. Kalp put it, the scientific study of these human minds hence became the "first matter of importance" in the teaching of speech.[26] The scientific study of the human psyche was to be where speech studies could find a grounding, seeking the "fundamental nature of man."[27] In such studies, as Virginia MacGregor argued in 1934, the study of speech was "at last unified" and became "more permanent and far-reaching in scope and less open to gross misrepresentation and misunderstanding."[28]

Rather than analyzing the individual character of a person or the psychology of a specific audience, the psychological study of the audience became the study of the human as an ideal—the study of the fundamental nature of the human subject. Irvah Lester Winter made the position unequivocal in his 1914 essay: "A knowledge of human nature and of human life, important to all teachers, is an essential to the successful teaching of this subject."[29] Here, in the scientific quest for general laws and unity of explanation, the question of how a speaker might dominate an audience became a search for how the mind is, by its very nature, vulnerable to domination. In other words, speech psychology was the study of how science might uncover the intrinsic weaknesses of the human psyche so that rhetors could more effectively exploit these openings in every audience's defenses. In such analyses, the search was for knowledge of "how we, and our fellows, think—on the ideal basis."[30] Rather than setting out to discover such knowledge through their own studies, American communication scholars such as J. Jeffery Auer largely turned to the theories of William James, Graham Wallas, John Dewey, and similar advocates of the scientific study of human thought. Dewey and James, in particular, were important figures for speech scholars, even making their way into the introductory texts and training materials.[31]

For a discipline consumed by concerns over its institutional legitimacy and its capacity to articulate its scientific basis to university administrators, psychology offered speech scholars a way to justify support for their discipline. Elwood Murray argued in 1938 that psychology offered the greatest possibility for speech to contribute to human life because "every failure in human relations, every barrier in democratic living goes back to failure on the insides of persons' minds—minds which are rigid, inflexible, inadjustable, and more or less resistant or closed to the ordinarily gentle and feeble insistences of truth and reality."[32] Likewise, speech could be characterized as fundamentally psychological in nature, serving, as J. Richard Bietry wrote in 1939, to reveal the social and emotional adjustment or maladjustment of a speaker.[33] Psychology and speech became intertwined, as speech could initially reveal a psychological state, psychological tests could confirm diagnoses, and a speech teacher could then use psychological principles to prescribe the "course of speech projects which is most valuable for each student."[34] The teacher of speech was now expected not merely to instruct upon good oratorical technique and to listen for students' successes and failures in deploying rhetorical technique but to analyze the mental state and health of the student on the basis of his or her speech. Then, on the basis of what was observed, the teacher was advised to confirm the diagnosis by testing the student's psychological condition. Finally, the education of the student was to be guided by the results of those diagnoses so that training in speech could aid in the proper mental adjustment or development of the student.

Speech Sciences and Mental Health

The primacy of scientific methods and the interest in making speech an applied psychology fostered attempts to construct purposes for speech education other than persuasion or transmission. As early as 1916, scholars were troubled by psychological theories challenging the view that audiences were reason-centered decision-makers.[35] Theories of the subconscious and of motivations that operate outside conscious decision-making conflicted with the view of speech as currency in a transaction between two parties. If audiences and interlocutors were not predominantly moved by rational choice or conscious decision, then the transactional view of reasoned exchange would have to yield to a more subtle notion of motivation, impulse, and inclination. If persuasion did not primarily occur at the level of conscious choice, then rational and deliberative speech would have to recede in importance.

Additionally, if speech psychology was to adopt an ideal model of the human mind, it also required normative psychological standards for mental development and health. For the study of the human mind to be a science, it needed a model of the mind that would be common, at least as an ideal or normative standard. Science could not approach the individual mind as each wholly unique without underlying common form. It was thus that speech scholars under the sway of psychology began to describe speech "as a means of mental development."[36] Speech could be connected to this normative standard or psychological ideal through its role in the development or adjustment of the individual psyche.

The panels and papers presented at conferences during the period reflected a widespread interest in the mental hygiene and social adjustment perspectives on speech, including a special two-hour session focused solely on the issue of "social adjustment" in speech training at the 1935 meeting of the Western Association of Teachers of Speech.[37] Wayne Morse expressed the clout of psychological sciences on early speech at the 1929 Eastern Public Speaking Conference when he commented that a change was overtaking the discipline as "increased interest in individual psychology is influencing our teaching."[38] Throughout the 1930s and early 1940s, speech scholars such as Bryng Bryngelson and Richard Bietry argued that speech was "a symptom of emotional health" and that "nothing more completely reflects our emotional state than our voice and speech."[39] If one spoke poorly, it was because one was mentally maladjusted. Likewise, if one was not in proper mental health, then one had no hope of speaking well until the mental defect was cured. The student who stuttered was a hysteric who converted a "mental conflict into a physical symptom."[40] Psychological theories led speech teachers to the opinion that, as Kalp put it, "a speech problem originates in a personality problem, or to put it more effectively, a speech difficulty may be a manifestation of a personality disorder."[41] Likewise, Murray wrote that "the well adjusted person . . . almost always has fewer speech deficiencies."[42] As such, the quality of one's speech was the quality of one's mental health. Teachers and students of speech were involved in a process of mental adjustment: the teacher's duty was to provide guidance to yield proper thought and speech, whereas the student's responsibility was to follow the advice so that proper speech could lead the student to proper mental states. If a student was unwilling to accept the advice of a speech teacher about his or her performance, then that student was said to be "suffering from a mental and moral maladjustment which must affect unfavorably his relations with men in his life work."[43] Thus, becoming of proper mental adjustment was a key component of being educated and learning to speak.

Of course, to teach toward proper adjustment or to ascertain a student's deviations from the ideal mental condition required a model of the correct mental state. Murray characterized the well-adjusted person along four axes: one must be "emotionally stable," must possess a "reasonable amount of self-sufficiency," must tend "to be an extrovert," and must be neither markedly dominant nor markedly submissive.[44] At roughly the same time, social scientists who sought to identify the character traits that made a speaker more effective at persuading an audience found a "definite *trend* to indicate that the best speakers tend to be (a) extroverted, (b) dominant (ascendant), (c) self-sufficient, and (d) more stable emotionally."[45] The model public speaker was the well-adjusted orator, and thus was likewise the effective orator. Noteworthy, however, is the claim that while the well-adjusted person must be neither markedly dominant nor markedly submissive, the most effective speakers were clearly dominant. The conflict between the mental health prescription against dominance and the empirical evidence of dominance in effective public speaking manifests repeatedly throughout the history of communication ethics, as we will see in the remaining chapters.

In addition to these four elements of proper adjustment, speech psychologists praised the capacity of interlocutors to take the perspective of the other person in a speech situation. Turning to mental hygienists such as Jean Piaget, W. H. Burnham, and Fritz Kunkel, Murray argued that a fundamental characteristic of the well-adjusted person was the ability called "mental objectivity." Murray defined mental objectivity as the "ability to take into consideration what is going on in the other person's mind."[46] The ability to step out of one's own perspective and to consider how the target of one's rhetoric might be operating mentally, Murray argued, was both a fundamental element of mental health and a critical component of effective persuasion. Failure to develop such an ability would be both a severe handicap in any speaker's endeavors and a fundamental mental defect that would impair every interaction in which one might find oneself.

However, the focus on developing proper mental health was not simply a matter of helping students to live better lives. It was also a matter of improving the broader society by improving the mental health of the general social order. Not only could mental defects be diagnosed, confirmed, treated, and cured, but they also could be exacerbated or even spread. This contagiousness of mental disease meant that social contact with the maladjusted could spread their views of the world, causing others to catch their opinions "the same way as we do the smallpox or measles."[47] Thus, part of the role of every teacher—and especially teachers of speech—became the prevention of an epidemic of mental maladjustment. Education was for the mental health of not only the student but society. Similarly, education for mental health provided the student with the tools to adjust the mind toward the ideal, equipping the student with the potential for a positive contagion, spreading the cure rather than the illness. As MacGregor wrote, "True education makes clear to the individual not only what he has but what he lacks. It should show him, too, how to acquire what he needs and should help him to do it."[48] The role of such a speech education would be both the mental hygiene of the specific student and also the development of the habits of that student so they might then spread as a positive force of mental hygiene throughout society at large. The contrary risk of failing this educational task was not only that the specific student would be unhappy or maladjusted but that the student would become a carrier of a contagious mental disease that could exacerbate the ills of the social world.

Speech Training as Personality Development

Many speech teachers took on this crusade with vigor. Since speech was fundamentally connected to the psychological and emotional state of the speaker, speech training became a critical path to mental and emotional adjustment. Indeed, Bietry argued that "nothing in the curriculum so closely affects the life of the student as speech."[49] Murray similarly held that principles of mental hygiene ought to guide speech education because "nothing with which the teacher may work is more intimate to the student than his speech."[50] William Farma had made a similar point at the 1929 Eastern Public Speaking Conference when he argued that speech situations were uniquely emotional for students compared to their other courses and could thus provide "an excellent measuring stick of the student's personality."[51]

From these beliefs, the speech teacher could be imbued with a unique capacity and responsibility. It was the speech classroom and speech education that was most able to affect the mental state of the student and thus also most responsible for having such an effect. Compared to writing, philosophy, or the study of psychology, speech was far more personal and more immediate and hence considered more revealing of the student and more powerful in that student's transformation.

Given this unique position, these new teachers of speech were not primarily concerned with the development of effective and efficient persuasion or transfer of ideas but focused instead upon how speech training might better the whole person of the student. Robinson wrote that the purpose of all education ought to be "the development of the whole personality so that the individual may make a successful job of living, and adjusting to his environment."[52] In place of Esenwein's notion of understanding the mind so that one could better persuade the minds of others, here the very purpose of speech is to bring the minds of those speaking and those spoken to in line with the norms of mental health.

This change required that the purpose of the basic course in speech also shift with the adoption of a mental hygiene perspective. MacGregor argued that if one considered the purpose of education to be personality development, then the introductory course in speech "does not assume as its primary task the over-night production of verbose platform sensationalists. . . . Its responsibility to the individual is of far more subtle and fundamental nature. Its object reaches below mere mechanics or external manifestation and concerns itself with the individual made manifest."[53] Murray wrote that this was the essential nature of teaching speech: always to teach the whole person, since "no single aspect can be trained apart from the personality."[54] Thus, a redefinition of the meaning of "speaking well" was underway. Morse articulated this redefinition well while retaining the connection between mental health and persuasion: "The principle of good speech is not one primarily of developing physical habits in the use of the speech mechanism, but basically is a problem in developing a state of mental health in the individual who desires to influence the behavior of others."[55] The question of how one might move others to share the speaker's opinion receded as the question of how one could speak toward a state of proper mental health took the foreground.

Training of the personality was intended to assist the student in adjusting to social life but also to instill an ethic grounded in that same personality training in the student. While Robinson called for the development of classroom experiences that would build "more capable, better adjusted" students and Bietry claimed that speech education should serve the role of "a social integrator," these same classroom practices and models of adjustment became the fundamental bases for how the discipline would understand its ethical responsibilities.[56] In 1935, W. Arthur Cable actually defined "ethical character" as "a development of the emotional processes, which forms a part of speech training, and their control by the thought processes."[57] Beulah Kite Wales and Chloe Zimmerman made a similar case but merely transposed the relationship when they wrote that emotional development included "all indices of adequate character traits or ethical character" and "manifest[s] itself in honesty, fairness, justice, and dependableness."[58] It was not merely that there were similarities between proper mental adjustment and proper ethical character. Rather, the ideal state of mental health became the model for ethics.

Similarly, speech scholars imported the means of achieving these goals from precisely the fields that established the normative standards for adjustment and integration: psychology and mental hygiene. These fields not only provided the model for ethical behavior but were likewise mined by early speech scholars for the methods by which students could be adjusted toward those norms. Murray proposed the adoption of "many of the principles and mechanisms whereby teachers may use speech training as a means of developing personality adjustment in its larger aspects" and pointed to specific mental hygiene principles and techniques that speech teachers might adopt.[59] Mental hygienists like Murray considered speech an ideal discipline for social integration and mental hygiene practices, and many of the speech scholars inclined toward psychology and psychological sciences echoed these views, even if they did not explicitly self-identify as mental hygienists. As Winter wrote, "Few teachers probably have so large an opportunity as the teacher of speech expression for exerting influence upon character."[60] Bietry wrote that speech provided the "principal tool which the individual uses in the adjustment process." This "adjustment process" was then elevated in importance by claiming that the "process of living is nothing more than a continued series of adjustments."[61] Robinson more explicitly made the case when he claimed that personality growth and social adjustment did not primarily occur through reading about society nor studying any of the social sciences but "from the standpoint of the individual, from actually engaging in these activities which man '*uses to make*' such growth and adjustments. These are fundamentally activities of communication."[62]

Murray continued this reasoning by proposing that speech training had two great values for "the therapy of mental hygiene or mental health." The first was that speech "affords means and opportunities for changing the faulty habits of thinking and feeling and attitudes which underlie maladjustment." The second was that speech "aids the student to obtain the all necessary objective and critical view of himself."[63] In the course of training a student in speech, a teacher functioning as a mental therapist could observe resistances, wastes of energy, and inefficiencies. For the mental hygienists and speech psychologists, these offered what Murray called "the most significant opportunity a teacher will ever have to help the student face his problem, understand himself, and gain release from the pressures that have been set up in his history which hinder smooth human relations at many points."[64]

It is likely apparent at this point that many of the therapeutic goals of mental hygienists and speech psychologists were incompatible with the ways in which speech was characterized by scholars who focused on the efficiency and efficacy of oratory, such as Esenwein and Woolbert. Speech training could not be the study of how to make knowledge palatable to an audience and how to overcome their resistances if such training was to serve the aims of personality development and social adjustment. Quite the opposite, mental hygienists called for a complete overhaul of the speech education process. As the focus on developing "verbose platform sensationalists" gave way to a concern for the development of the "whole person," the normative standards of mental health became criteria for prescribing curricular changes in speech education. Consider Bietry's argument: "If speech is to function as a social integrator, our conventional standards in forensics and public speaking must be revised. In this field, certainly, our methods and attitudes reflect the philosophy of 'rugged individualism,' a philosophy which contributes to personality distortion."[65]

Regardless of their scientific bases or their rising connection to political and social causes of the time, advocates of mental hygiene did not displace the central importance of efficacy and efficiency in speech classrooms. Instead, they were consistently confronting the importance of these values in both journal publications and conferences. In order to overcome the objections of speech scholars and teachers who predominantly valued the efficiency and efficacy of communication, mental hygienists argued both from their psychological foundations and from scientific experiment that effectiveness and mental health were interdependent. It has already been seen that mental health was considered to be a prerequisite to effective oratory. The corresponding relationship was that effective oratory was a key to the development of mental health. Murray claimed that if a speaker was successful, then his or her tendencies for a healthy mental life were strengthened, whereas if not, then maladjustment would certainly be intensified. It thus became critical that teachers of speech simultaneously teach principles of effective speech and "principles of a healthy mental life."[66] Kalp likewise argued that in order to "stabilize the pupil emotionally, promote clear thinking, and stimulate the constructive use of the imagination," speech teachers had to use principles of psychiatry and mental therapy to put students in "the right kind of speech situations."[67]

Objectors to the mental hygiene perspective toward speech pedagogy argued, among other points, that speech teachers were not sufficiently equipped to serve as therapists. R. L. Irwin wrote in 1942 that "the business of repairing the mentally ill is an enormously complicated matter, even when the problem appears to be only that of straightening out a mistaken notion."[68] Such calls, however, only solidified the unique expertise claimed by the social psychologists and mental hygienists in the speech discipline. As far back as 1918, scholars had noted that, as J. M. O'Neill argued, "a person who has not had thorough and careful training in this work should no more be allowed to treat defective voice or speech than he should be allowed to treat a broken arm or typhoid fever."[69] The contagious potential of defects of the mind and voice only emphasized that experts in repairing the human psyche ought to be the only teachers entrusted with the tasks of determining not just the norms of mental health but also the methods by which a teacher of speech ought to assist students in their own normalization. Manifesting their faith in scientific expertise, many speech scholars chose to import the psychological theories and therapeutic practices developed by social scientists in other disciplines. In extreme cases, those that mental hygienists and speech psychologists would call "cases of a psychopathic nature," the speech course was the most likely place for the maladjustment to be revealed, but the speech teacher was advised to seek "close cooperation" with a skilled psychiatrist.[70]

The connection between mental health and effective oratory did provide the opportunity for objectors such as Irwin to argue that a good speech class did not have to focus upon the therapy of each student's injured psyche in order to have substantial therapeutic value. Irwin contended that if the goal was the social integration and adjustment of the student, then exposure to a speech class, even without the use of mental hygiene techniques, would accomplish much of this task. In abandoning the psychological probing and standardized tests, Irwin wrote that "it is frequently more expedient and just as helpful categorically to demand that [the student] slow down and speak up if he knows what is good for him."[71] Even proponents of the mental hygiene approach sometimes confessed that "speech training in itself may serve as excellent personality therapy."[72] There was practically no question of whether speech training had any connection to personality development or moral adjustment, nor was there a question of whether communication scholars ought to rely upon the methods and theories of the social sciences, but only questions of how the teacher of speech ought to respond to a maladjusted student. By the 1940s, the idea that speech ought to serve the function of adjusting the whole person of the student to social life was rarely questioned. The issue now was far more whether and how the traditional means of teaching speech were to be altered in order to accommodate therapeutic ends.

Self-Mastery through Speech

One of the central themes in the advocacy of mental hygiene and psychiatry in speech training was the need for students to develop self-mastery if they wished to become effective speakers. In being reasonably self-sufficient and adopting mental objectivity, the good speaker would develop awareness and control of himself or herself. Self-mastery per se was not new to speech education. In 1902, Esenwein wrote that "the mastery of the self in thought, in feeling, and in will is essential to mastering an audience."[73] However, with the emergence of psychological models for speech, this principle was both amplified and altered. Whereas the question for Esenwein was one of how the speaker might control thought, feeling, and will, in 1932 George P. Krapp turned the attention of speech teachers to a kind of knowledge that would be a prerequisite to self-mastery. He wrote that "the philosopher's injunction '*know thyself*'" ought to be modified to '*know thy speech and thou wilt know thyself and thy neighbor.*'"[74] For Krapp, a speaker must understand the fundamental, timeless principles of the human psyche in order to master the self. This model of self-mastery was predicated upon a knowledge of the self as an abstract ideal—not merely in one's own particularities or concrete practices.

The concrete practices of one's speech were where the psychologist and the mental hygienist made their diagnoses and determined personality disorders, but they were not themselves manifestations of the ideal human psyche. Self-mastery, to the mental hygienist, meant the capacity to conform one's concrete practices to the ideal vision of mental health as established in the normative claims of psychology. Speech revealed to the attentive listener—which might be the speaker himself or herself—more than the intended overt content of the words spoken. As MacGregor wrote, it revealed "the more specific truth that 'as a man speaketh, so is he.'"[75] Thus, speech education might yield two forms of knowledge essential to self-mastery: first, the particular knowledge of who the individual speaker is, and second, the abstract knowledge of the normal and properly adjusted human mind that the speaker might strive to become. That is to say, according to the mental hygienists and speech psychologists, speech training, when properly conducted, developed those characteristics essential to self-mastery, confidence, and poise. As one student wrote to MacGregor of his experience in speech training: "I am learning to observe and to interpret things in the light of myself as a person. I am, consequently, learning to know myself, for each time I speak or read aloud, I reveal to the world what I am and what is behind me. Whether this is of strong or of weak foundation, of beautiful or gross appearance, profound or shallow depends on me. I am discovering that we cannot lead the world to believe we are that which we are not."[76] MacGregor and similar teachers of speech counted the value of such self-knowledge and self-mastery as threefold: first, the increased well-being of the student, who would be better acclimated to lead a "normal mental life"; second, the greater efficiency and efficacy of the student's speeches, with the subsequent gain in the personal rewards for being persuasive; and third, the possibility that a world of better adjusted individuals would promise substantially improved political and social relations. The first two of these advantages have already been discussed, but the third claim extends beyond the personal gains that speech might offer the student.

As an advocate of scientific methods and psychological theories in speech scholarship and pedagogy, Gray criticized Greek oratorical theory for being solely concerned with the well-being of the State or the "greater organism." Gray articulated a fundamental premise for the mental hygienists' claims to social and political benefits when he wrote that "a care for the whole naturally looks to care for the parts."[77] From this view, if one is concerned with the broader social order and relations, then one must give attention to the health and adjustment of those individuals who make up society. A student needed a certain education and training before the student's speech could serve society. MacGregor warned that before a speaker is "ready to give the world his own thoughts, let him mature and enrich those thoughts that they may be more worthy of utterance."[78] Still, her position was not that of the Socratic imperative to study oneself deeply before engaging in politics and then throughout one's life. Rather, it is that speakers must know in what ways they fail to fit the normative standards established by psychologists so that they might better adjust to these norms before speaking. Such sentiments made their way even into the official California State Department of Education statement on the place of speech in the educational process: "Good speech is that which gives an accurate indication of an integrated, self-reliant, alert personality. It is an expression of mental adjustment, physical poise, and emotional balance."[79] The concern for the California government and the speech sciences was that such an integrated personality could yield a better world, a world in which fewer individual mental maladjustments would mean fewer broad social conflicts. Bryngelson represented the progressive faith that fueled the mental hygiene movement when he wrote that many social ills would disappear "if people at large would understand their superior-inferiorities and their defenses for them. I wager that strikes, wars, and destructive social programs such as we have today would be extremely difficult to promulgate were talking man more adequately adjusted and thus more honest with himself."[80] This honesty with oneself was that kind of self-awareness that could allow one to find his or her deficiencies and work to bring them to proper adjustment, to train oneself to conform to the psychological ideals.

Reason's Arbitration of Mental Conflicts

In some ways, we can understand this "honesty" that one must have with oneself as a principle of self-governance, by which an individual masters base elements of the psyche with a higher form of thought. At the very least, the speech psychologists and mental hygienists called for each person to settle any internal mental conflicts. In 1902, Esenwein considered this to be "harmonizing your feeling with your thought."[81] For Esenwein, this harmonization was necessary to restrain "undue excitement" while maintaining a level of passion needed for an entertaining and stimulating delivery. However, mental hygienists and speech psychologists in the 1930s and 1940s viewed this harmonization rather differently. For them, it was not the bringing together of two useful and separate elements but rather the coordination of an intrinsic conflict between the two countervailing forces of reason and emotion. F. W. Lambertson, writing in 1942 of Hitler's oratorical style, said that reason and emotion are mutually exclusive; to increase one is always to reduce the other. Maintaining the dominance of reason in speakers and audiences, Lambertson argued, would require that emotions be restrained and governed by the intellect.[82]

While Lambertson and others came to argue that Hitler's oratorical success was a paradigmatic case of emotions trumping reason, it was not Hitler's example that established the dichotomy between these two elements for speech scholars. In 1934, Pellegrini had already argued that speech teachers and public speakers had a social obligation to minister to "a need more abiding and permanent and less likely to change than the needs of the immediate present."[83] He then defined that more abiding and permanent need as "a passion for intellectual honesty and the life of reason." Sixteen years prior to Pellegrini's essay, Glenn W. Merry voiced a belief in the zero-sum relationship between reason and emotion and stressed the moral priority of reason when he wrote that "the spoken word may light the fires of passion and unreason or it may inspire to highest action and noblest sacrifice a nation of freemen."[84] Woolbert had similarly insisted in his own 1914 statement of ethical principles for public address that "he who actually does not know how to reason well has no right to offer himself as leader of the thought of others."[85] Lambertson, Pellegrini, Woolbert, and Merry all made it plain that not only was it for efficiency and efficacy that a speaker must use reason to govern emotions, but it was likewise a moral and social duty—whether for political reasons or for reasons of mental health. The speaker who appealed to reason not only inspired Merry's "highest action and noblest sacrifice" but also provided a "constant, unyielding appeal" that Pellegrini identified as "the only way to hasten the life of reason."[86] Thus, reasoned argument was prioritized and valorized, whereas emotional argument was positioned as its opposite and its predator. By practicing this priority of reason in one's discourse, one could inspire the elevation of reason in others, whereas the use of emotional appeals threatened to dominate or extinguish reason.

Thus, in Pellegrini's 1934 credo for public speaking instructors, the second principle was that "in a speech there must always be intellectual honesty and the appeal to reason." Pellegrini was adamant about this position. He argued that "a conclusion must stand or fall on its own logic."[87] A responsible orator could never exploit the prejudices or emotions of an audience but rather had to strive to remove all prejudices, explain away all biases, and lay out only those arguments that utilize logic as their foundation. If reason could not hold the day, then the position must yield.

Lambertson extended Pellegrini's call by outlining certain techniques that could be used to keep the emotions in check and to maintain the dominance of reason. For example, in Congress, our lawmakers benefit from three "safeguards" that help to keep them "critically minded." First, they have full, voluntary control over their physical motion, which maintains their individuality and prevents them from engaging in a moblike physical movement. Second, they do not speak out of turn but follow rules that permit orderly discussion. Third, they are seated apart from one another "so that the contagion of emotions will not spread."[88] In this analysis, emotions became akin to a viral infection, both threatening and awakening reason's immune response. Emotions were a contagion that could be spread by contact. Proximity became a determinant of the communicability of the emotion-disease. To communicate emotionally was to communicate against reason—to weaken reason—and the communicability of the emotions was the communicability of a threat to reason. This mental disease, which was both threatening to and cured by reason, was a political and ethical failing to the speech scholar. For speech scholars of the first half of the twentieth century, the scientific, psychological, political, social, and ethical doctrines intersect in a call for a self-mastery that represses the emotional response through a governing intellect of logic and reason.

This convergence of the core motivation of efficacy and efficiency with scientific and psychological theories of mental health that privileged reason and self-mastery set the stage for a new politics and a new discourse of democracy to take hold in speech. As the next chapter demonstrates, this convergence brought a shift away from the training of the elite for exceptional service to the Republic through platform oratory and toward the training of every citizen for direct participation in democracy through their daily conversations and participation in local discussions. This became a logical extension of the principles of science and self-mastery that were grounded in the early-twentieth-century convergence of democratism and scientism.

2 Rhetoric, Discussion, and Character

If one were to listen only to the political discourse and the civic education of today, then one might never imagine that it was not until 1913 that citizens nationwide could vote for their federal senators or that the Nineteenth Amendment did not nationalize women's suffrage until 1920. It is hard to imagine, by today's standards, that there was a time when an almost incalculably small minority had even a dream of receiving a college education. Even educated Americans often are unaware that these first few decades were a time of active and strong Communist and Socialist parties in the United States, both locked into conflict with government agencies while also fielding candidates for the presidency.[1] Many would be surprised to learn that this was a period when people who spoke out against the draft might find themselves in prison labor programs or deported.[2] It was during these first few decades of the twentieth century, in a time of change and turmoil, that speech teachers and scholars took up a movement toward a broader and more inclusive democracy and the subsequent education that would be required for citizens to participate. It was exactly during this conflicted period that many in the early field of speech found justification and guiding principles for their pedagogy and scholarship. By defining their field broadly and connecting it to national and political purposes, teachers and scholars of speech articulated what was likely a distinctively American attitude toward communication in the early twentieth century. It was full of difficulties and even contradictions, at once embracing a wide and deep form of democracy and also supporting domestic propaganda efforts. In these first few decades, there was already a rich discussion of some of the most vexing and important questions that had and would continue to plague rhetoric and speech.

This chapter begins with a study of how the breadth of speech gave scholars a wide focus in their teaching and scholarship. That breadth, combined with the shifts in the purposes of speech education, pushed teachers of speech toward a concern for educating the general citizenry. In large part, this was due to the perceived connection between education in speech and the capacity for every citizen to participate in democracy. However, the commitment to democracy and broad scope of the discipline also gave rise to more nationalistic service by speech teachers and scholars. This chapter continues with a documentation of how speech studies and training were deployed as military assets. The capacity for speech to be pressed into service in wartime leads into a discussion of the difficulties in the distinction between speech and force, a difference that has long been vital to ethical positions in the discipline. In an effort to resolve some of the increasingly complex ethical and political difficulties that speech education was encountering, the operation and education of moral character became a vital concern for the discipline.

The Breadth of Speech

If speech was a communication not only of the content of the speaker's mind (the idea or thought) but also of its health (the relation of reason to emotion), then any communication event in any context became important to the scholar of speech. If proximity and duration determined the communicability of reason or emotion in communication events, then those events that were most intimate and pervasive became most important. Consequently, the study of speech from a speech psychology perspective could not focus upon the rare moments of grand oratory but had to shift attention to questions of everyday communication of people living their lives. By 1934, it was not even terribly controversial for one to stand up at a convention, as John R. Nuttal Jr. did, and say that "speech should be considered a social art and should be developed for use in a wide variety of simple every day human relations."[3]

Even speech scholars who focused primarily on politics found that they could not sustain an overriding interest in events of platform oratory. J. Jeffery Auer, while conceding that nineteenth-century politics were dominated by "demonstrative oratory and formal debate," argued in 1939 that these modes of communication were not adequate for the politics of his day and could no longer be considered "the most effective bases for determining collective action."[4] In 1932, George Krapp had argued that "the day has gone by when public opinion in the United States can be determined from the platform."[5] The claim here was simple, straightforward, and imminently practical: formal public speaking was no longer the model for political deliberation, nor could it continue to serve as the means by which political positions would be won or lost.

This was not to argue that there was no longer any place for the study of or for training in public speaking. However, as Krapp noted, this was no longer the focal point of public politics or citizenship. Rather, he wrote, "its place is strictly in professional study as preparation for a special activity."[6] By professional study and special activity, Krapp was referring to those specific fields where the capacity to make a public speech might still be important to one's position or duties, such as the practice of law or running for political office. Speech scholars increasingly characterized the difference between the late nineteenth century and the early twentieth century as a movement from an era when citizenship and business demanded a capacity for public oratory to a time when public oratory was no longer relevant either to the practice of democratic citizenship or to most people's professions. Giles Gray argued that in most of the professions in which students of 1923 would work, public oratory "would be sadly out of place."[7] The status of public oratory was threatened enough that in 1935, J. Fred McGrew dedicated an entire paper to arguing that "the world is not tired of public speaking."[8] This contestation over the status of public speaking continued, though less vociferously, in later decades, even though undergraduate pedagogy at many universities took up formal speech-making as a central part of undergraduate education. Part of what is intriguing about the 1920s and 1930s was the widespread call for a shift in both scholarship and pedagogy away from oratory, putting the public speaking teachers on the defensive.

In place of public oratory, speech scholars began to place increasing emphasis upon the everyday practices of communicating. Krapp argued that even if one conceded to public oratory the "utmost degree of importance," one still had to recognize that "training for platform speaking must sink into insignificance in comparison with training in speech as part of the daily life of man, woman, and child."[9] Joseph F. Smith, D. Mack Easton, and Elwood Murray actually ranked the order of importance of speech contexts in the introduction to the 1935 Western Speech Association convention proceedings, placing conversation first, discussion second, public speaking third, and interpretation last.[10] It is worth emphasizing this order and the shared characteristics of the top two priorities. In both conversation and discussion, we see the valorization of local and personal communications in private, semiprivate, and business settings; in small groups and one-to-one meetings; and in family, friendship, and community. Likewise, there is a necessity of interplay, a multidirectional communication in conversation and discussion. On the other hand, in both public speaking and interpretation, the communication model is primarily in public settings, with large groups and audiences, where the primary model of communication behavior is unidirectional and the interplay between speaker and audience is subdued in favor of making the speaker the centralized point of attention and the primary source of information. This prioritization, then, was not merely a transformation of scholarly interests or pedagogical focus but reflected a change in the constitution of social relations and civic society that would value local interactions and multidirectional exchanges. Krapp, Gray, and others of their time were beginning to express something of what Lennox Grey in 1944 would say: "Communication is the basis of all human community—the basic factor in all education, in all human relations, in all national union, in world federation."[11] It was, then, a part of the progressive movement for transformation of civic life that dreamed of building union and federation through a more equitable and interactive model of political dialogue.

While it may be argued that Grey took a broader perspective than Krapp and Gray—embracing communication rather than simply speech—it is also important to recognize that, in their time, these speech scholars often did not make such a distinction. The idea that "speech" as an academic term referred to platform oratory in the first half of the twentieth century is at best anachronistic. In fact, Karl Robinson wrote that when speech scholars "refer to *speech*, we use the word in its generic sense and intend it to include those processes by which we express and communicate our ideas to other individuals and groups."[12] In 1939, James Winans noted that speech "includes everything involved in the utterance of meaningful sounds."[13] Smith, Easton, and Murray clarified that "by a speech situation is meant all the circumstances surrounding an occasion in which two or more persons have come together for fellowship, for clarification of thinking, for making a decision on a matter of policy, for carrying out a plan or adopted course of action, or for an impressive experience."[14] Herman Cohen has argued compellingly that if there was a split to be found in the type of communication to be included in the early speech discipline, it usually resided in the split of speech from English, assigning to the first all things related to the oral and to the latter all things related to the written. However, as Cohen noted, even this distinction was often muddled and crossed in the process of teaching and research.[15] The study of speech, by and large, operated as the broad study of communication in a wide variety of forms, including theater, radio, and interpersonal dialogue, as well as platform oratory.

While this breadth of thinking pervaded the academic study of speech from at least the 1930s forward, part of what speech scholars of the time saw as the unique change in the meaning of speech was a reprioritization of the modes of speech as political communication. What was emphasized by the shift from public oratory to everyday speech was a concern for the most banal and the most intimate of communication events. Marjorie Gullan wrote in 1941 that the focus of speech teachers and scholars must become "the daily interests as well as the daily speech. . . . We must link up their being articulate for the sake of a communicating of daily needs and the sharing of daily experiences."[16] In 1939, Richard Bietry had argued similarly that "the private speech, the everyday conversation in the ordinary life of the student, must become one of the points of principal emphasis."[17] While it may be tempting to leap from these kinds of comments into contemporary studies of interpersonal communication, one should be cautious about drawing too much similarity between the largely humanistic and civic-minded advocacy of studying private speech during this period and the later development of relational and familial studies that would blossom under the quantitative and laboratory research models of the later twentieth century.

The shift to the rhetoric of the everyday was not a move away from the importance of politics, but, as was suggested by Krapp and Gray, it followed political discourse from the realm of public oratory to the everyday speech of each individual. The work of the first half of the twentieth century turned to private speech because it understood this as a key site for political communication and civic relations. C. C. Trillingham wrote in 1939 that as speech education shifted away from formal speech activities and "toward the more informal types of self expression and social communication," it did so in an "attempt to serve democracy further."[18] Two years earlier, H. A. Wichelns had argued that speech education at the time focused on "the normal person" developing the "ability to communicate with others in the ordinary affairs of life." Such ordinary affairs were "understood to include civic and aesthetic interests as well as concerns of business."[19] In short, it maintained the strong connection between the psychotherapeutic discourses of mental hygiene and speech psychology and wedded these to the Deweyan political motivations toward participatory and democratic models for communication. The psychological and therapeutic models existed, first and foremost, to serve a civic function.

Bringing Speech to the Masses

In the transition from a focus on public oratory to the everyday speech of citizens, speech scholars likewise were shifting from a concern with a few elite public orators to a concern for each individual in his or her everyday life. Even speech scholars who maintained the centrality of public oratory noted the importance of an increasing concern with every individual in society. Halbert Greaves argued in 1938 that "the first obligation of a speech curriculum is to the every-day, practical needs of every student, through guidance in self-expression (chiefly public speaking)—not to the special artistic skills of the talented few."[20] In 1932, Krapp had characterized this shift as a move "away from technical and professional disciplines and towards a broad, general and elementary treatment which may be regarded as national in extent and character."[21] Wichelns referred to a move "from concern for the gifted few to concern for the many."[22] Of course, these kinds of shifts did not occur in the speech discipline alone or present themselves ex nihilo. As with the impetus toward a scientific articulation of its identity, the need for a certain degree of populism reflects a broad shift in the purpose and structure of higher education in America during this period. William Keith has thoroughly documented some of the connections between these transformations in early speech and American education, especially as they related to the rise of Deweyan models of democracy and education.[23]

These two joint movements—the shift from public oratory to everyday speech and the shift from the gifted few to the speech of every person—were inseparable from a diminution of the status and influence of the individual platform orator. Wichelns put it particularly well when he wrote that "interpretation of speech as communication among ordinary citizens prevents us from exaggerating the personal force or accomplishment of the speaker."[24] This may have been precisely the kind of "corrective balance" that was called for in the same year by Donald C. Bryant when he declared "the fault of the history of literature and oratory" to be "to let the study of figures obscure or blot out the study of forces and social movements."[25] It was in the movements of masses of people through coordinated conversations and networks of communication that Bryant saw the transformation of history and the possibility of political action. Such social movements and forces could not be found in the great orators and oratory. Rather, in a focus on the everyday event of speech, communication was oriented more toward informal discussions or dialogues than toward the monologues of the orator. One participant at the 1929 Eastern Public Speaking Conference stood and declared bluntly, "The time for the public speaker, a person whom we used to think of as a public speaker, has gone and the time for a man who can sit around a table and discuss has arrived."[26] This was not to say that there would never be need for a speech again but that these speeches were becoming less important to the deliberative function, no longer being the means by which people formed opinions, took up allegiances, or changed their views. Instead, those kinds of persuasion were found in properly conducted discussions.

A concern with proper modes of effective discussion and the distinction between dialogue and monologue had been present in the discipline since at least 1924. Joseph Mosher had explained that discussion was to be understood as "a communing of disinterested, non-argumentative minds" and that such communication "plays a considerable part in life. As employed in ordinary conversation it bulks large in the world's utterance."[27] While Gray, Grey, Krapp, and Wichelns had recognized a certain political necessity to the study of the everyday speech of the citizen, speech scholars interested in discussion and dialogue saw moral and social duties in their concerns. Angelo Pellegrini argued that "communication with other minds" was a true social value, while "there is no social value in demagoguery or in a piece of brilliant salesman-ship, or in any speaking for personal gain, because in such performance there is no true sharing."[28] Here the ethical claim is made quite explicit, and one can see a change in the way that good communication is structured around a sharing and communing that not only would take priority over oratory but would cast an ethical pall over all those modes of communication that sought to move others toward a preestablished conclusion.

This is not to say that between the 1920s and 1940s, monologic and ora-torical styles were not taught and advocated. Quite to the contrary, as Auer noted in 1939, most teachers of speech were concerned only with training students "in the field of formal debate, to the entire exclusion of consideration of contemporary patterns of public discussion."[29] In their 1935 assessment of the current state of the discipline, Smith, Easton, and Murray wrote, "In the social sciences, discussion techniques are largely ignored; in speech, the stress is still very much upon competition instead of cooperation, the central principle in discussion."[30] However, in roughly these three decades, there was a constant call in the scholarly literature to move away from the formal modes of adversarial debating and traditional public oratory. In laying claim to a mode of communication that would be called more socially responsible and more mentally healthy, proponents of discussion and dialogue argued, as James H. McBurney did, that formal debating and the logic often attached to it were "shackles which hinder the progress of thought."[31] In a more moder-ate tone, James N. Holm simply asserted that if the advocacy of the orator is necessary for a cause to be heard, then "discussion is equally necessary [so] that problems be solved and that information be made freely available."[32] Holm's belief in the importance of making information available through discussion was likewise reflected by Evelyn Konigsberg and her colleagues when they asserted that "group discussion" is superior for such purposes to any "lecture by an expert."[33] In short, whatever ground was retained by public oratory, it was made dubious and even a little dirty, a characterization it re-tained in differing forms throughout the twentieth century. Its virtues were transferred to other modes of communication, and its vices were attached to its core defining qualities of persuasion and monologue. Whatever vital functions speech-making could serve, discussion and conversation would claim to do better.

The need to disseminate information and develop effective means of discussion can easily be connected to the move from a concern for the grand orators to the everyday speech of the citizen. Auer wrote in 1939 that he hoped a progressive step was "the attempt to treat argumentation, discussion, and debate as tools of social inquiry and to synthesize them in a course which will better prepare our students to lead and participate in the contemporary patterns of public discussion."[34] It was such a "progressive" movement that led Konigsberg and her colleagues to hope that effective discussion would offer "a desirable, peaceful means of arriving at conclusions."[35] The hopes of Auer, Konigsberg, and others required that discussion take a radically different form from the modes of communication and politics for which they blamed many of the troubles of the second and third decades of the century. In Aristotle's *Topics*, McBurney found such a difference: the distinction between "discussion in the spirit of competition" and, here quoting Aristotle, "those who discuss things in the spirit of inquiry."[36] The former was left to the debaters and political speakers clinging to the old models, while the latter would be assigned to the new models of communication grounded in the scientific ethos and conversation.

Discussion could thus obtain a stronger foothold in the grounds of reason than could those modes of communication with which it was contrasted. While conceding the more formal logical rules to the debate method, speech scholars situated discussion as more properly dialectical and more properly designed to maximize the human capacity for thought and decision-making. Yet, even in the social and ethical justification of discussion, scholars drew heavily upon their faith in science. Echoing the works of John Dewey, McBurney expressed a faith that in discussion, we could "procure for group deliberation that co-operative tendency toward consensus which marks inquiry in the sciences." McBurney compared the discussion method to scientific method, hoping that discussion would secure a "consensus in the formulation of what has been called *evaluational judgments of fact*, and in the determination of *generalized conceptions as to what should be done*."[37] It is not merely the case that the advocacy of scientific thinking was similar to that which Dewey also advocated. Archival research conducted by Keith has provided strong evidence that the early advocates of discussion theory were likely directly connected to Dewey and his students by university affiliations and association with political and social organizations.[38]

As a cousin to scientific inquiry, discussion could not be a loose and free-flowing process. If it was to make the claims to reason and dialectic that would ground its legitimacy, it had to be fitted out with certain rules and structures. McBurney wrote that the most important problem for proponents of discussion was "the development and clarification of the logical principles upon which it proceeds."[39] The first of these would return to a standard principle for speech scholars: truth. Murray wrote that "the essential element is the meeting of minds on the basis of truth."[40] Truth, of course, requires that speakers express themselves truly and thus likewise entails the burden of honesty but also a commitment to the discovery of what might be best known as the truth by being open to the exchange of arguments without being unwaveringly committed to a particular position or outcome. Honesty and truth, then, were commitments that required speakers to approach each other as disinterested in any specific outcome and as deeply interested in finding that outcome that could lay claim to the greatest truth value.

As such, proponents claimed that reciprocity between interlocutors was essential to proper discussion. Emery W. Balduf argued for "a workable two-way flow of ideas and opinions."[41] Konigsberg and her colleagues maintained that "group discussion, properly conducted, should serve to train students in respect and tolerance for the opinion of others."[42] In contrast to the model of the orator unloading his or her mind into the mind of an audience, discussion proponents asserted a reciprocal agency for audience and auditor while shifting their roles as the discussion ran its course. Balduf wrote that it is the mutual and reciprocal participation in discussion that allows each person to "figure things out" for himself or herself. Such discussion, he continued, allows one to reach "a point of personal conviction that is far more conducive to intelligent voluntary action than the sometimes fleeting auditory impressions given him by a speaker in direct address."[43] Note that the outcome for Balduf is not only the better truth of the matter but that a truth arrived at through these means is more politically functional; it better enables those who reach it to act voluntarily on the basis of that truth than do those opinions they might form after listening to a rousing orator.

Here we see how connecting the basis of truth to reciprocity allowed the political practicality of discussion to be grounded not only in following politics into the realm of everyday conversation but in the assertion that the free dissemination of information and open, reciprocal exchange of ideas were synonymous with modes of democratic deliberation. Auer even contended that free public discussion is "perhaps the only form of force which distinguishes democracy from dictatorship."[44] Konigsberg and her colleagues likewise claimed that it was largely through discussion "that people learn to live together in the democratic way of life," and Milton Dickens argued that "democracy requires that the thinking of the individuals become reciprocal."[45] The reason why discussion is important, the real value of truth, and the vitality of reciprocal exchange was grounded in the value of democratic participation and life. Discussion and even the science upon which it was grounded were good and necessary because of their political capacities and ethical qualities.

While this faith in discussion as a superior form of communication and decision-making was clearly tied to a faith in democracy as a form of government, discussion could not be a willy-nilly free-for-all. It still relied heavily upon rules—certain principles of reasoning—that would help it to yield the proper results. A significant number of the rules of proper discussion were based on a clear distinction between reason and emotion while holding reason above the emotions. Discussion had to be reasoned, without undue emotional attachment or investment, if it was to produce the results it promised. F. W. Lambertson articulated the position well: "In a democracy one of our gravest dangers is that the average citizen shall not think. If he is controlled by his prejudices and urged by the lunatic fringe of the populace and by the demagogue, we are in a bad way. Co-operative problem-solving is the hope of our nation, not the dogmatic utterances of a dictator. Therefore, to the extent that any speaker robs his listeners of their critical faculties, he is undermining the foundation stones of democracy—critical and discriminative thinking."[46] Similarly, Earl W. Wiley connected the cooperative mode of discussion to the governance of reason, arguing that "democratic utterance originates at the point where, on the basis of reason, the man speaking relaxes his egoism in deference to public purposes." Such purposes, Wiley continued, relied upon understanding that the "primary function of speech is to make co-operation respectable."[47] Cooperation, speech, and discussion relied in significant part on a basis of reason—a grounding in rational rules and principles—that was also connected to a faith in scientific inquiry.

If reason and science grounded proper methods of discussion, speech, and cooperation while mental health inspired its ethical legitimacy, then it was the faith in democracy that gave these forms of communication their political and societal imperative. Not only was discussion the expression of democratic principles and the proper method of democratic deliberation, but, as Earl Kalp wrote, discussion was supposed to help bring about "true democracy." By true democracy, Kalp meant "the active participation of every individual up to the limit of his capacity in the conduct of all his affairs."[48] Dickens extolled the virtue of representative democracy and its "recognition of the indispensable function of group discussion in the democratic process." By placing democracy and discussion so close together, proponents of discussion and dialogue would likewise argue that propaganda and monologue were inappropriate in democratic societies. As Dickens wrote, "The characteristic role for individuals in a democracy is participation; in a dictatorship, obedience. The chief technique for securing participation is group discussion; that for securing obedience is propaganda."[49] Note how Dickens positioned two polarized modes of communication, given each side emotional charges, and left open for persuasive platform speaking really only a status of propaganda for securing obedience. While hyperbolic, this stark oppositional view produces a sharp depiction of what was at stake in discussion theory.

Given these depictions, it is certainly no surprise that the rising emphasis on discussion was not universally embraced. In fact, it met with significant opposition from many speech teachers. While the publication of pieces opposed to the discussion perspective diminished substantially in the 1930s and 1940s, Mosher's 1924 article stands out for its polemical rejection of discussion and dialogue. Mosher argued three points that essentially represent the major position of speech scholars who opposed discussion and dialogue. First, Mosher asserted that some issues are simply "bilateral" and that only a very small, elite group of people might be able to argue those positions in a disinterested manner essential to reciprocal discussion.[50] That is to say, on topics such as labor relations or United States involvement in war, most people would be too emotional or too personally invested in the issue to engage in proper discussion. Second, dialectical opposition of two positions in a contested debate was the only proper route to the "ultimate truth" of any policy proposition. Thus, the "yes or no attitude" is essential to deciding issues of public policy.[51] Similar to the defense of the American trial courts, Mosher's position was that in policy deliberations, the debate contest was an essential test of the truth of the competing positions. Finally, Mosher argued that only in a "world of universal culture, unanimity of view, and perfect altruism" would it be possible for discussion to achieve the status that its proponents expected.[52] While likely overstating his position, Mosher was contending that the goal discussion advocates sought in social relations would have to exist first before discussion would work, whereas the advocates of discussion saw it as a means of reaching a more broadly shared culture and viewpoint.

Speech as Training for Democracy

However, what Mosher and the discussion advocates agreed upon without question was the belief that good speech was duty-bound to serve democracy. Democracy (and by this was meant the United States of America's form of government) was inseparable from the social values and normative psychological standards to which students should be adjusted in their speech training. It was an essential function of all education, and most certainly of speech education, to train students in proper democratic participation.

Murray wrote that the end product of education ought to be a "citizen who is a well-adjusted, critically minded cooperator."[53] The Virginia Plan for Secondary Education noted that "American secondary education has its orientation in the ideals of democracy."[54] W. H. MacKellar wrote that schools and colleges could only justify their existence and financing insofar as they served as "centers, from which are going forth armies of men and women to oppose all the cults of wrong."[55] The explicit connection between the expanding educational system and the enculturation of citizens into the American democratic model was common in the discourse of this era, but speech teachers and scholars were finding a specific and powerful connection between their discipline and these objectives.

The equivocation of democracy and the American system of government and the connection between democracy and speech enabled speech education to claim a certain indoctrination into the political and social values of American government. Trillingham argued that speech education must serve every student because "all citizens are expected to participate intelligently in the affairs of a democracy." This education, for Trillingham, was essential so that the American citizen might "merit freedom of speech"—that is to say, might be sufficiently prepared to contribute to democratic deliberative processes.[56] John D. Hansen likewise maintained that training and experience in speech would serve students well "when they are called upon later to perform important duties of citizenship in a democracy."[57] Thus, a political belief in democracy grounded not only discussion but speech training in general. Interestingly, these beliefs also presume that one must be taught how to be a proper citizen. Students, to be worthy of participation in American democracy, had to learn the right ways to speak, listen, and think so that they could then serve that democracy effectively.

This celebration of democracy in the 1930s and 1940s gave further credence to the discussion advocates' claims for cooperative modes of deliberation, reinforced the mental hygiene standards, and further undermined the position of traditional platform oratory. The priority of listening in the democratic system served as a fulcrum point for these positions. Holm argued not only that it was the important skill of self-expression that gave freedom of speech and democracy their significance, but it was equally dependent upon the inclination and ability of every individual to listen to others.[58] After all, for discussion to occur, there had to be an interplay and sharing between the disinterested discussants, which required that they listen to one another. Trillingham likewise wrote that the obligation of speech teachers was not simply to produce good speakers—those who could skillfully and articulately express themselves—but also, if speech teachers wished to perpetuate and improve democratic life, to ensure "that those who are on the receiving end of speech activities are intelligent listeners."[59] Students would need to be mindful and critical in their reception of messages so as to contribute to the conversations and discussions that they may encounter.

With listening given its due, the value of the full sharing of information, and the promotion of the primacy of reason, one could ground a faith that democracies produce optimal decisions. The faith that the full sharing of information produces the best decisions was expressed best by James Innes in 1945: "If the common people know the facts, we can trust the judgment of the common people to stand by the right principle."[60] Connecting proper decision-making and understanding of information to the ethical and psychological standards of honesty and reason was a long-standing tradition in speech studies. Charles Woolbert had made it a central feature of his ethic of public address in 1914, writing, "Honesty plus the vision to trust the force of truth inevitably overcomes trickery and slippery methods."[61] Thus, the sharing of information and the honesty of that sharing again returned to the priority of truth as a key component of ethical and politically responsible speech. The extraordinary power of this point of view is its capacity to adapt and interpret every event to support its faith. All failures were sufficient proof of their own poor practices, while every success could be ascribed either to good practices or to the fortunate grace of a proper outcome even in light of erroneous communication. Every historical instance could be taken as an example of the importance of teaching and following the principles of honesty and truth.

This desire to train students to become responsible participants in the American democratic process likewise reflected both a faith in American governmental systems and a perception that a certain crisis of faith or legitimacy was threatening those systems. Carrie E. Church expressed this fear well in her 1934 presentation at the Western Association of Teachers of Speech Convention: "America is facing a crisis. The future may be intelligently democratic or arbitrarily fascist. Either we train good leaders or we accept bad ones."[62] Alfred Westfall wrote in 1943 that "too many young people have grown up with no faith, or too little faith, in the American form of government. Our task is to give them an understanding of democracy and an abiding faith in the democratic way of life."[63] This was not quite the same thing as the nearly incessant cry of the decline of morals among the youth, repeated ad nauseam from ancient times onward, but rather was an expression of a real challenge to the American political and economic systems during the 1920s and 1930s. As Keith has noted, many people in the twenty-first century have forgotten that in the 1920s and 1930s, there were many options besides American-style democracy that were actively in play, even here in the United States.[64] Communism, fascism, anarchism, and other structures of economic and political life were all still contesting the future of the nation. Teachers of speech took a definitive side as allies of American democratic government, understood to require broad participation of the citizenry, and expressed a strong faith in that government to be able to better the lives of all its citizens.

Part of this faith was a belief that democracy, as Trillingham put it, "contains within its own ideology and within its own machinery the opportunities and means for its own improvement. It encourages change. It promotes the quest for truth."[65] From such a faith in democracy, one could also establish certain principles that would both distinguish the form of government from others and identify the proper modes of communication in a democratic society. A. F. Wilenden outlined three basic assumptions required by faith in democracy: "First, that all folks either are or can be interested in really studying the problems that confront them; second, that if average folks are provided the facts on all sides of a case and are given free and ample opportunity to study and discuss them, we can trust their decisions; and third, that in arriving at public policies we prefer the slow and often painful educational method rather than the quicker executive action."[66] From this faith in American democratic governance, speech scholars articulated a variety of differences between democracy and its nemesis, dictatorship. Kenneth G. Hance praised democracy for permitting speechmaking by citizens even when the nation was at war. It was, for Hance, particularly noteworthy that in a democracy, "all of us are talking—not a few actual or self-styled leaders or a body of propagandists."[67] Propaganda was separated from speech and allied with dictatorship. Dickens wrote that propaganda was "the most important single measure of the efficiency of a dictatorship." In no small part, this was because Dickens held that dictators relied upon their ability to secure "obedience to policies which would ordinarily be unpopular."[68] Thus, the key defining factor of democracies was that everyone could speak; contrary and opposing voices were given their space. The definition of propaganda and dictatorship was that it could not permit the expression of contrasting positions. So, in Dickens's view, the defining quality of despotic and nefarious societies is their intolerance for unpopular views. This is not merely the idea of government control and restriction but, more important, the fact that a democratic society listens to a wide range of voices, whereas non-democratic societies hear only the voice of the propagandists.

In Dickens's description, it is obvious that speech could thrive only in democratic settings. Earnest Brandenburg, in his article on Roman orator and teacher Quintilian, wrote that "eloquence flourishes only in democratic surroundings." Brandenburg continued his argument by claiming that "every orator of sufficient prominence to be considered in the area of statecraft has been a champion of democracy."[69] Perhaps, in part, such claims could be made without substantial controversy because the standards for prominent oratory were already infused with democratic ideals. Trillingham explicitly argued that "in a democracy, all avenues of communication should likewise serve to perpetuate and improve democracy."[70] So, only communication that improves and perpetuates democracy was worthy or good communication; thus, it is quite easy to discard any communication outside of democracy as incapable of being healthy or ethical.

In this way, the function of speech in a democracy paralleled the scientific and psychotherapeutic models advanced by the mental hygienists. Murray made the connection explicit in 1938 when he wrote that "speech has a threefold function: (1) it must facilitate warm, friendly relations, (2) it must result in clear understanding, meeting of minds, and cooperation, and (3) this meeting of minds must, as near as possible, be on the basis of a content of scientific fact. This functioning of speech is the foundation for progress in democracy."[71] Democracy, mental hygiene, and scientific method all required a form of speech and argument that did not involve the loading of minds or the domination of the audience but, as Auer put it, the presentation of an idea "so that audience may make rational judgments as to its validity and desirability."[72] The importance and pervasiveness of this connection was well expressed by the stated theme and purpose of the second annual convention of the Western Association of Teachers of Speech in 1930. The convention program listed the theme as "A Program of Speech Education in a Democracy," while the stated purpose for the conference, printed immediately below the theme, was "The Fullest Development of the Speaking Personality."[73] This was the meaning given to speech that might distinguish it from the act of propaganda. It was thus that the model of the big-game hunter would become antithetical to the study of speech and the marked dominance that some found effective in speakers would be labeled a deficiency in character and in mind. Speech was regarded, as MacKellar put it, as "the crowning achievement of the human mind and the cementing principle of civilization."[74] The ability to engage in the healthy, proper, democratic, ethical practice of communication—that which would set itself apart from propaganda—would require an entire disposition and style of communicating, a self-discipline and a governing logic that would engage reciprocally with interlocutors. Such a method of communication not only would express democratic values and mental health but would likewise promote both. As

Lester L. Hale argued in 1948, democratic freedom is only possible for "those who seek for it in the expressions of his total person, in his services and in his habits of life."[75]

This convergence of methods and perspectives reflected an impulse toward generating a system of ethical standards or rules for communication. This was a movement toward a view of how communication ought ideally to be undertaken and in what modes one ought properly to engage in the daily practice of living one's life as a communicating being. Such a convergence was dependent upon linking together views ranging from the psychology of mental hygiene to the political faith of early-twentieth-century proponents of American democracy. However, the proponents of democracy held that speech could serve another purpose for the American government, a purpose that would conflict with these ideals and ethics: speech would play a part in war.

Speech as Military Strategy

During both World War I and World War II, speech teachers claimed that speech education and the practice of speech-making could play critical roles in American victory. B. C. Van Wye claimed that "the work of the teacher of speech is eminently essential in the great task of winning the war. . . . It offers extraordinary opportunities for genuine patriotic service."[76] Such services ranged from the analyses of Axis power war rhetoric by the U.S. government during World War II, to the importance of speech to soldiers (especially officers) in both world wars, to the speeches made at home in support of the war effort and the soldiers' service.[77] In 1940, the interest in such projects was reflected by the large number of conference panels on speech in wartime and on speech as a component of national defense, as can be seen just by perusing the conference program of the Western Association of Teachers of Speech that year.[78] While the broad clamor over the possibilities actually diminished after 1942, the war did serve throughout the early 1940s as a central focus for a significant portion of American teachers of speech.

For example, in 1943, William Norwood Brigance and Ray Keeslar Immel published a textbook specifically designed for training military officers in public speaking and speech. By that date, Brigance had already been teaching a course in speech for officer candidates for some years and had consulted on speech training for both the army and the navy. Brigance and Immel laid out their case for the importance of speech training for military officers in the first few pages of that text: "The ability to speak effectively is essential to personal military leadership. Men do not respect officers who speak in a weak, apathetic manner."[79] This valuation of speech training for military service was not one-sided. The military likewise reflected this concern with communication training, as Brigance's consultation and his and Immel's text demonstrate. Even more telling is that the military drafted a few speech teachers into active duty specifically to make them serve as teachers of speech for the officers. Glenn R. Capp resigned his position in the southern region's speech association in 1942 because he was drafted "without any application" in order to serve "as an instructor in public speaking to Army officers."[80]

For some speech scholars and teachers, no draft was required. They eagerly sought out ways to aid war efforts and encouraged their colleagues to do likewise. Balduf listed three of the ways that speech teachers and students might most directly involve their skills in the war effort: reach people with war information, train volunteer speakers, and keep the community in high spirits.[81] These tasks found the greatest application during World War I and reflect the difficulty in distinguishing between democratic speech and propaganda. Merry quoted the U.S. Director of the Speaking Division of the Committee on Public Information in 1918 as calling upon the "National Association of Public Speaking Teachers" to attain "that universal education absolutely necessary for the winning of the war, for in a democracy fullness of information and intelligent participation by each citizen is essential and this can be effectively secured only through the spoken word."[82] What is most interesting is that "fullness of information" meant the effective expression of the government's position on the war. Van Wye called directly for "speakers who can interest and enlighten, speakers who can put before audiences the wishes of the Government in a brief and appealing way."[83] Franklin H. Knower, in asserting the role of speech departments in World War II, claimed that it was "training in the presentation of the propaganda or morale-building message—spoken, read, or acted" that uniquely qualified speech teachers and students to assist the war effort.[84] In contrast to the discourses of listening and discussion and the valorization of open dissent in democracy, here we see the prioritization of government positions being put forward and people being moved to the task of supporting the war, not engaged in critically minded discussions of it.

Perhaps the most concrete and organized example of these practices came during World War I when the American government, with the cooperation of teachers and departments of speech, organized a program called the Four-Minute Men. As Merry explained it, this organization was composed of men who would speak for four minutes or less in movie theaters before each showing, "carrying the gospel of patriotism." These speakers would receive topics and facts bimonthly from the nation's capital, from which they would then assemble a short speech.[85] In cities such as Cincinnati, a teacher of speech would be one of the members of a committee that would hear the would-be speakers who volunteered for the program and ensure that they were of high enough quality to perform the duty.[86] In 1918, over twenty thousand men were enrolled in the program, delivering the message of the national government in movie houses across the country.[87] Democracy required its propagandists to put forward the government's position.

While the belief that speech could aid the war effort was again advanced by many speech scholars during World War II, there also was a group of articles that began to challenge both the propriety and the effectiveness of speech-making on behalf of the government. First, there was the extension of the mental hygiene argument that wars, strikes, and social unrest were caused by mental maladjustments and poor communication. Grey argued that World War II was due, at least in significant part, "to the failure of communication among some peoples."[88] Likewise, the "fullness of information" would take on a different significance as scholars such as Hansen argued that the duty of speech teachers and students was not only to repeat the government position but to "obtain and impart information not readily gained by the general public through the daily news, to keep critical issues continually before them, and to ensure a sturdy morale by protecting people from the warping effects of misinformation and propaganda."[89] The distinction between speech and propaganda would legitimize the infusion of information not commonly available, and such an infusion would occur under the name of democracy, allying it with the war effort at its base.

The more complex model of democratic discussion and deliberation represented by Hansen's position was also reflected in Everett Hunt's claim that there could be no grand oratory on American involvement in World War II. In part, this was because the war was seen as "the result of a series of selfish, stupid, preventable mistakes, with justice and injustice so inextricably intertwined" that any "lofty pretensions" would only be met with suspicion. Hunt argued that in 1943, most of the sources of grand war oratory were simply not persuasive. Among those he listed as being dubious were "boasting, heroism, the hills of home, a holy cause, joy in the destruction of the enemy, and, in a softened civilization, even the sweetness of dying for the fatherland."[90] What Hunt was describing was a relatively common dissatisfaction with the extension of the American involvement in the war onto continental European soil. It was not for many years to come that a broad consensus would form in America on World War II. Thus, for Hunt, the war lacked the kind of central values or issues that could be used by propagandists to rally the American public behind the cause, which he believed had occurred during World War I. Whether or not his assessment speaks well of him or his age, it does help to demonstrate a shift in the thinking about the propriety and function of governmental communication campaigns surrounding war efforts between the earliest decades of the twentieth century and the 1940s. That change was also connected to changes within the discipline of speech and its attitudes toward persuasion and discussion.

Speech and Force

Part of what was playing out in Hansen's and Hunt's claims about World War II was the difficulty that speech scholars had in distinguishing reasoned discourse from force. Mental hygienists and democratists had held speech and especially discussion above propaganda and threat because speech and discussion could more properly engage the reasoning capacities of the interlocutors and allow each individual to make up his or her own mind on a subject. Trillingham expressed this view when he wrote that language "gives men the means to substitute intelligence for force."[91] Communication offered the promise of transcending conflict-oriented politics and social organization while offering the hope of democratically "getting along." Claude E. Kantner even laid the responsibility for developing such communication processes squarely upon the teachers of speech.[92]

However, it was also the case that conflict and force were implicit in the practice and training of speech. In his study of effective public speakers, Clyde W. Dow noted, as others had before him, that while mental health asserted that one ought to be neither markedly submissive nor markedly dominant, the best public speakers were markedly dominant. Dow observed that though this may make people difficult to live with, enhancing the dominance of our students will also enhance their efficacy as public speakers: "It probably would not be very pleasant to live with a definitely ascendant person, but the indications are that this ascendant person is likely to be a good public speaker. It seems reasonable to suggest, then, that in our attempts to train young men and women to become effective public speakers we should try to develop in them this trait of ascendance or dominance."[93]

Additionally, some speech teachers, such as Angelo Pellegrini, threatened that if ever a student should engage in inappropriate speech practices such as charlatanism, the teacher would "rise and tongue-whip him into the dust."[94] These practices made dubious the distinction between speech and force, advocating both that forcefulness and dominance were traits essential to effective oratory and that force and threats were appropriate methods of speech. Recall R. L. Irwin's statement that those with speech or mental defects might best be cured by telling them that they should slow down and speak up if they know what is good for them.[95]

The distinction between democratic discussion and force was perhaps most thoroughly critiqued by William E. Utterback in his 1940 study of the appeals to force that underlie democratic discussion. Utterback noted that while citizens might "possess a body of truth which can be employed as the basis of political decision" and that "unfettered public discussion is a part of the democratic philosophy of government," these truths and the outcomes of these discussions rest largely on force. He agreed that democratic discussion relied upon certain "political truths" that were regarded by the interlocutors as having "universal and permanent validity," but Utterback's examination of these political truths found that "most, if not all of them, appear to have originated as formulae for the adjustment of group conflicts. . . . The terms of the compromise were dictated by the balance of power between the two groups." The truth of these political principles was thus neither universal nor permanent but rather could be maintained only so long as "that balance of group power which generated it remains substantially unaltered." Thus, when discussants rely upon a shared political truth as a premise to their argument, "its ultimate reference is to force." Government by debate and by conference would thus both hold force as "the ultimate determinant of legislative action."[96] The order of speakers, the burden of proof, the status of presumption, the acceptable and unacceptable forms of evidence, the value of certain practices or norms of communication, and even the prioritization of certain social goods were all built up over time through contestations involving power relations and were dependent upon power for their maintenance or possible alteration.

Despite such critiques, the distinctions between speech and propaganda and between speech and force were essential to how speech scholars legitimized not only their own discipline but also American politics, especially during World War II. While probably no single orator has gained as much attention or extended study as has Adolf Hitler, it was largely after World War II that such writings really began. During the war, comparatively little on Hitler was published in speech journals. Of note, however, is Lambertson's 1942 essay, which grappled with the fundamental problem that would obsess speech teachers for decades to come: how could someone whom speech scholars believed to be so thoroughly evil and lacking in any proper mental health, moral character, or respect for democracy be such a profoundly effective speaker? While in more recent years some have tried to solve this problem by asserting that Hitler was in fact not an effective speaker, Lambertson immediately argued that the opposite was true. He quoted a variety of sources to establish that Hitler was, in fact, one of the most effective orators of the first half of the twentieth century.[97] The question was, what could explain this phenomenon?

Given the dominance of the social scientific and psychological perspectives in speech scholarship of the 1930s and 1940s, it should be of little surprise that Lambertson turned to social psychology to explain Hitler's ability. In keeping with the mental hygiene perspective and with the proponents of discussion, Lambertson asserted that Hitler used excessive emotional appeal rather than reason to move his audiences. He wrote that Hitler's belief was that "to reason with people was futile and absurd, but to make them feel deeply concerning his ideas was to gain action." Hitler, according to Lambertson, also tried to "stimulate the emotions" in the early part of his speeches because emotional responses tended to make the audience "more credulous, suggestible, and non-critical." Similarly, he criticized Hitler for playing upon the "hopes and fears and hates of his listeners." The idea of a speaker dominating the audience was likewise part of Hitler's appeal. Lambertson claimed that this idea was essential to any speaker, but because Hitler was especially skilled at dominating his audience, he wielded the "greater power." This combination of emotional suggestion and domination of the audience was described by Lambertson as Hitler's ability "to place both himself and them in a hypnotic state."[98] Here, emotion is not only opposed to reasoning but opposed to will, choice, and voluntary actions, with emotional motivation equated with hypnosis.

In sum, Lambertson concluded that three factors primarily determined Hitler's success as an orator: "1) his ability to make men mob-minded, 2) his intuitive grasp of the hopes and fears of the audience, and 3) his fanatical sincerity." Hitler's rhetorical power, then, could be separated from rhetoric and speech under the democratist and mental hygiene models and could be set in opposition to any argument grounded in good character or sound reasoning. The problem, of course, is that Hitler's persuasive strategies, decried as foul by most speech scholars of the period, were highly effective. Hence, in the midst of examining the techniques of one of the most persuasive orators of his age, Lambertson took a moment to pause and ask whether a speaker could be "ethically justified" in using Hitler's techniques. The ethical question arose, at least in part, in response to this dilemma: while certainly highly persuasive to his target audience, Hitler did not fit the normative standards for mental health, he favored the emotions over reason, and he espoused no faith in democratic governance. To explain this, his effect had to be attributed not to his abilities as a platform speaker but to his grasp of "crowd psychology" and his ability to strip people of their proper reasoning faculties by seducing them into a "hypnotic state."[99] His ascendancy and capacity to move people were themselves transformed from merely ethically dubious qualities of successful speakers into the eradication of choice and agency in his audience. In Hitler was found the worst possible kind of speech: a drug that could rob the listener of his or her very capacity to think and choose.

Alternatively, when similar methods were used by Winston Churchill or Franklin Roosevelt, these speakers were praised as skilled orators. Joseph W. Miller, in his 1942 study of Winston Churchill, wrote that his skilled speech displayed "vigor, imagery, turbulent driving rhythms, and potential sweep" that suggested "Milton, Burke, and Macaulay." His ability to use emotion was thus characterized as "skilled speaking" or referred to as "amplification" and praised as reflecting Cicero's theory of oratory. Churchill was said to "mingle proof with emotion; the effective desires he uses vary with the circumstances, but he appeals chiefly to self-preservation, patriotism, love of God, fair play, justice, common sense, and duty." He was praised for adapting his speeches well to his audiences and held a reputation for "enchanting his listeners." Regardless of the similarities between the praise for Churchill's methods and the condemnation of Hitler's oratory, Miller not only did not question the ethics of Churchill's methods but advanced the view that Churchill's speaking was an "ethical proof." Miller wrote that "Churchill invests his speeches with an ethical proof unsurpassed by any other Englishman who might aspire to be Prime Minister. Each occasion for a speech imbues the utterance with implications crucial to the Democratic world."[100] This is not to say that Hitler's oratorical style and Churchill's were identical but rather to point out that in those cases in which emotional appeals could be seen as benefiting contemporary democratic governments, particularly in the Allied war effort, these emotional appeals could be praised even while also referring to them as "enchanting" the audience. It was not, then, merely the issue of emotions per se that seemed to tilt the critics of public address one way or another but the underlying ethical and political practices of the speaker.

Harold P. Zelko made a similar analysis that same year of Roosevelt's speaking style, expressing no hint of a concern for the ethics of his methods and also praising highly his capacity to move audiences to rally behind the democratic cause. Zelko applauded Roosevelt's "splendid vocal quality" and "rare charm" while attributing both to his "rare rhythm that is attained in the structural development of sentences and ideas throughout the speech."[101] Roosevelt was commended neither for his capacity to marshal reasoned argument for his cause nor for engaging in a democratic discussion with his audience. Instead, his methods were appreciated for many of the same qualities that brought praise to Churchill and condemnation to Hitler. If Roosevelt was able to lift the nation up and inspire its citizens to great acts, it was in many ways by virtue of tapping emotional motivations through rhetorical strategies, charming them and rallying them, not by convincing and reasoning. This is the Hitler problem for rhetoric and persuasion: that those strategies for persuasion condemned in Hitler's oratory are simply extreme versions of those more mundane strategies generally found to be at the core of effective persuasion. Lambertson hit squarely upon the Hitler problem when he tried to answer the question of whether a speaker could be ethically justified in using Hitler's techniques; he wrote, "Every good speaker does—to a degree."[102] This conclusion, however, could not be widely affirmed for speech training to lay claim to proper mental adjustment and social well-being. Instead, clear divisions and safeguards would need to be placed between the rhetoric of the demagogue and good speech.

Speech Education and Moral Character

The belief that eloquence required proper mental health, sound democratic beliefs, and a certain moral character would not yield to the persuasiveness of Hitler but instead was rallied into a kind of hyperactivity by events that challenged its veracity and functionality. Brandenburg noted the prevalence of this position when he wrote that "writers of textbooks in Speech, when they comment on the subject, seem agreed that the liar, the cheat, the blackmailer, the fraud, cannot be acknowledged a great orator. The highest excellence in public speaking is not a specialized skill which a person can acquire and use, regardless of his moral character."[103] Just as the mental hygienists had envisioned speech as an outward expression of mental health, so too did many American teachers of speech, at least since the turn of the century, consider that true eloquence was inseparable from "a high and noble attitude of mind," "lofty truth," and "unselfish service."[104] As Mabel Platz had put it in her 1935 history of speech education, "Those speakers have reached the greatest recognition and wielded the most influence who have had sincerity of purpose and a high moral quality."[105] Speech would, eventually, reveal the speaker's true qualities, and the audience would see the soul or psyche of the speaker, beyond any flourish or skill. This was by no means a new idea. In 1902, J. Berg Esenwein had written that "modesty, sincerity, naturalness, earnestness, and all other personal characteristics as revealed in style, cannot be taught by rhetoricians, but must be the outward expression of an inward character."[106] It was only with the proper preparation of character, what Lyman Abbot in 1918 called "moral preparation," that one was supposed to become "an effective speaker."[107] At the beginning of the twentieth century, we see this focus on character and moral training as prerequisite to effective speech. By the mid-1930s, these terms had been redefined into mental health standards but still retained much of the same content: "sincerity, humility, and confidence."[108] The earlier educators for moral character and the later educators for mental health had similar ideas about the general values and dispositions that such education would instill.

However, unlike the mental health that the teacher/therapist might offer, the cultivation of moral character was considered to be not a skill taught by a teacher but something that one would cultivate as "the work of a life."[109] Nonetheless, speech training had a vital part to play in the development of character. The general qualities espoused by those speech scholars and teachers who focused on moral character in communication resonate with the mental hygiene standards, bearing a strong substantive similarity but holding a very different tone in their consideration of morals and spirits instead of health and minds. MacKellar considered the ideal effect of education to be a "growth of the soul."[110] Robinson wrote that the fundamental aims in the discipline of speech included "the development of integrity, sincerity, friendliness, a sense of humor, courtesy, and tact, all of which are so essential to success in speaking situations."[111] The American Council on Education even stated that training in "the seeking of information" and "discussion in its various forms" was intended to "serve the formation of stable morals in all citizens."[112] Thus, speech education under the moral character model did not bear so much the mark of science and health but an earlier ethos of morality and integrity. Education was about personal standards of conduct grounded in moral traditions that had not yet found their justification in a scientific discourse. As Kantner wrote, the most important goal for speech teachers was to promote the student's development of "a sense of social responsibility that will lead to high standards of sincerity of purpose and honesty in speech."[113] This was a tradition more grounded in the humanities, in the study of the "great works" of literature and oratory as paradigmatic examples from which one should draw moral lessons. In 1914, Woolbert explicitly connected these questions of ethics to the study of literature when he wrote, "The ethics of speech has been a subject that has interested men since the beginning of literature, and every text book dealing with speech methods has its say as to what is proper and what is not in public address."[114] Thus, while we certainly can say that during the first part of the twentieth century, many of the substantive standards for what made good speech remained relatively constant, the grounds for those standards shifted significantly from an education in literature and the humanities for the purpose of moral character to an education that would instill scientific principles of good thought into students so that they might more effectively adjust to healthy, hygienic, and proper mental habits.

Yet, despite all such avowed concern and the constant prodding of the previous four decades of mental hygienists, democratists, and moralists, in 1946 Carroll Brooks Ellis argued that too little attention had been paid to "the moral and ethical responsibilities of the speaker."[115] Two years later, Robert D. Clark blamed this perceived failing on speech scholars' paying "too close attention to the science of speech," thus producing a "partial view" of the discipline that was focused upon "the most easily measured aspects." Clark asserted that speech scholarship and education were obsessed with how one might most effectively persuade and hence were focused solely upon "the means of achieving it; and having omitted the social content in the statement of the goal, we ignore it also in the treatment of means."[116] Earl W. Wells had similarly complained that "many in our profession complacently dismiss these problems with the smug assertion that their business is not to 'preach,' to philosophize, or to moralize to their students, but to teach them *how to speak*."[117] Yet, it was the scientific concepts of the speech psychologists and the mental hygienists that served as the basis and justification of the communication ethics that Ellis and Clark put forward. In his explication of the ethical principles that he attributes to Quintilian, Ellis repeatedly draws upon and references the mental hygiene literature to legitimize those ethical principles. Ellis wrote that "a speaker is approaching Quintilian's definition when his conclusions come as a result of observation, study, and scrupulous objective thinking."[118] These are terms and values far more closely allied to the mental hygienists than to Quintilian, but with a slight bit of interpretive finesse, the ancients could be justified by making their thought reflect the dominant ethical systems of 1930s and 1940s mental hygienists.

Thus, whether starting from the ancients or from early-twentieth-century social sciences, the development of the explicit study of the ethics of speech turned to mental hygiene and social psychology for the structures of proper ethical and moral character. To be well adjusted mentally—to fit the normative standards for mental health—was in effect the same as being of sound moral character. Ethics and mental health became one and the same. The teachers of speech incorporated these principles of mental health and faith in American democracy into the moral and ethical structures that might be taught in the classrooms and defended in the journals. Teaching speech was expected to "demand of the student that he grow in mental and moral stature."[119] Such a pedagogical obligation likewise placed certain duties upon the teachers of speech. In order to effect such an education, Hale argued that the teachers themselves would have to be exemplars and thus "should be the most cultured, refined, and normal people in the world."[120] The official introductions and statements of both the 1933 and the 1935 annual conventions of the

Western Association of Teachers of Speech placed similar obligations upon the teachers of speech. The 1933 introduction of the convention theme stated, "Our teachers must, therefore, be more than experts in speech and mental hygiene, they must be society's representatives, consciously developing in the young socially desirable attitudes, ideals, and interests—they must, in other words, become missionaries of human good will and cooperation."[121] The 1935 Western Association statement of principles on the integrated speech program similarly declared, "The ideal speech teacher would probably be among the most intellectually and emotionally mature members of the faculty."[122] In our current context, it is hard to read these comments without a raised eyebrow or slight chuckle at their self-aggrandizing tone and evangelical social projects, but the importance and vitality of these movements should not be understated. To dismiss the central role that mental health models and social psychology played in the formation of communication ethics and the missionary zeal of communication scholars requires that one set aside yards of archival materials and volumes of early publications in the field.

The drive to present standards for ethical speech to students and to adapt their behavior to these normative mental hygiene principles became the defining center of some curricula, overtaking an interest in performance or persuasion. Holm said that Kent State University in the early 1940s had accomplished precisely this transition, "stressing the more ethical side" in an effort "to give the students a feeling of 'why' as well as 'how.'"[123] Kent State had redesigned its course offerings, requirements, and in practice the very purpose of its teaching in less than a dozen years to effect this new ethics education. That kind of transformation, while most marked perhaps at Kent State, was occurring in the teaching and scholarship of many in the speech discipline during this period. The hope was that such a change would allow a teacher of speech to "quarantine" the contagion of "foul and base" thinking by teaching proper ethical principles such as "personal responsibility coupled with self-respect."[124] The primary goal of speech education was not, by this model, persuasive or compelling speech, nor even speech with socially responsible ends, but the training of speech that would by its very form and model be more conducive to healthy thinking and socially benevolent relations.

The imposition of normative standards of mental hygiene and of democratic ideals as ethical rules likewise affected the critical study of oratory. Critics of speech were told that they ought to take greater concern with "whether or not the speaker was interested in accomplishing the greatest possible total good," in addition to the speaker's success in oratory. Critics of rhetoric were asked to pay close attention to the desirability of truthfulness and to consider carefully the "moral character of the speaker."[125] While criticism and public address studies were quite a minor part of the discipline during these first few decades, as the conference programs and journals well evidence, even here the priority of ethical judgment rose above that of moving an audience to the speaker's desired ends.

Thus, over these few decades, a number of key transitions and shifts in speech studies were grounded in no small part on the ethical and political commitments of its scholars and teachers. In early-twentieth-century speech training and scholarship, the principles of mental hygienists and democratists became the values that supported the ethics espoused by communication scholars. These values were derived first and foremost from the psychological and political analyses of the psychotherapeutic movement in speech and from a faith in American systems of government. Yet, the importation of those visions of proper mental health and ethics into speech communication relied upon an acceptance of scientific models of human nature and a faith in American governmental structures. As such, communication scholars in the first half of the twentieth century engaged in the application and enforcement of normative value structures.

As the following chapter shows, the conflicts and tensions of this period, such as the effectiveness of ascendant and dominant attitudes deemed to be unhealthy and unethical or the tense difficulty of distinguishing demagoguery from good rhetoric, were highly productive sites for scholarship and in many ways were the most important openings for the expansion and development of the humanistic and philosophical tradition of the 1950s and 1960s. That period would at once both break with the early field's near unanimous adoration of science and also generate an extensive argument about the importance and capacity of reason in the ethics and politics of speech. As the approach became more humanistic, the sites of conflict shifted from wars and national politics to domestic strife and the discipline's own internal conflicts.

3 From Speech Science to Rhetoric and Philosophy

Just as the earlier ethics, which were derived from the social sciences, undermined common assumptions about the centrality of efficacy in speech communication and the "great orator" model of historical change, so too did emerging philosophical understandings of communication in the 1950s and 1960s continue to cast doubt upon some of these same suppositions. With the investigation of philosophical perspectives, the very possibility of a stable ground for communication ethics became more difficult, the importance of truth in ethical communication was called into question, and the idea that a speaker is able to exercise an independent will upon an audience became dubious. As theorizing about speech became increasingly complicated, rhetorical studies replaced a crumbling foundation with an unstable and shifting field of ethical and political questions that reflected the complexity and indeterminacy of the study of rhetoric itself. However, these difficulties were not limitations, excesses, or contradictions within speech communication so much as they were extensions of the questions and methods that made it possible for rhetorical studies to become something other than a psychotherapeutic or a social-scientific field. Indeed, the dilemmas and questions generated by the philosophical study of communication invigorated rhetorical studies and made acceptable the idea that diverse rhetorics—perhaps too diverse even to find a common definition—required the acceptance of diverse and even contradictory modes of study.

While similarities with the scholarship of the earlier twentieth century persisted, the ways in which many scholars constructed and understood human agency changed between the early 1950s and the mid-1970s. During this time, philosophical concerns and a desire to establish the grounds upon which critics might base ethical judgments turned many speech communication scholars away from the social sciences and toward humanistic, rhetorical, and philosophic approaches. At the same time, many speech communication scholars believed that social sciences were losing touch with ethical concerns and focusing solely upon questions of efficacy and efficiency. As a result, speech communication developed a mode of inquiry—or more properly, many modes of inquiry—that were quite different from those that had dominated the previous fifty years. During the 1950s, 1960s, and early 1970s, rhetoricians within speech communication not only continued a humanistic tradition but also developed a broader and more complex philosophical understanding of their subject. In so doing, rhetoric raised its status from that of a lesser art to become a sibling of philosophical studies and, in a few fleeting cases, also had the potential to establish itself as the governing discipline and to position politics, philosophy, and even the sciences as both subordinate to and dependent upon rhetorical studies. Part of this movement disclosed rhetoric's own capacity to establish itself as the most appropriate way to study and advance ethical questions. Rhetoric became a discipline not synonymous with ethics but inextricably bound to ethical studies.

This chapter focuses upon four major themes in rhetoric's rise to prominence during this period. First is the perception of an ethical crisis both within speech as an academic discipline and within communication as a social practice. That perceived crisis mobilized rhetorical scholars to develop an ethic for rhetoric, but in so doing they were confronted with the problem of grounds for that ethic. That led to the second major theme, which is the problem of moral criteria. Trying to find or establish moral criteria for communication gave rise to a body of rhetorical study that would largely replace social-psychological principles as the source of ethics. Third, in that body of study we find a return to reason as the grounding principle for communication ethics. This was not a reason primarily or most often based in science but instead in philosophy. However, and this is the fourth theme for this chapter, the turn toward a more humanistic and especially philosophical mode of inquiry posed as many problems for reason and for moral judgment as had any prior scientific or psychological position. Indeed, during the 1960s and 1970s, existential philosophy not only challenged some of rhetoric's presumptive principles but spurred a wide range of scholarship on rhetoric and communication that spanned the range of philosophical positions.

Speech and the Ethical Crisis

Philosophical studies in the United States and the discourse surrounding ethics changed during this period as well. Rather than describing an epidemic of mental imbalances or problems of mental hygiene, speech communication scholars now more commonly perceived what McDonald W. Held called "a breakdown in moral standards."[1] For some speech communication scholars, this breakdown could be located most acutely in the presence—no matter how small or new—of European existentialism in the United States. S. M. Halloran made obvious reference to European philosophy when he described the crisis of ethics in terms of experiencing all values as "unstable and fragmented" and human experience as "absurd."[2] For some, such as Held, the perception of such a crisis in ethics gave rise to a desire for "a more clearcut, definite value system to guide the decisions and actions of members of our society."[3]

Since many speech communication scholars believed that communication is central to the development of the whole person, the perception of an ethical crisis was not to be taken lightly. Just as previous scholars had described the relationship between communication and mental health, so did Halbert E. Gulley argue in 1970 that "communication is central among the factors creating moral climate."[4] Almost twenty years earlier, the centrality of the ethical question was highlighted by the Western Speech Association's twenty-fifth anniversary conference theme: "Responsible Speech—The Challenge of Our Time."[5] However, unlike the focus on mental health established through proper speech training, speech communication scholars, and especially rhetoricians, began to consider communication's ethical function to be its role as the means by which one comes to be an individual with agency in the world. This transition was by no means trivial. As the communication ethics literature moved from explicit social scientific and mental hygiene foundations toward rhetoric and philosophy, the range of possible ethical questions and ethical standards likewise shifted.

The opinion that an individual's personality is both reflected in and affected by how he or she speaks had been present in the discipline for decades, and the view expressed by E. C. Buehler in 1960 was similar: "I believe speech is essential to the growth and flowering of the human personality and provides a way for self-discovery and self-renewal."[6] However, there is a fundamental difference between the opinion that one's speech is both a symptom of and path for cure of mental defects and the belief that communication is the method by which personhood is established. Many speech communication scholars of the 1950s, 1960s, and 1970s believed that in the process of learning to communicate and then of participating in the process of communicating, one "develops into a personality, a speaking and thinking creature."[7] It was not merely the kind of personality but the possibility of any personhood at all that was now attached to communication.

Speech scholars of the previous fifty years had often held to the belief that mental defects, manifested as personality defects, could be cured through proper speech training. They believed that to learn to express oneself properly would likewise teach one to think and behave in a healthy and normal way.

That sentiment was converted in the 1950s and 1960s into a belief that character and personality were not "in-born" but rather were "all shaped pretty much by the society in which we grew up."[8] Perhaps the most important of the subtle differences in these views was that rather than viewing speech training and the style or method of communication as indicative of one's mental health, every act of communication, from a campaign speech to an interpersonal argument, was believed to have "the personal function of influencing the fulfillment and growth of the selves of the people in the transaction."[9] In 1970, Edwin Black put it quite directly: "The quest for identity is the modern pilgrimage. And we look to one another for hints as to whom we should become. . . . The critic can see in the auditor implied by a discourse a model of what the rhetor would have his real auditor become."[10] The two critical moves here are the establishment of a malleable social character, in which personality occurs only in communication and then is under constant change through communication, and the function of criticism to uncover how an event of communication sought to change the character or persona of those it spoke to and spoke about.

Positioning communication as increasingly responsible for individual character and for the perceived moral crisis in American society gave speech communication scholars an impetus to argue that communication, and especially rhetoric, must play a crucial role in ethics. To some extent, rhetoric would share the blame for the failure of contemporary ethics. Speech communication scholars' prior obsession with science was blamed for directing their attention away from ethical concerns. Ralph T. Eubanks and Virgil L. Baker, in bemoaning the perceived "value-illness of twentieth-century man," argued that rhetorical education would now have to take the central role in turning the morally and ethically deficient person into "a fully civilized human being."[11] In order to have such an effect, rhetorical education would have to be far more than simply training in good speech. In contrast to many of the mental hygienists of the 1920s and 1930s, the later communication ethicists argued that speech training would not be sufficient to cure the value-illness of the ethically deficient person unless it is accompanied by direct training in character. Claude Kantner perhaps most clearly articulated the shift that was already inchoate in 1951 when he wrote that "skill in speech as such possesses no virtue, as we have ample occasion to observe in the daily conduct of public and private affairs. In fact it may be, and often is, a *public menace unless it is bridled by reason and good character.*"[12] Speech could be viewed as a neutral tool of great power, requiring it be reined in by ethics.

Whereas poor mental health and the capacity to misuse group psychology were the predominant explanations for Nazi persuasion in the late

1930s and early 1940s, by 1963 the specter of Hitler had a new role for speech communication scholars: "a warning of what can be done . . . and a constant reminder that a good speaker must be a 'good man,' one who is pleasing to the gods."[13] In the new rhetoric, then, the specter of Hitler was a warning of what could be done if training in speech was not governed by some ethic, a proof that rhetoric needed ethics to temper its excesses.

We should not overstate this shift. In many ways, the blossoming communication ethicists connected themselves to the mental hygienists who had come before. In attempting to produce a synoptic view of the discipline, Douglas Ehninger argued that "the seeds of a rhetoric dedicated to the promotion of healthy and productive human relations rather than to the cultivation of the arts of persuasion were sown in the early decades of this century."[14] While many in communication now focused on ethics rather than on mental health, the moralizing and the moralistic educational doctrine of the mental hygienists continued. Ilse Schweinsberg-Reichart in 1968 sounded much like a mental hygienist when she wrote that "speech education, properly understood and in the hands of well trained, responsible teachers, means training people to use language *responsibly*, thus promoting better language, better speech for a liberal education, and perhaps a more effective social and political life."[15] The belief that ethical communication education would produce a better social and political life shares with the mental hygienists and the advocates of discussion a belief that, if properly done, speech education could help to give a people or a nation unity and purpose. The potential for communication education to achieve such unity was a core justification for its growth and importance. Many speech communication scholars expressed the view, as Henry Nelson Wieman wrote in 1961, that the philosophical significance of speech was its contribution to social unity, especially unity in basic values, and that such unity was central to what makes a culture possible.[16]

Given that communication was considered a force in shaping and sharing these basic values and that a perception of ethical crisis was common in the discipline, rhetoricians were well poised to advance the importance of rhetorical education as a cure to moral decline. The centrality of shared values to culture, the perceived crisis in ethics, and the centrality of communication to values all came together, and by 1976 it was almost trite for Donald K. Enholm to justify the importance of rhetorical studies by claiming that "when a culture disintegrates, words become central for the very reason that systems of meaning are breaking down."[17] In short, over this roughly twenty-five-year span, rhetoric displaced social science as the root of communication ethics while laying claim to a central role in all ethical inquiry.

Contrasted to the view that communication education might ameliorate the decline in social values, some speech communication scholars were still enthralled by the belief that it was not properly the role of speech communication to examine the ends of political or social action. For these scholars, the evaluation of what political or social goals were desirable was properly conducted well beyond the purview of speech communication in disciplines such as political science and philosophy. Instead, rhetoric was still viewed as a lesser art—as merely a means that could be used to produce benevolent or malevolent ends. Accordingly, the focus in communication ethics had to be on the importance of using ethical means to achieve whatever ends might be sought.[18] The obverse of the conversation is that just as ethics were becoming a central concern for speech communication scholars and as rhetoric was emerging as an independent field of study and theory, communication and ethics were increasingly viewed as being interdependent. Communication was used by some scholars as a proving ground for ethical theory, holding a special obligation to "provide the ground of 'right action' in the sociopolitical realm."[19] After all, if ethics were about the self living well with others, then communication would have to bear in large part if not completely contain the ways that we practice or fail to practice such living. Similarly, James W. Chesebro in 1969 wrote that for a number of years, it had been "a relevant assumption in communication theory that ethics must occupy a prominent position in the theory and practice of oral discourse."[20] If one were to be engaged in studies of speech, and most especially in rhetorical studies, one was required to engage in the study, or at minimum the application, of an ethic of communication as a mode of social or political activity.

Similar to the social and behavioral scientists' moralizing under the rubric of preventing a plague of mental maladjustment, so too did later speech communication scholars moralize in their teaching and criticism. Such overt application and enforcement of particular ethics or value systems was necessitated by precisely the problem represented by the specter of Hitler: rhetoric was perceived as being at best morally neutral and at worst connected to demagoguery and charlatanism. Charles W. Lomas, for example, argued in 1961 that "the kinship between rhetoric and demagoguery imposes obligations upon the teacher of speech to demand ethical use of facts to support intelligently conceived ideas." This kinship was a function of the fact that the demagogue makes use of the devices of rhetoric as a means to distort the truth. Hence, Lomas argued, in order to spare rhetoric from the condemnation deserved by demagoguery, the rhetorician not only must distinguish rhetoric from demagoguery but also "must learn to identify and condemn demagoguery wherever it appears."[21] While there is a mirror here to the earlier dilemma of unhealthy or unhygienic communication being the most persuasive, we should note two important changes. First, discourses of health and hygiene had by this point almost entirely dropped out of the disciplinary conversation. Second, critical study of communication was pushed to the foreground, overtaking pedagogy as the primary concern of scholars and teachers of speech communication.

Of course, teaching was still the lion's share of the work done by professors of speech communication, and so the unique obligation posed by rhetoric's precarious position was of great concern to communication education as well. The teacher of speech was expected to provide and employ "sound basic principles for determining when a speaker's attitudes and methods are ethical."[22] In providing such principles, the teacher of speech was expected to instill in his or her students a set of morals or values that would provide for proper ethical action and create a better world. This justification for moralizing, combined with the perception of a crisis in the values and morals of society, led Harry W. Bowen to argue in 1960 that moral education in the communication classroom was duty-bound to "take over the job of instilling proper values into the systems of recalcitrant youths who are often products of amoral or at best nominally moral homes."[23] What Gulley perceived as the "drift toward irresponsibility in contemporary communication" meant that courses in communication were given the duty of restoring moral order—an obligation to contribute to reversing moral decline.[24] As such, speech teachers would be admonished to avoid teaching rhetoric as a tool for personal gain in favor of a communication education that would enhance the unity of national values. Communication education, and especially rhetorical education, was expected to encourage the student to replace personal benefits or individual values with beliefs and standards that would, as Bowen put it, "benefit the lot of his society."[25] As teachers, members of the speech communication discipline had a duty to produce responsible speakers rather than to train demagogues and needed a means to make such an education effective.

In order to relieve itself of its association with demagoguery and the image of Hitler, communication education had to do more than simply assert that proper moral education might turn rhetorical strategy to the unification of national values and the reversal of moral decline. Such moral education might be conducted without teaching students the rhetorical techniques that could be used to distort truth and promote demagoguery. The justification of rhetorical education required a unique bulwark against the potential reappearance of a figure such as Hitler, a safety mechanism that would provide a check against the possibility that a well-trained orator of ill intentions or unsavory moral character might turn the tools of rhetoric to antisocial ends. Communication educators and critics met this need by extending the moralizing function of rhetoric from pedagogy to criticism. A key function of and justification for rhetorical criticism as a field of study and as a form of scholarship was that, as Fred L. Casmir argued in 1963, "when one has decided what makes a man good, he is then faced with the problem of how one can adequately judge this goodness within a short period of time."[26] This was likewise Lomas's central question in his 1961 study of rhetoric and demagoguery: "How may we identify and combat demagoguery when it arises in respectable quarters?"[27] The response to the problem had already been stated quite simply by Edward Rogge in 1959 when he wrote that "the critic must be a moralist."[28] In the capacity to pass moral judgment through rhetorical criticism, one could instill in the study of those rhetorical devices an ameliorative capacity for the moral ills of the age.

The study of rhetoric and of public address existed in the discipline of speech communication well before the 1950s, but both tended at their best to be subordinate features of a discipline dominated by discourses of science and at their worst were merely extensions of sociological and psychological principles grounded in a faith in scientific method. It was not until the 1950s and 1960s that rhetorical studies, as a field within the discipline of speech communication, developed methods and theories that would move away from scientific justifications. That separation meant in many ways that rhetorical studies needed a new grounding, focus, or central concern. This grounding or centering role was served by moralizing. Anthony Hillbruner in 1975 wrote that "the most important function of the critic is to act as a moral guardian of civilization."[29] Almost twenty years earlier, one of the leading figures in communication ethics, Thomas R. Nilsen, had similarly argued that "if criticism is to be socially responsible as well as intellectually responsible it must continually relate speeches to their social consequences through the application of principles that reflect the values society seeks to realize."[30] Many rhetorical critics between the 1950s and 1970s embarked on such projects, viewing rhetorical criticism, as Wayne Flynt wrote, as an investigation of "the methods of a speaker to determine if the persuasion is ethical and democratic."[31] It was the moral and ethical duty of criticism that gave the exigency for rhetorical studies to blossom and become a significant portion of the speech communication discipline in the middle of the twentieth century.

The belief that making moral or ethical judgments of rhetorical acts was a central duty of rhetorical criticism was not a simple admonition that the practice of rhetorical criticism should change. While many of the earliest essays on rhetoric had taken their purpose to be the discovery of which rhetorical devices were most effective at moving an audience, for rhetorical critics after the 1950s to "run out on their duty to examine and pass judgment on a speaker's dialectical and axiological bearings" was considered generally unacceptable.[32] Black wrote that there is something "acutely unsatisfying about criticism that stops short of appraisal." This dissatisfaction is an expression of an incompleteness but also an expression of a sense of disorder. For Black, the judgment of the oratory is not only a duty and an ethical commitment but a means by which a critic brings order to history.[33] Such an order was not simply logical or aesthetic but also ethical, giving to historical events an ethical and moral structure.

The Moral Criteria Problem

The nagging problem for rhetoricians was determining the grounds on which they might be able to base such judgments. The right or privilege of moral judgment, if it was to be exercised by rhetorical critics, required that rhetoricians establish a set of criteria that would empower them, as Douglas G. Bock put it, "to say 'this is of value' because that statement has been related to what we know in terms of values."[34] When Chesebro in 1969 looked back on the prior two decades, he noted that the increasing emphasis on ethics in speech communication had been "primarily upon the development of *standards* for evaluating oral discourse." These standards, he wrote, needed to be grounded in such a way that they could be justified as "universally agreed upon by most men" if they were to have validity and force in establishing a moral project that would enhance national unity of values, permit the moral appraisal of the speech of public figures, and promise the redemption of American moral character.[35] Rhetoric needed ethics that would allow it to make moral judgments about communication events, to determine good speech from bad, even though the practical concerns of speech were still strong in the needs of both teachers and students.

The importance of efficacy and efficiency in speech communication was not wholly displaced by the interest in communication ethics. Rather, a tension developed within the discipline—not unlike the tension between mental hygiene's belief that dominance is unhealthy and the social scientific finding that dominance is highly effective in persuasion. Many communication ethicists and moralists, such as James R. Andrews, perceived a longstanding tension between the developing ethical concerns and "the strong urge to succeed."[36] As theories of communication ethics developed, they were forced to account for the desire to succeed and to permit the student or practitioner of rhetoric enough leeway in method to have an opportunity to move an audience toward his or her position. Even the overt call for the moralization of communication and rhetorical studies in Robert T. Oliver's writing was qualified by his claim that "our defense of ethics cannot ignore the insistent demand for efficiency. Every man and every group has goals and wishes to achieve them."[37] Most speech communication scholars still perceived the desire for efficacy in communication to be a legitimate and primary concern of rhetorical education and criticism.[38] Thus, one could not simply dismiss efficiency and efficacy as less important than ethics but had to find some way to make these tense drives compatible.

This tension was confronted and managed—though not resolved—by means quite similar to those used by most mental hygienists to manage their comparable dilemma: ethical speech was argued to be prerequisite to effective persuasion. In an attempt to offer a rhetorical theory that could promise both efficacy and ethicality in persuasion, the 1960s saw the promotion of the belief, perhaps most clearly expressed by Oliver, that "what is ethical and what is efficient in persuasion are fundamentally the same thing."[39] In contrast to the simultaneous recognition that every rhetorical device has the potential to be turned toward antisocial persuasion if not properly tempered by moral character, some communication ethicists positioned ethical argument as central to effective persuasion.

One avenue for such an argument can be found in Karl R. Wallace's emphasis on the role of values and value-judgments in "the substance of rhetorical proof." Wallace argued that "the basic materials of discourse are (1) ethical and moral values and (2) information relevant to these."[40] If a rhetorical act were to be effective, if it were to be persuasive, it would have to resonate with ethical and moral values in order to move the audience to agreement. Ethical argument, for rhetoricians like Wallace, displaced the emotions evoked by a speech and the logic of an argument as the key mechanism by which a speaker might move an audience to agreement. This was exactly the view expressed by James W. Corder, who, after arguing that sincerity fails to move, that emotiveness is already excessive, and that logic can often confound, concluded that "on most issues, at least those that disturb us most, what we require is ethical argument."[41] In light of reason's impotence and emotion's dubious history, ethics could claim the central place as the route of good and effective persuasion.

Whether one holds that persuasion is dependent upon ethical argument or that ethical standards are a necessary check upon rhetorical excesses, in either case speech communication needed defensible standards for ethical argument that could be taught to the would-be rhetor and the would-be critic. Since communication education was dependent upon ethical standards for both its efficacy and its own ethicality, ethics took on a central role in speech communication between the early 1950s and the late 1970s. As a force for socializing "recalcitrant youths," rhetorical criticism took up the mantle of guarding society against the immoral uses of rhetorical devices and made the very possibility of persuasion contingent on shaping solid ethical arguments. In every aspect of rhetoric's emergence within the larger discipline, ethics became central. As such, it should be of little surprise that the search for stable ethical standards would become a major component of the scholarship in the discipline's journals.

Speech scholars of the first half of the twentieth century had often turned to social sciences or scientific principles to ground their theories, and their faith in science certainly did not suddenly disappear at the middle of the century. Many speech communication scholars continued to argue that science and scientific methods were central to the meaningful study of human communication. In 1962, A. Craig Baird argued that the core of the discipline was still largely "a compound of William James' pragmatism and of John Dewey's logical reconstruction—with strong scientific overtones."[42] Similarly, in the late 1970s, even Halloran, a speech communication scholar and a self-proclaimed humanist, wrote that he felt "virtually compelled to be a scientist as well."[43] Given science's well-established position as a common method in the discipline of speech communication, it should not be surprising that some believed science might serve as the ground for an ethic of communication. The scientific method had been clearly proposed by Robert Redfield in 1953 as the foundation for a communication ethic, since "the mental habits of science and scholarship are peculiarly adapted to the formation and utterance of responsible opinion."[44] The belief that the scientific method was, as Arthur A. Eisenstadt wrote in 1959, the "embodiment of sound thinking" made it easy to continue arguing that it not only should be the governing method of the discipline but also should govern how communication ethics are established and evaluated.[45]

From this faith in science, some scholars concluded that the study of communication ethics itself should be considered a scientific enterprise. Wallace characterized ethical inquiry as a science, and Bowen argued for "the wedding of scientific methodology and ethics."[46] Bock likewise wrote that if we must evaluate the ethics of a speaker, then this too could be assessed through scientific methods. Bock thought that one might be able to determine which values are timeless or universal by applying "the objective approach to axiology" in order to weed past societal changes.[47] There was an emerging scientific project to use social scientific methods to isolate universal principles that could be assigned to all peoples in all places. By utilizing such scientific methods, many early communication ethicists believed they could discover the stable foundations upon which to build ethical systems and base moral judgments.

Science also offered communication ethics the possibility of inculcating these newfound values into society. Many speech communication scholars who maintained a central focus on efficiency and efficacy were largely following or mimicking social scientific methodologies. Ralph A. Micken and other similarly oriented researchers argued that rhetoric needed science in order to work toward making "social control through speech more effective, more scientific, more predictable."[48] The possibility of such knowledge being derived from the scientific study of speech meant that teachers of communication might use these methods of social control in order to make their classroom moralizing more effective at shaping students' values. Turning to modern psychological sciences, Bowen believed that speech communication educators might find a way "to present these values and make them stick in our students."[49] For those scholars who maintained a faith in the social sciences and the scientific method, science could serve not only as a potential groundwork for an ethic of communication but also as the means of gaining broad acceptance for that ethic. Thus, social scientists in the discipline developed a two-pronged approach to a science of communication ethics. Along one prong was the establishment of true universals by demonstrating either that there were no known exceptions in anthropology (no society had existed without those universal values) or that there was at least an overwhelming dominance of certain values across cultures, geography, and time. Along the other prong was the isolation of those means of persuasion that might instill these same universals into the recalcitrant or deviant individuals, who always represent a significant number of students. The obvious tension between the presence of such values as "universal" and the need for a method to inculcate those values into deviant or recalcitrant persons seemed hardly to be noticed by those communication scholars who were following these scientific projects.

However, not all communication scholars and certainly not all rhetoricians were enamored of the social sciences and scientific methods. In fact, most rhetoricians expressed at best an ambivalence and more often outright skepticism about the rising social sciences. During the 1950s, 1960s, and 1970s, the social sciences and their methodologies were especially criticized for their inadequacy in dealing with ethical questions. Part of the reaction and the volume of the critics of science may have been spurred by the booming emphasis on science in public school funding and federal education programs during the 1950s. Fearing a trend in education that would completely supplant the arts and humanities with scientific studies, the Speech Association of the Eastern States issued a rare public resolution in April 1958, expressing a belief not only in "the basic communication skills of speaking" but also in the importance of "art, music, theatre, and other fine arts."[50] By the late 1960s, many speech communication scholars were arguing that, at best, the scientific method was properly considered to be one of many different ways to investigate communication and, at worst, that it was inappropriate to the construction of rhetorical theory. In 1970, Karlyn Kohrs Campbell argued that "if neatness and order are the criteria, analytical and empirical perspectives are clearly preferable, but they are . . . constraining and incomplete when adopted as the exclusive bases for theorizing."[51] Campbell was not arguing that the social sciences do not have value in the study of communication but rather that there are certain aspects of communication that are not most fruitfully investigated empirically and especially from scientific perspectives.

The inadequacies or incompleteness of the social sciences perceived by many speech communication scholars were due in part to their inability to account for phenomena important in the study of rhetoric. For example, Campbell argued that behavioristic theory "is likely to ignore discourses which do not produce measurable or observable effects, a criterion for recognition which is problematic."[52] In his 1964 essay on the value of existential philosophy to rhetorical studies, Robert L. Scott made a similar observation, bemoaning the fact that rhetorical scholars were "coming to say, with logical positivists, that we shall limit our study only to that which can be empirically demonstrated. . . . The danger lies in the obvious implication that what we cannot treat positivistically is unimportant."[53] A year before Scott's essay, Otis M. Walter argued that the mistake of making rhetoric "the tool of the experimentalist" reflected the "scientism" of the age and the "desertion of philosophical analysis."[54] The perception of the trend toward scientism and the increasingly empirical and quantitative forms of social scientific inquiry led Everett Hunt to go so far as to make the hyperbolic claim that one who specialized in social scientific studies would never be "much more than a statistical calculator of tests and measures."[55] Of course, this depiction is a gross oversimplification, but it also reflects some of the ways in which the social scientific methods that were on the rise during the 1950s were still very immature and underdeveloped.

Part of the perceived inadequacy of scientific methods was their failure to contribute to the establishment of ethical standards for evaluating oratory. Regardless of claims made by Bock, Bowen, Chesebro, Wallace, and other advocates of science, some speech communication scholars concerned with ethics and value inquiry argued that scientific methods made it, as Halloran wrote, "difficult to establish clear norms for judging performances."[56] Hunt was slightly kinder in his assessment of the failures of science in the field of ethics. He argued that, whereas "the social sciences were once concerned with the good life," by the mid-1950s most social scientists had "repudiated any responsibility for value" and had come to identify "more with the development of scientific technique."[57] The perception of the social sciences' dismissal of ethics, combined with the rise of science and the abandonment of philosophical analysis, all contributed to the belief, as Mark S. Klyn wrote, that "as psychological theories of motivation are popularly interpreted . . . they contrive to steal the thunder of morals and metaphysics."[58] Science was simultaneously failing in the vital function of producing compelling ethical theory and unseating those methods that provided alternative routes to such theories. A perceived crisis was emerging that rhetoric was being primed to address.

By the 1970s, the perception that the sciences were poorly equipped to study issues of ethics and a belief that rhetoric needed a more philosophical method of inquiry were strongly held and clearly expressed by many speech communication scholars. Moreover, such perceptions strengthened rhetorical studies' independence from the growing quantitative social scientific study of communication. Looking back in 1975, Ehninger recognized that the development of the study of rhetoric had "grown out of a realization that so far as the promotion of harmonious human relations is concerned science has served us poorly." Thus, the failure of social scientists to consider ethical questions adequately had made the scientific method a poor choice for communication ethicists. Such failure also led Ehninger to consider the idea of patterning methods of decision-making on the scientific method "not merely as misguided, but as subversive of the public good."[59] Such a claim would have been incoherent forty years earlier, when science was the very model of reasoned deliberation and discussion, but with the social sciences of the 1970s increasingly technical and specialized, with almost slavish attention to the empirical and measurable, Ehninger's position could have been simply intuitive to many rhetorical scholars.

In part it was through the failure of the social sciences to address ethics adequately, in part it was through the perceived need for philosophical inquiry into human communication, and in part it was through the belief that scholars have a duty to develop knowledge that might advance the social good that rhetoric found its legitimacy and role in speech communication. The question, thus, was not whether rhetoric and ethics were related—for the very foundation of rhetoric was built on its relationship to ethics. Nor was the question whether rhetoric ought properly to employ philosophical methods and perspectives—for rhetoric was not simply an *antistrophos* of philosophy but became consubstantial with a certain part of that sibling discipline. The major arguments in rhetorical theory and communication ethics in the 1950s, 1960s, and 1970s focused on determining which philosophical perspectives might best inform rhetorical studies and what might be the proper relationship between rhetorical and philosophical studies.

Rhetoric Reasoned

In the search for a philosophical ground for rhetorical studies and communication ethics, many rhetoricians turned to familiar forms of reason or rationality. From neo-Aristotelians' faith in the innate rationality of the human soul to democratists' view that reason is central to responsible democratic decision-making, many rhetorical scholars and communication ethicists had long relied upon reason to substantiate their rhetorical theories. Lawrence J. Flynn, in his exposition of neo-Aristotelian communication ethics, argued that when confronted with questions of ethics and morals, "man's reason is his guide without positive aid of divine revelation."[60] Baird extended the centrality of reason not only to the grounds of communication ethics but to all rhetorical criticism, teaching, and research.[61] Thus, if questions of ethics, as Wallace defined them, were signaled by a concern with what one ought to do, then ethical theory must be the study of "the rational and reasonable responses that human beings make to the question."[62] From these positions, there was an innate capacity or at least an inchoate ability to reason in every person, and the adjudication of the ethical and right could be found in the activation of that innate quality.

Grounding communication ethics in the value of human reason provided an additional benefit to rhetorical scholars. By using reasoned and rational decision-making and argumentation as the basis for communication ethics, one could claim that vigorous and effective advocacy of a particular position was perfectly ethical so long as the advocate "is committed to rational methods rather than victory at all costs."[63] Reason could serve as an ethical ground for neo-Aristotelians, democratists, and even scholars inclined toward psychology. This connection between many of the perspectives in communication ethics was perhaps most clearly represented by Franklyn S. Haiman's argument: "If the speaker can do it through rational means, which by their very nature are respectful of the psychological integrity of the listener and which can be successful only if the listener accepts them in full awareness of what he is doing, the speaker has remained in full accord with the democratic ethic of free rational choice."[64] Competitive or bilateral debate and persuasive platform oratory, which had been so badly battered by discussion theory and mental hygiene, could now ground their ethical legitimacy in their focus upon reasoned argument to move audiences, a defense especially potent for argumentation and debate scholars. In the judicial model and the rules of evidence, they could find a hypertrophic analogy for ethical debate and persuasion writ large.

Such a faith in the ethicality and efficacy of reason required that rhetoricians and communication ethicists be able to maintain a distinction between reasoned or logical argument and emotional or pathetic appeals. Since the former was to serve as the grounds of ethics and the latter would be assigned the lion's share of the blame for unethical speech, the distinction was essential. The separation of reason and emotion could not be absolute, since studies of persuasion in both the sciences and rhetoric had shown them to be interdependent, but as Lomas argued, even if such a connection was unavoidable, the distinction might be found in those rhetors emphasizing "emotional reactions at the expense of thought."[65] Even so, some communication ethicists and rhetoricians continued to view reason and emotions as mutually exclusive, trading off in a zero-sum relationship. Flynt argued that a rhetor who "appeals to emotions which short circuit the auditor's normal critical faculties uses unethical and undemocratic methods."[66] The structure of the emotion-reason relationship was largely inverse, so that no matter how much one might concede the utility of emotion, it always came at the expense of reasoning, as a short-circuiting, a disabling, or an interruption of the more proper and ethical mode of logical persuasion.

Rather than surrender this position to the growing belief that emotional and logical appeals are inseparable if not indistinguishable, scholars most wedded to the rationalist view of communication ethics argued that instead "we must devise more sophisticated methods of distinguishing the rational from the emotional message."[67] In response to the problems of efficacy and competition between reason and emotion, Nilsen argued that even though it was true that audiences were often moved by the irrational and that modern psychology had largely shown irrationality to be a significant element of the human psyche, "all the more do we need to make a deliberate and continuous effort to increase the amount of rationally controlled behavior, based on democratic values, in all our areas of common concern."[68] Toward such an end, rationalist speech communication scholars had to argue not only that the distinction was possible but also that one could meet the ends of both ethics and efficacy through the dominance of reason.

Yet, modern psychology and the social sciences did much to obstruct such a view of human motivation. In attempting to reassert the status of reason, Haiman implicitly recognized the difficulty in trying to resolve the problem: "I think I can assert with the full support of psychology behind me that it *is* possible to move men to belief or action on the basis of *enlightened* self-interest; that it is not necessary to stir their emotions."[69] Haiman's protestation and appeal to the social sciences were an attempt merely to show that it is possible to persuade by reasoning, regardless of how comparatively weak might be such reasoning. However, for the rationalist view to fulfill its role in ethical and effective persuasion, the power of reason to move an audience had to be seen as being stronger than that of emotion. If rhetoric was to use reason as the ground of both its ethicality and its efficacy, then rational discourse would have to be capable of combating or correcting the unethical speech of the demagogue or charlatan who would play upon an audience's emotions. When emotions carried the day, Dennis G. Day argued, "the ethical culpability rests on those who fail to counter them with rational appeals."[70] The role of reason was not merely as the more ethical alternative mode of persuasion, but it was supposed to be able to defeat less ethical rhetorical strategies whenever necessary.

For many rhetorical scholars and communication ethicists, the distinction between the rational and the emotional was thus also the distinction between the ethical and the unethical. The sanctity of reason meant that it would not be associated with unethical uses of rhetoric, regardless of whether one could isolate a particular structure or a type of logic in their operation. For example, Wayne Brockriede condemned seductive rhetoric, but he confined the mechanisms of seduction to *pathos* and *ethos* bedazzling an audience, leaving *logos* unmarred by the potential for being seductive.[71] Similarly, Lomas's condemnation of demagoguery did not consider reason as a rhetorical tool that could be used to distort truth but characterized the demagogue as one who "plays upon traditional fears and utilizes words which evoke conditioned emotional responses."[72] In fact, it was the deviation from reason and "critical thinking" in communication education that Haiman argued was ethically questionable. He found dubious "the entire gamut of devices recommended by the textbooks for rendering an audience or listener suggestible, . . . deliberate omission or minimization by a speaker of evidence and arguments, . . . [and] the use by a speaker, with conscious intent, of emotional and ethical appeals designed to short-circuit the listener's critical thinking process."[73] Anything other than the rational support for one's position was by its very nature unethical and to be avoided. That teachers instructed their students in the use of such means was as much an ethical failing as a pedagogical one, regardless of how effective such strategies might have been.

In the early years of rationalist communication ethics, it was unclear what constituted this reason and where it came from. It certainly had to be innate, or at least an innate potential, and a universally shared form of reason and not simply how a particular audience might reason. Yet, it likewise had a certain vulnerability or a possibility of not being realized or practiced. For these communication scholars, who placed their faith and grounded their ethics in the power of reason, the human mind had to be naturally rational but yet was also easily corruptible. Somehow reason could fall away at the insistence of emotional appeals. To resist the emotional appeal and to discipline oneself to uphold the highest form of rational thought required training or skill—preferably training in rhetoric. Just as the mental hygienists had to view the human mind, in its natural and healthy state, as a source of correct thought and action, so too did the rationalist ethicists have to believe that each person is imbued with at least the potential to reason properly and that this ability needs only to be activated or educated or invigorated by proper discipline in order to see past emotional appeals and to make the right choice: the choice that, by virtue of reason, is both ethically and practically superior.

This primacy of reasoned discourse also required a separation that was perhaps even more problematic than the distinction between reason and emotion. If reasoned argument was to be the path to truth and morality, then it would need to be clearly separated both from emotional argument and from other forms of persuasion that were considered to be ethically corrupt by nature, such as coercion or force. Herbert W. Simons noted in 1967 that "peaceful persuasion is the method rhetoricians understand and characteristically prescribe."[74] Invoking the emotional corruption of reason as the explanation for the persuasiveness of Hitler and Nazism was a primary mechanism by which the discipline repeatedly attempted to exorcise the specter of Hitler, though his figure has refused to leave us in peace. Hitler is perhaps the single most persistent ghost to haunt post-1940 rhetorical studies. However, this defense was not so easily leveled against the claim that reason itself was wedded to the use of threat or force as a means of persuasion. If reasoned rhetoric was to be ethical, then it would have to be able to distinguish itself from threats and force, which were presumed to be both emotionally charged and ethically suspect.

Rhetoricians not only separated force from persuasion but also argued that force was fundamentally contrary to the proper functioning of reason. For example, Dwight Van de Vate wrote in 1975 that when individuals engage in reasoned argument, "threats and what they threaten are ruled out from the very beginning, and everyone knows this, just as everyone knows that tipping over the checkerboard is not merely another way of playing checkers."[75] Reason and rhetoric were positioned as, at minimum, separate from force and were more often considered antithetical to the use of force or threats to gain compliance. Even scholars who recognized, as Malcolm O. Sillars did, that "much persuasion has implied force within it" still wanted to separate the "raw acts of force" from persuasion.[76]

Force, threats, violence, and coercion were characterized as unethical because the reaction to them deprived their targets of free, rational choice. If ethical rhetoric required the persuasion of auditors by means of reasoned argument, then the desired outcome of ethical rhetoric was the auditors' decision to agree with the arguer based on reasoned consideration. To threaten a person with a gun or with unemployment was undemocratic and unethical, according to Haiman, "because we feel that force or the threat of force does not allow the individual on the receiving end to make a free, rational choice."[77] With the acceptance of social psychological views of stimulus-response behavior and of human susceptibility to emotional motivation, even techniques of propaganda that are not explicitly threatening or violent were considered coercive and unethical because they interfered with free choice. For example, Patricia Lynn Freeman condemned the rhetoric of Glenn W. Turner on precisely this charge: "Turner's persuasion is also unethical because the means employed commonly include various propaganda devices. . . . In effect, his methods constitute coercion, an interference with free choice."[78] The spoken word was imbued with a kind of capacity for producing Pavlovian conditioning, causing people to have psychological reactions no more within their control than the stimulus-response behavior of machines or single-celled organisms, stripping them of the capacity for choice.

Many believed that free choice and rational choice were inseparable. If an auditor made a choice due to succumbing to the emotional prodding of a speaker, then the auditor acted in a way that was not "free," since his or her ability to reason about the choice had been short-circuited by the speaker. Indeed, from this viewpoint, only reason could be the ground of freedom of thought or action, even though reason would purport to lead one closer to the most true and most right choice. Threats, violence, coercion, and force were all the result of a breakdown in reason or, as Hal Howard put it, "a failure of talk."[79] When communication functioned properly, it enabled the reasoning person to make a choice for himself or herself on the basis of rational consideration of the facts.

Such a faith in reason and the condemnation of those rhetorical strategies that departed from logical argumentation left little room for social and political resistance to structures, organizations, or paradigms that had insulated themselves from reasoned argument. The juxtaposition of the rhetorical advocacy of reason and the perceived impotence of reasoned argument during the social crises of the 1960s made clear not only the biases of a rhetoric based on reason but also the coerciveness or force that already operated within such reasoned discourses.

Perhaps the most extensive criticism of the distinction between reason and coercion during the mid-twentieth century came from Parke G. Burgess. In his analysis of crisis rhetoric, Burgess wrote that rhetorical strategies deemed to be noncoercive still operated on the same principles as those seen as coercive. At the simplest level, Burgess noted that "each exploits the symbolic power of persons to respond to events in the physical absence of those events—to respond to the has-been or not-yet as if it were here-and-now." Threats could be found even in "non-coercive" rhetoric: "One rarely observes significant political, commercial, or international rhetorical address that does not bristle with 'dire consequences' swiftly to follow if one elects the wrong candidate, fails to purchase the right product, or continues a foreign policy of dangerous initiatives."[80] Indeed, coercion or threats, Burgess argued, are rhetorical attempts at persuasion since they attempt to persuade an audience to one course of action as opposed to others through a representation of force in language in the absence of actual force.

To say that coercion or threats operate as rhetoric is not in itself sufficient to answer the claim that such modes of persuasion are unethical because of their illogical or unreasoned nature. Hence, Burgess attempted to explain how coercion and threats can be based on entirely logical appeals. Consider that even in the most blatant instance of coercion, such as when one says, "Your money or your life," one is confronted with a choice: "Only the audience addressed can decide whether compliance is reasonable under the circumstance and can be forced in no way to that decision. The coercer surely depends on the assumption that his audience will decide as most persons would (choosing 'life' over 'money'), but that decision is theirs, not his."[81] To ask an audience to choose between two paths, one posing great personal risk and the other resulting in minor financial loss, is to ask the audience to engage in a simple cost-benefit calculation and to decide as one expects them to decide, that is to say, to make a rational decision. Thus, coercion and even overt threats of direct physical violence do not so much necessarily diminish an audience's capacity for reasoned decision as much as they weight one side of the equation to make the choice obvious. Audience members are still free to choose, but they are now placed in a situation that takes advantage of the values they hold to weight the choices in such a way that one path becomes radically more desirable than another.

Kenneth Burke similarly noted in his 1952–53 series of essays in the *Quarterly Journal of Speech* that threats and promises are flip sides of a single rhetorical strategy. Indeed, he wrote that "any promise is in function a threat if it can be withheld."[82] The withholding of a promise is the loss of what one might have otherwise gained, and the greater the potential gain, the more substantial the loss that is felt when the promise is revoked. Thus, the promise, Burke argued, is in form a threat to refuse to give what might otherwise be gained.

In addition to coercion's function as a rational argument, Burgess contended that coercion at times may be a political and ethical necessity. Characterizing coercion as outside the realm of the rhetorical or as an unethical form of persuasion risks denying what Burgess called coercion's "potentially justified role in crises, no matter how limited that role should be, particularly when 'relative forces' as conventionally conceived are as illegitimate as they are intransigent."[83] The advocacy of reasoned, calm, and rational debate rendered illegitimate some methods of resistance that were deployed in efforts to challenge dominant social and political structures and paradigms. For Burgess and a few other scholars of his time, this meant that communication ethics based on the primacy of reason, and especially those democratic ethics that held calm, reasoned discourse to be the only ethical means of persuasion, were fundamentally antithetical to full social and political participation and perhaps to the possibility of an inclusive democracy. Haiman recognized this same problem when he wrote that "if the channels for peaceful protest and reform become so clogged that they appear to be (and, in fact, may be) inaccessible to some segments of the population, then the Jeffersonian doctrine that 'the tree of liberty must be refreshed from time to time with the blood of patriots and tyrants,' may become more appropriate to the situation than more civilized rules of the game."[84] Haiman's position should not go unnoticed, as here he openly advocates violence, the spilling of blood, as a necessary part of good, ethical, and democratic rhetorical enterprises.

While this was an extraordinary and compelling contestation of rationalist ethics and rhetoric, reasoned persuasion still remained the preferred or more desirable method for both Burgess and Haiman. For Burgess, coercive methods were more ethical and acceptable only because they resemble reasoned decision-making. In short, coercion could capture the legitimacy of reason. In Haiman's case, only when channels are "clogged" so that reason cannot function properly did he see a legitimate opening for forceful or coercive persuasion (or more radical means) to remove this blockage. Even in these arguments against the distinction between reason and force, reason still held a higher position as the moral preference.

There was, however, a far simpler problem during this period that significantly undermined the authority of reason in persuasion and in communication ethics. Just as many of the social psychologists of the early twentieth century had recognized that persuasion often occurred through avenues other than reasoned argument and that in many cases reasoned argument was the weaker of the forms of persuasion available to a rhetor, so too did some rhetoricians in the 1950s, 1960s, and 1970s find that the meaningful study of rhetoric required that one take seriously the power and legitimacy of emotion and character in persuasion. The argument here was decidedly pragmatic. As Casmir noted, a focus on reason in rhetorical studies leaves scholars unable to provide satisfactory explanations of persuasion and social movements because these forms of analysis "do not tell us all we need to know about people and events."[85] This pragmatic problem, at least as much as any ethical or theoretical concerns, opened an opportunity for a broad reconsideration of the philosophical foundations of the field of rhetoric. The primacy of reason in the common neo-Aristotelian philosophy that circulated in the period meant that if rhetoricians were to seek a more adequate account of persuasion without returning to the social sciences, then rhetoric would need a different philosophical perspective.

Rhetorical Studies as Philosophical Inquiry

There were a wide variety of possible ways that rhetoricians could have used earlier theorists of rhetoric and communication to develop an alternative philosophy to rationalism, but romanticism and most other previous schools were unlikely candidates for broad scholarly enthusiasm or acceptance in the middle of the twentieth century, though a few did try. Instead, between the 1950s and the early 1970s, it was existential philosophy that made a strong appearance in the discipline of speech communication and developed significant sway in the field of rhetoric. This rise of existential philosophy, concurrent with the rise of rhetoric itself as a field within the discipline of speech communication, directly challenged the primacy and functionality of a rhetoric based on logic or reason. Myrvin F. Christopherson noted this convergence between existential philosophy and rhetorical studies in the early 1960s, arguing that the writings of existentialists such as Kierkegaard and Sartre and the work of rhetoricians such as Charles Woolbert made it difficult for scholars to maintain a distinction between "logical and so-called emotional arguments in discourse."[86] In breaking down the distinction, emotions were neither made to follow a particular logic nor subsumed within a structure of stimulus-response that might be mapped or charted, as social scientists were doing. Rather, for rhetoricians emerging as independent from the social sciences, the recuperation of emotion and the de-privileging of reason opened a space for passion in and about rhetoric that was similarly well presented in existential writings.

In 1967, Scott published what is perhaps the best-known essay on the convergence between existentialism and rhetoric, "On Viewing Rhetoric as Epistemic." In addition to clarifying a conception of rhetoric as a method of truth-production, he argued throughout the essay that the primacy of reason in speech communication not only handicapped scholars' abilities to examine and discuss rhetoric but also was fundamentally anti-rhetorical and anti-democratic. Scott phrased the dilemma faced by a reason-centered philosophy thusly: "The art of persuasion is granted sufferance only on the grounds that men are not as they ought to be. Were all men able as some men are to reason soundly from true premises, then rhetoric would be superfluous."[87] At heart, Scott's argument points out that the primacy of reason as a means of arriving at true and right belief makes rhetoric useful only as a means of repairing the flawed reasoning of those who have arrived at the wrong conclusion. Perhaps most interesting is Scott's recognition of a certain dilemma in rhetorical theories based upon reason: if one needs to use reason to guide others to the correct conclusion, then how can one have faith that reason will move those who have already reasoned incorrectly? If the problem of disagreement and the need for rhetoric arise because some cannot or do not reason rightly, then on what grounds can one believe that these persons will be correctly moved by reason? If one believes that in some persons the ability to reason is corrupted or inadequate, then one must doubt the capacity for reason to move these same persons to a desired conclusion.

As Scott and Donald K. Smith later argued, even if all the presuppositions of traditional models of rhetoric were sound, "they can no longer be treated as self-evident."[88] Accordingly, many rhetoricians of the 1960s and 1970s questioned not only the relationship of reason to rhetoric but also the role of reason in the human psyche and in human relations. Existentialism found interesting allies in some psychological and sociological theories. Even in the movement away from social scientific explanations for human relations and communication, rhetoricians sprouting from the soil of existentialism could provide support for their claims by looking at the results of psychology and sociology. For example, in his effort to undermine the primacy of reason, Scott noted that in psychology, the role of reason in human motivation "seems fundamentally a subordinate one." Similarly, Scott saw sociology as a field of study in which "society is organismic" and in which one "cannot grant to individual, rational man sovereignty over his physical and social environment, nor over himself."[89] Theodore Clevenger Jr. similarly appealed to empirical studies of persuasion and communication. Clevenger argued that the empirical evidence offered strong support for the conclusions that "personal conviction can distort the reasoning process, that prejudice frequently precludes persuasion, and that people do not employ reasonableness as the basis for the acceptance or rejection of arguments."[90] In proposing a rhetoric that might operate independently of the social sciences, many rhetoricians would still concede an authority to scientific inquiry, though science would come to imply conclusions that themselves undermined the authority of the reason upon which scientific methods had relied.

Faced with the dual challenges of the existential rhetoricians questioning the legitimacy of reason as a ground for rhetoric and the social scientists undermining the efficacy and primacy of reason in human relations, rationalist theorists found themselves unable to deny that nonrational appeals are effective. Campbell noted that rhetorical theorists who insisted upon the primacy of reason deployed ethics as means by which one could "condemn these effective uses of language as unethical and propound instead a form of rhetorical appeal which is widely believed to be less efficacious."[91] George I. Mavrodes in 1968 pointed out the dilemma when he wrote that the fact that "an explanation is correct or that an argument is sound does not at all guarantee that it will be accepted or believed. The rejection of such explanations and arguments is commonplace."[92] Similarly, Haiman noted that many of the most popular forms of rhetoric during the 1960s and 1970s, such as "sloganeering, folksinging, and draft-card burning fall into a category of persuasion that hardly passes muster by the standards of rational discourse."[93] Hence, for those rhetoricians who exalted reason, the options were to be unethical by abandoning reason in favor of efficacy, or to be ineffective by maintaining the ethical commitment to reason.

If reason lost much of its privileged status, or if at the very least the primacy of reason was called into question by rhetoricians of the 1960s and 1970s, then communication ethics and rhetorical theory required new grounds. While communication scholars of the first half of the twentieth century turned largely to psychologists and other social scientists for their groundings, rhetoricians coming into their own found a need to connect to ethics, politics, poetics, and philosophy. Prior to the late 1950s, though some communication theorists made occasional use of philosophical texts, especially classical Greek works, little attention was paid to contemporary philosophy, and almost no attention was given to continental European philosophy. At most, rhetoricians referred to American or British philosophers who were also considered to be psychologists or sociologists, such as John Dewey and William James.

The separation of speech communication from philosophy was well articulated by Walter's 1963 argument that for too long, rhetoricians had overlooked the contributions of philosophy, which are, he argued, "perhaps the richest sources for rhetoric." Unlike many of his colleagues, such as Campbell and Scott, Walter was not advocating that rhetoricians ought to consider the viewpoints of a particular philosopher or philosophical school but rather that *"every* philosophical system has rhetorical implications—implications that are somewhat different from that of the well-known and perhaps overused (but still incomplete) Aristotelian system."[94] Similarly, William S. Smith argued in 1962 that rhetoricians, as professionals and academics, "need to devote time and energy investigating the philosophical foundations of our field."[95] However, neither Smith nor Walter were advocating that rhetoricians ought uncritically to adopt the conclusions or systems of philosophers in the same way that earlier speech communication scholars had often imported the thinking of Dewey and James. Rather, both believed that a great deal of philosophical thought was already implicit in rhetorical studies, occasionally poking its head above the surface, as Smith put it, but with the great body of rhetorical philosophy lying hidden below. The goal was not just to import new thought from philosophy but also to allow rhetoric itself to take on philosophical inquiries. As Walter put it, the need was not for the mere translation of philosophical thought into rhetoric but for the uncovering of starting points, the judgment of the value of rhetorical systems, and the intelligent critique of the philosophical foundations of rhetorical studies.

More specifically, Walter argued that while many rhetoricians deployed or referenced the writings of Protagoras, Plato, Isocrates, and Cicero, there was almost no discussion among rhetorical scholars of the metaphysical foundations of these rhetorical theories. It was this failure to critique fundamental premises, this inability to grapple with the metaphysical issues that motivated rhetorical theories, that Walter blamed for the failure of rhetorical studies to "uncover new doctrines or modify its old ones in the way that contemporary thought has burst old limits."[96] If rhetoric was to grow, to mature, and to become a body of scholarly literature, the rhetoricians would have to produce a body of philosophy capable of serving as the backdrop and foundation for their methods and their theories.

The movement to connect rhetorical studies and philosophy was also well represented by the development of cross-disciplinary publications. Not only was the journal *Philosophy and Rhetoric* founded in 1968, but philosopher Henry W. Johnstone published notable essays in the *Quarterly Journal of Speech* from the mid-1960s through the 1970s.[97] Johnstone attributed rhetoric scholars' newfound interest in philosophy and philosophers' renewed interest in rhetoric to the fact that "the orderly processes through which people are normally able to persuade one another" had gone awry and could no longer be counted on. More specifically, he noted that the association of persuasion and virtue, carried from Aristotle forward, had "come unstuck." The presence of significant persuasive abilities "in the hands of those who could not by any reckoning be counted as virtuous" pushed both rhetoricians and philosophers to reassess the relationship between the fields and the foundations of rhetorical theory.[98] Here, the example of Hitler could return again, without him ever being mentioned, as the kind of rhetorical practices for which he was the archetype were politically commonplace.

The turn away from the sciences and rhetoric's rising interest in philosophical studies were not merely a change in the source from which rhetoricians drew the premises for their studies of oratory. Rather, they altered the role of the rhetorical theorist in the production and critique of theory. Just as the rhetoricians could not become involved in the production or critique of premises derived from social scientific study without themselves becoming social scientists, so too did the rhetoricians who inquired about and interrogated philosophical systems become philosophers themselves. As Walter put it, "When we locate old starting points, criticize them and discover new ones, rhetoricians may accurately be said to be thinking philosophically."[99] This kind of "thinking philosophically" was the essential key to rhetoric being more than a practical art or a handmaiden to philosophy. As rhetoric developed independence from the sciences, rhetoricians such as Scott chastised the discipline for being too quick to "absorb with no significant thought a little of the phraseology of existentialism" and challenged their colleagues to look harder at the philosophies that they studied, allowing them to "shake the edifices of rhetoric."[100] The very project of the rising rhetorical studies was to take up philosophical thinking about speech and communication to build a whole new body of thought, not merely to validate or repeat the work of philosophers or previous speech scholars.

It was perhaps in the writings of Scott more than in any other place that the connection between the existential philosophies and the persistent interest in communication ethics was clearest. In contrast to those rhetoricians who placed their faith in the functioning of reason, whether public or private, to ground their systems of ethics, Scott argued that the certainty sought and ostensibly produced by reason mitigates one's responsibility for actions. On the other hand, the uncertainty inherent in existential thought demanded a higher level of responsibility for the one who acts.[101] Contrary to the common argument made against existentialism by those who grounded their ethics in reason, Scott noted that the responsibility created by the need to make choices in the face of uncertainty did not mean that one who chooses not to act might be relieved of responsibility. Rather, Scott wrote that it was precisely the burden of participation that called one into action and placed a certain ethical duty on each person to act even in the face of unknowability.

The disjunction between the existentialist philosophies of rhetoric, such as Scott's, and the reason-based modes of ethics proposed by scholars such as Nilsen was that while Scott's writings articulated certain grounds on which we might argue that one bears an ethical duty and even provided some guidelines for how one ought to make choices in communication, his epistemic view did not lend itself easily to assessing the ethicality of a speaker's act. Rhetoricians such as Nilsen, who sought to use ethical systems to pass judgment on the communication behaviors of others, considered Scott's work less useful and less coherent than neo-Aristotelian ethics. Nilsen viewed the study of rhetoric and the rendering of moral judgment as inseparable and believed that the rhetorician's duty to study philosophy was largely aimed at enabling the rhetorician to pass moral judgment upon others.[102]

What was shared by Scott and Nilsen was the recognition that in order to discuss rhetoric, to engage in rhetorical criticism, and especially to investigate communication ethics, one must be willing to engage in philosophical work. A large part of that drive toward philosophy was the rising need for a revaluation of the ethics of rhetoric. Bruce E. Gronbeck argued that if rhetoricians wished to engage in the practice of giving advice, then the study of rhetoric "would demand a more thorough and explicit examination of valuative premises."[103] Eubanks similarly wrote that if communication scholars desired to establish "a fully rounded ethic of rhetoric," then they ought to go beyond mere dicta and "include the principles by which the valuative presuppositions of social and philosophical doctrines may be tested."[104] Rhetoric had to take itself up as a philosophical enterprise, as an endeavor that could build its own theories, premises, and ethical models that would pay attention to surrounding disciplines and studies but be beholden to none but itself. It would then be capable of standing as the source and the testing ground for the question of good speech. Thus, the rise of the philosophical attitude in rhetorical studies found its opportunity for emergence in a combination of the retreat of science from the field of ethics and the perception of a dire need for new grounds upon which one could base not only decisions of what one ought to do but also judgments of the morality of the acts and words of others. The potential of philosophical and humanistic studies to answer the problem of moral criteria gave rhetoric its opportunity during this period to ascend to a higher position of scholarly, ethical, and political significance.

As the next chapter documents, this move found its strongest foothold in a return to the question of the nature of the human mind, but taken up now as an ontological philosophy that would push rhetoric to grapple with its own limits, its conception of dialogue, and the status of truth. As cries of the collapse of moral systems escalated and existentialism gained prominence among rhetorical scholars, both ethics and rhetoric found even greater importance and potency in the study of speech communication. This was a formative and defining period for communication and rhetoric in America, and scholars were well aware that the task of definition was upon them. In response, a significant movement emerged in the discipline to mark out the boundaries of rhetoric and establish a core identity for the discipline of communication. Likewise, that movement evoked a vocal opposition who saw rhetoric's value to be dependent upon its shifting scope and porous borders.

4 Humanism, Rhetoric, and Existential Ethics

The necessity that rhetoric engage in philosophical work and the relative weakness of reason as a ground for ethical theories or moral criteria pushed rhetorical studies and communication ethics in the middle of the twentieth century to take up ontology, the study of the nature of being. This period saw an explosion of rhetorical theory that paid little attention to questions of persuasive technique and far more attention to the structure and meaning of human communication, the very core of what it might mean to be a human communicating or persuading. This was in some ways an extension of the early-twentieth-century promise of discovering the nature of the human mind, revealing both the most effective means of persuasion and also the standards for an ideally healthy mental state. However, unlike their earlier counterparts, many speech scholars of the 1960s and 1970s—most notably those associated with rhetorical studies—turned away from science and toward philosophy. In that turn, they brought with them the concern for questions of the true nature and ideal manifestation of the human mind or soul but now sought an alternative route by which to approach the question. As such, rhetoricians were immediately attracted to those schools of philosophy most directly focused on the innate and true nature of the human being.

At the same time, the infusion of existentialism into American philosophy and humanities pushed rhetoric to reconsider its own limits and definition while simultaneously emphasizing greater degrees of responsibility and the vitality of ethics even in moments where ontology and humanism broke down. The struggle between humanism and existentialism during this period cut across a broad range of theoretical questions, but interestingly almost no one in either camp doubted the centrality or importance of ethics to their projects. Instead, they contested each others' claims to the grounds or forms that ethics might be given.

This chapter starts with rhetoric's focus on ontology and the search for a unifying essence of humankind that could serve as the first premise for rhetorical theory and for an ethic of communication. It then examines how that attempt to define the meaning of being human is in many ways mirrored by and intertwined with the attempts to define rhetoric and communication during this same period. Partially as a response to the rising controversies over the study of being and in part as a response to new institutional and professional pressures, the discipline of speech communication and the field of rhetoric struggled with their own boundaries and identities. While defining the discipline of speech communication has been a Sisyphean task, this chapter concludes with the argument that if there is to be something like a core or a definition for rhetoric, it might be found in the fact that it has been persistently concerned with questions of ethics and politics, even if—or perhaps precisely because—it cannot produce conclusive answers to those questions.

Rhetorical Theory as Ontology

In meeting the requirements of a more complete philosophical foundation for communication ethics and rhetorical theories, most major rhetorical theorists of the mid-twentieth century relied upon a particular view of the nature of humankind, an ontology of the human being, that could serve as the first premise for their theories. Even some scholars who were closely associated with existential philosophies of communication focused on the ontology of rhetoric and engaged in a rhetoric of ontology. For example, Karlyn Kohrs Campbell argued that all rhetorical theories required the assumption that human beings are "by nature subject to and capable of persuasion." The differences between many of the perspectives, she wrote, come from how they explain this innate capacity for persuasion: "Traditional theory explains that man is rhetorical because he is rational; behavioristic theory explains that he is rhetorical because he has certain basic, unlearned drives; theories of symbolic behavior explain that he is rhetorical because he is the symbol-using or signifying animal."[1] Kenneth Burke had developed much this same point, captured in 1953 by what would become a sound bite of rhetorical theory: "man, the symbol-using animal."[2] What Campbell and Burke pointed out was a more developed and complicated explanation of Ralph T. Eubanks's own argument that "rhetoric is grounded in the very nature of man."[3] Shared among these scholars of speech communication and rhetoric was the belief that some innate nature of the human being, some essence of humanness, was at the core of communication and persuasion.

The threat to rhetoric that traditional theorists saw in existential philosophy was not so much its reliance upon philosophical inquiry but rather its denial of any such unifying essence in humanity. It was the "loss of an adequate theory of man" that Eubanks blamed for rhetoric's failure to produce and maintain a theory of persuasion "appropriate to the human condition." The answer to the anxiety and uncertainty of the existentialist age, Eubanks wrote, was not to trace out where thoughts of anxiety and uncertainty might take us—as Robert Scott tried to do—but to look more deeply into the psyche or soul in order to identify "those valuative propositions which undercut man's essential nature."[4] Thus, Eubanks pitted against the existential views of Scott and similar rhetoricians the humanistic views of his own philosophy of human nature and those of neo-Aristotelians such as Lawrence Flynn. In their adaptation of Aristotle's work, these neo-Aristotelians grounded both persuasion and ethics in the study of "human nature and human society."[5] It was as a conserving response against the perceived threat of existentialism that neo-Aristotelian rhetorical theory and communication philosophy matured into a developed and complex body of literature.

The threat posed by the existential proposition that there was no essence to humanness or that existence precedes essence was significant, for if the stable essence of humanity was shaken, then the very foundation of neo-Aristotelian rhetoric and ethics shook. Existentialist views of rhetoric and communication posed the idea that any individual's "nature" and any society's structure were the results of, rather than the origin of, communication. Henry Wieman argued that the very possibility of being an individual, the very capacity to call oneself a human, was not embedded in the structure of the soul or the innate psyche but was an effect of communication. To be human, Wieman contended, requires four characteristics: "(1) capacity to expand indefinitely the range of meanings conveyed by the signs used, (2) intimate and prolonged association of parents and children so that children acquire the art of creative interchange, (3) culture, and (4) history."[6] All of these elements, Wieman wrote, are acquired only through communication. Humanness and anything that might be later called "human nature" are products of communication giving form to the human individual. If such a "nature" was a product, then it lost its priority as natural, its dependability as stable, and hence its capacity to serve as the first premise of any ethical or rhetorical theory.

Reliance upon some form of humanism, some faith in a grounding essence to the human being, could be found in most any ethic or rhetorical theory that relied upon human reasoning. As Scott pointed out, "the act of invoking *rationality* ordinarily suggests that man *has* an ability that distinguishes him from other animals and that he *should* depend upon it."[7] The neo-Aristotelian focus on reason is an excellent example of this ontology of reason. For the neo-Aristotelian, an act cannot be said to be truly human unless, as Flynn wrote, it "proceeds from a rational agent who knows what he does and freely chooses to do it."[8] If one's reasoning capacities are in any way impaired or obstructed in the decision-making process, then by neo-Aristotelian standards, the choice made cannot reflect one's full humanness and is less ethical due to its lack of reasoned grounds. Teachers of argumentation likewise offered a view of reason that placed it at the center of human nature. Dwight Van de Vate wrote that instructors teaching logic do not really teach the student to reason or make the student into a reasoning being, but rather they "find logical autonomy already in him."[9] Here we see reason placed as an innate capacity, but not always fully developed or realized. Thus, one needed proper education to transform that inchoate capacity for reasoning into a realized practice.

While not universal, the belief in a human essence was widespread among rhetorical theorists and communication ethicists. Even many of those who would posit that humans are essentially role-taking or role-playing creatures, following out a certain aspect of the dramatistic view of rhetoric, advocated that a human core or essence was still present beneath those roles. As John Poulakos wrote, "We cannot escape the more basic reality of a Real Self who must perceive the available roles, choose a particular one, interpret it, and act it out."[10] Poulakos's position posited a preexisting agent, some base substratum of a human being with will, who then later is placed into social and communicative situations and chooses roles and makes decisions in those situations. Even that very basic notion of the preexisting human agent carried substantive implications for the form of both communication and ethics, providing a kind of soft first premise for later conclusions. Most dramatistic and even many dialogic views of rhetoric and communication ethics likewise continued the trend of grounding theories and presuppositions in at least this minimal kind of human essence or nature.

Democratic communication ethics also appealed to humanist grounds for their authority. Though democratists appealed directly to the political system for their ethical and rhetorical foundations, the legitimacy of democracy and the coherence of democratic ideology relied upon, as Nilsen put it, "a belief in reason as an instrument of individual and social development; self-determination as the means to individual fulfillment; man's fulfillment of his potentialities as a positive good."[11] In no small part this was connected to the value of democracy as the collective opportunity for the expression and choice of reasoning persons to determine their own destinies, embedded in the relationship between free, rational choice and ethics. Continuing the trend started in early-twentieth-century speech communication literature, many rhetoricians and communication ethicists proposed democratic governance as the model for ethical communication. Virgil L. Baker and Ralph Eubanks, for example, suggested that communication scholars should adopt as their "value-touchstone the democratic ideal of the fullest possible development of human potentialities."[12] David L. Lawrence noted that, in part, this connection between communication ethics and democracy was an outgrowth of the perceived historical connection between public speaking and politics.[13] Such a perspective did not, however, elevate rhetoric to an art in its own right but rather viewed it through a neo-Aristotelian scheme that ranked it as subordinate to many other fields of study, including politics. From this view, as Karl Wallace explained, the proper aims and ethics of rhetoric would be left to the political scientists, whose "master art" would set the controlling ideas for the "instrumental art" of the rhetorician.[14]

Many of these democratic models of communication ethics were antithetical to the elevation of the study of rhetoric and communication ethics as academic disciplines because they demanded that the free will of the majority be the source from which all standards of value should be derived. From this view, as explained by Edward Rogge in 1959, all those who would support democracy would "insist that standards of value should devolve from the people, not from a 'higher authority.'" Combining democratic faith in public decisions with Ciceronian political sentiments, Rogge warned rhetoricians and communication ethicists that "what the multitude approves must win the approval of experts."[15] To refuse to accept the faith in public deliberation or to question the righteousness of the majority view was to deny the value of democratic government. Theodore Clevenger noted that if one admits that the public is unable to make the wisest decisions in every case or doubts that the public will adopt the wisest possible methods for carrying them out, then one must "admit our unfitness to govern ourselves and to argue strongly for the rule of the ignorant masses by the enlightened few."[16] One should notice the political and social context of these views in the 1960s when they were published. To claim that majority opinion should always win the day had significant implications in the political movements of the era, especially surrounding segregation and racial discrimination, which would have been unacceptable to liberally minded speech communication scholars.

In part because of their potential to support politically contentious and disturbing positions, these democratic views had to be qualified by Clevenger and others to include only those situations in which the audience might have full access to information and contending viewpoints. Just as Parke Burgess had noted that reason could not always govern public discourse, so too did he point out that democracy could not always function well. For Burgess, democratic government and deliberation work well only "when relatively free from divisive conflict and strife."[17] Similarly, Franklyn Haiman pointed out that techniques of persuasion falling outside the realm of sound logic or genuine public deliberation can be defended ethically only in those situations where "the norms of democratic process may be inapplicable."[18] Just as Burgess and Haiman maintained the primacy of reason by attempting to raise emotions to the status of reason and to provide exceptions to the governing rule of reason, so too did their exceptions to the democratic view of communication ethics reinforce the centrality of democracy as the governing value structure for ethics. In making exceptions, they established democratic standards for communication ethics as the norm from which one could deviate only when already released from the obligations of democracy by the antidemocratic structure of existing social circumstances or deliberations.

In contrast to the democratic views of communication ethics, which largely subordinated rhetoric and speech communication to political philosophy, many communication theorists in the 1960s and 1970s took interest in philosophies of language as starting points for communication ethics and rhetorical theory. While still often relying upon humanist appeals to the nature of humankind, they sought to unseat rationalism and the kind of universal vision of reason in favor of a first premise that would prioritize rhetoric and communication. Rather than demoting rhetoric to the status of a lesser art, theorists such as Barry Brummett argued that "the most ethical world view is one with rhetoric at its center."[19] While a certain self-importance can easily be read into these views of communication ethics, they were grounded most commonly in an understanding of rhetoric or language as the defining core of human being. Taking a broader view of rhetoric than merely as public advocacy and deliberation about issues, rhetoricians and communication ethicists who focused on the linguistic nature of the human viewed rhetoric as "the study of men as they possess and are possessed by their language."[20] The possessiveness of this phrase is telling in the relationship between the human and language. Most rhetoricians and communication ethicists had described language as a power, capacity, or possession of the human being. For Eubanks, "rhetoric is a function of *human purposiveness*, or that feature of life the Greeks termed *telos*."[21] Similarly, Robert Oliver's view that "man is essentially the talking creature" placed symbol systems and languages within the human brain as "a power possessed by no other living organism."[22] To ignore, denigrate, or diminish this essential human nature as "the symbol-using animal" was unethical and even "nihilistic."[23] It was, essentially, to deny the fundamental and unique nature of the human being.

The importance of language in human nature, however, indicated that a certain element of language exceeded any capacity of the human to possess or control it. Humanness itself, the capacity to be a person, was predicated on a prior imposition of language that would give one the capacity to think and to say "I." Language could not merely be a tool at our disposal but had to take on a certain animism, a force in which it could do things to us. Henry Wieman and Otis M. Walter argued that, without some symbols, "we cannot develop into *human* beings; we can only become animals that are biologically human but psychologically no different from other animals."[24] This biological humanness is not where most rhetoricians and communication ethicists located the human capacity for language. Unlike advocates of reason who often followed Aristotle in placing reason at the apex of the human soul, advocates of language ethics came closer to an existentialist position in arguing that language came before the individual human, making him or her into a person before the person could ever be said to possess or control language. As Burgess wrote, personhood is not determined by body or brain nor by the capacity to perceive and react to signals. It lies instead in the learned capacity to "conceive and respond within symbolic space."[25] Thus, the language-centered ethics developed a kind of constructivist humanism, with perhaps a human nature but a constructed nature, built up by the imposition and repetition of language and our communication capacities.

In contrast, the neo-Aristotelian view that language and reason are conjoined and are possessed by the human soul was well represented by Eubanks, who found the mingling of reason and language in the term *logos* a key point of intervention against the existentialist language ethics.[26] However, this view was constantly contested by understandings of language and humanness that posited the former as being prior to the latter. Rather than positioning the human as agent and owner of language, Douglas Ehninger argued that the human being "is inevitably and inescapably a rhetorical animal."[27] The *being* of human being is determined by language, is predicated upon language, but language does not originate within the human. It is not possessed by the human but makes the human, is inseparable from the humanness of the human, and is consubstantial with the human. Donald K. Enholm called language a "second nature" that determines humanity as much as, if not more than, nature or biology.[28] While again posited as an essential quality of the human being, language rises to be the defining capacity, giving reason its shape and possibility. Communication, then, could be the study of that which makes it possible for a person to be a person.

It may seem odd that Kenneth Burke has been only occasionally mentioned up to this point in the discussion. Indeed, it is true that many of the previously mentioned rhetorical scholars either drew upon or responded to Burke's work. While Burke had been producing books on rhetorical and literary theory since the 1930s, he was largely known only in the discipline of English at that time and did not emerge in the discipline of speech communication until the early 1950s. His most significant appearance occurred in 1952–53 when the *Quarterly Journal of Speech* published a four-part series of essays on his dramatistic view of language and theory of the negative. These essays explicitly connect the origins of language, the nature of the human, and the quality of a moral act through an examination of what Burke called "the negative."

The concept of the negative, represented simply by "No," is not found in the phenomenal experience of reality but resides as a concept only in the realm of language. Language, Burke argued, must thus derive not merely from history or from human experience but from a realm that transcends the linguistic, "the realm of a 'more-than-language,'" and in that transcendent realm there must exist the concept of the negative. The origin of language, then, lies in something that is at once grounded in "Reality" and yet is not found directly in human experience of the phenomenal world. It is this condition that led Burke to claim that the negative in language is a manifestation of a "transcendent motive."[29] This transcendent realm could then provide a ground for the establishment of a free will for the human. For Burke, there is no sensible notion of will without freedom, for "a will to be a will must be free." Burke grounded that freedom in a realm that must at once be "*beyond nature*" and also a "scenic freedom."[30] Thus, the human will finds freedom because it exists in a reality that is governed by a transcendent motive of the negative that provides a causality beyond both language and nature. Free will is thus universalized to the human nature while finding its grounding in something that transcends human experience.

With language and human will being thus positioned, Burke sought to answer the question, "What, then, is a moral act?" The answer takes Burke on a path reminiscent of German idealism: "It is an act in which man himself freely lays down the law." Burke explained that he is referring to acts of "self-legislation" in which "one asks of others only what one, in principle, finds it just to ask of oneself."[31] Note that this is to ask of others not only what one also would ask of oneself but what one *in principle* would ask of oneself, which is to say that one legislates, establishes laws of action, based upon a hypothetical extension of that legislation to self and to others.

While Burke represents perhaps one of the discipline's earliest, most extended, and most detailed discussions of the origins of language and their relation to human nature and moral action, we should not understate the significance of other scholars, such as Campbell, Enholm, Scott, and Ehninger, who mark the moment of rhetoric's rise to the status of a distinct and independent field that need not subordinate itself to the social sciences, philosophy, or politics. Here, for perhaps the first time in the twentieth century, communication ethics and rhetoric were fully mature fields within speech communication that could both inform and be informed by fellow disciplines of poetics, politics, psychology, and philosophy but that did not need to serve a subordinate role or accept the findings of these disciplines as unquestioned premises.

Delimiting Rhetoric

With this rise of rhetoric as an independent discipline and with the transition of journals such as the *Quarterly Journal of Speech* to an almost exclusive focus on rhetoric came the disciplinary preoccupations with domesticating rhetoric, defining its boundaries, and standardizing its canon. It would be difficult to say too much about the arguments over the definitions of speech communication and rhetoric in the middle of the twentieth century. Indeed, one could write volumes just on how the transformation of the names of academic departments and organizations was connected to events in scholarship and teaching.[32] As S. M. Halloran wrote, "From the beginning rhetoricians have differed from each other on the limits of their discipline." The enormous diversity of thought about the proper role and limits of rhetoric led Halloran to conclude that "if there is such a thing as a rhetorical tradition, it cannot be successfully defined by either the kind(s) of discourse it deals with or the precepts for discourse it offers. There is just too much disagreement in these areas among the people whose writings are supposed to articulate the tradition."[33] Regardless of this diversity of views and difficulty in defining the term, or perhaps precisely because of them, rhetoricians would continually return to the task of defining rhetoric, for the problem, as Scott put it, "seems irresistible to rhetoricians."[34] From the moment that rhetoric came into consciousness of itself as a field of study, there has been a steady flow of arguments over its proper scope and definition.

This definitional task is not simply a desire to assay the field as it exists at a given time or had earlier existed. Rather, in the task of defining speech communication and rhetoric lies the choice of what will and will not be considered a legitimate part of the discipline. This means not only what might be considered an acceptable topic of discussion among scholars but what might make its way through the peer review process and into journals or conferences, what can be considered legitimate topics for seminars, theses, and dissertations, and what will be allowed into the canon of great writings.

In the 1960s and 1970s, what Halloran and Scott viewed as a lively and rich diversity of views was considered by such scholars as William Smith as a "problem of splintering in the speech field" that would best be remedied by clearly stating a central and defining "philosophy of speech."[35] In placing limits on the study of rhetoric and giving it definitive shape, Smith hoped to corral those scholars who viewed communication and rhetoric more broadly. The futility of such efforts seemed only to lend to the advocates' perceptions of their exigency. The constant problem of trying to produce a synthesis, a common denominator, or a direction for the discipline was only exacerbated by the booming scholarship and the increasing complexity and variety of methodologies. This was certainly not a new issue in this period but one that had consumed enormous amounts of time and energy on the parts of scholars and the leaders of the speech communication associations for decades. For example, Joseph W. Baccus, then Western Speech Association president, engaged in a sustained correspondence with leading teachers and researchers in the discipline over the question of disciplinary definition throughout 1948.[36] Twenty years later, the difference was the rate of new development, the broad-based reconsideration of the premises and purposes of speech and rhetoric scholarship, and the rise of these studies to a maturity and independence of thought unfamiliar to the earlier era.

Speech communication was exploding with possibilities, in no small part due to the adoption of philosophical views that would, at least in theory, elevate rhetorical studies to a significant place among the humanities. For example, even if rhetoric was loosely defined as persuasion, it still could be said to contain the study of all human interaction or, at a minimum, all communication, for as Scott wrote, "In communication, necessarily stressing man's relation to man, *mitwelt*, there lurks always the shadow of persuasion."[37] Even this, though, was too narrow a view for many rhetoricians. While Charles W. Kneupper observed the "controversy among major modern theorists about the central focus of rhetorical theory," he argued that the major theorists in rhetoric recognized that one could not restrict the field to persuasion, since "rhetoric has multiple functions."[38] Indeed, confining rhetoric to persuasion not only was an uncommon view in this period but was also considered, as Walter put it, a "distorted view" and often even "an unintelligent view."[39] At a minimum, Kneupper argued, rhetorical theorists were expected to take a broad view of their discipline and to consider everything about the structure and function of language as being germane to their studies.[40] Even the simplest acts of language, such as the assignation of a name to an object, were considered rhetorically important. As Campbell claimed, "In naming, man not only draws arbitrary boundaries about an event or object, but goes beyond it to speak of the event or object in terms of what it is not, a word, by which he codifies his experience into meanings which reflect his and his group's perspectives and attitudes."[41] One single event, such as pointing at an object and calling it a "chair" or "soft" or "tan" could take on rhetorical significance if that simple act of naming a perception was deemed important enough to its context.

Campbell's expressed concern for elements of rhetoric that exceeded or preceded the particular conditions of a speaker and an audience, extending into structures of language, social values, and broad conditions surrounding and giving rise to communication events, reflected a tendency of many rhetoricians to shy away from the neo-Aristotelian focus on the intentions of the orator. Even relatively traditional scholars such as Nilsen found that their examinations of rhetorical ethics led them to the opinion that "the effects a speech *has* are more important to society than the effects it was or is *intended to have*."[42] In the evaluation and criticism of rhetoric, the intentions of the orator counted for much less than the actual effects a rhetorical event produced.

If intent no longer governed the evaluation of a communication act, neither could intent govern the psychology of the speaker or the meaning of a communication event. William B. Hesseltine argued that in the interpretation of speech events, one found not so much the intent or psychology of the speaker but rather "the culture of both the speaker and his auditors."[43] Drawing from Sartre's writings, Campbell expressed a similar view of the function of criticism, in which, she wrote, one "interprets the context and audience broadly in order to view discourses as part of an ongoing cultural dialogue influenced by persuasive forces which include other discourses, persistent social conflicts, and cultural values."[44] While these views of rhetoric and criticism maintained a focus on interpreting speech texts in order to determine their effects and meanings, the de-privileging of intention that was common to many rhetoricians of the 1960s and 1970s unshackled questions of effect and meaning from the interpretive moorings upon which neo-Aristotelians had for so long insisted. In many ways, the authority of the rhetor-as-author over the effect and meaning of his or her oratory were not discarded but instead diminished to the status of merely another variable in a long list of elements that might contribute to a critic's interpretation and evaluation.

An emerging shift in the understanding of the relationship between communication and action was also taking place in the 1950s, 1960s, and 1970s. While communication scholars of the first half of the twentieth century often characterized speech as something that preceded an action, led up to a decision to act, or explained an action, communication itself was not most often considered to be a form of action. In contrast, a small number of communication scholars began to identify communication as an act with no less significance than any other. While some theories of symbolic action gave to communication a certain status as a lower-order act or would take act as a metaphor for communication, rhetoric scholars such as Malcolm Sillars made plain that "the critic should regard oratory as an act as much as he so regards throwing rotten eggs or pressing the trigger in a Mannicher-Carcano rifle."[45] Sillars's reference to the Mannicher-Carcano rifle, the make of rifle that Lee Harvey Oswald used in the assassination of John F. Kennedy, while obscure today, emphasizes the force and weight of rhetoric as an act in a way that leaves no space for a conception of rhetoric as a lower-order act or as a less substantial act than any other. As an act in itself, no longer merely a predicate or prerequisite to action, rhetoric demanded not only a greater scrutiny but also a greater gravity.

Yet, none of these strategies produced a definition of the discipline of speech communication or of the field of rhetoric that would be unanimously accepted. The same problems of definition that had haunted the discipline for the first half of the twentieth century persisted well into the 1970s, with scholars continuing to debate issues as fundamental to the boundaries of the discipline as the centrality of the spoken word.[46] Nor was there any consensus on research methods that might give the discipline focus. In contrast to the broad faith in science that motivated the search for a common method in the 1930s and 1940s, speech communication by 1970 could be best described by Gregg Phifer as a discipline in which "no research method has a monopoly on the good, the beautiful, and the useful. Nor is any method without its flaws."[47] Speech communication and rhetoric were indefinable, or, at a minimum, any definition that might be provided would fail to account for the diverse and contradictory body of work that composed them.

This lack of a definition, however, was also a source of productivity that provided a unique power and value. If rhetorical studies were unrestrained and if they lacked a common focus or method, this permitted rhetoric to become a site for the connection of previously unconnected ideas and thinkers. In failing to define itself as a field, as Anthony Hillbruner wrote, rhetoric was empowered to "transcend disciplines in an eclectic manner, borrowing from each certain salient aspects and unifying them into some cohesive whole."[48] Rhetoric's most unique and attractive element would not be its subject matter nor its methodologies but its less disciplined boundaries. As Baker and Eubanks noted, the value of rhetoric lay, in no small part, in its capacity to facilitate "the discovery of the complex relationships among various areas of knowledge."[49] Indeed, the move against defining, against "the world of complete conformity," was a preservation of this breadth of study and the capacity to cross over and join fields of knowledge.[50]

Campbell considered the fuzziness of the boundaries and the wide horizons of rhetorical studies to be "the price we shall have to pay in order to have the latitude needed to theorize about and examine the many language acts which do not fall easily into neat classifications of purpose."[51] However, the depiction of the breadth and indeterminacy of the limits of rhetorical studies as a price paid in order to attain this unique power continued to privilege neat borders to thought and limits to disciplines. There is a sense in which Campbell and many other rhetoricians in the 1960s and 1970s argued that we should accept the loss of distinct boundaries in order to gain some alternative advantage. Ideally, it seems, Campbell would prefer both distinct boundaries and the latitude she describes. That is to say, many rhetoricians still desired a clear definition for their field but were willing to accept the lack of such clarity in order to maintain the broad focus and diversity of methods that were both enriching and empowering their work.

On the other hand, a few rhetoricians were eschewing the very value of definition and depicted the difficulty of setting limits to the discipline not as a lack, loss, or cost but as an indication of a newer and richer view of rhetoric. Scott wrote in 1975 that in order for rhetoric scholars to "see more clearly," they had to stop "looking for *a* definition of rhetoric, i.e., a single set of attributes that will serve to mark off the limits of rhetoric once and for all."[52] The very term "rhetoric," as a mass noun, came under fire for perhaps the first time during this period. Oliver argued that scholars would soon have to abandon the term as a singular entity and begin to adopt a plural form: "I think that the facts of life indicate that there is not just one rhetoric—instead, there are many rhetorics."[53] This plurality reflected the incredibly divergent approaches to studying rhetoric and the contestation over the scope of what is and is not rhetorical.

Rhetoric and Communication Ethics

Perhaps only one aspect connected all the rhetorics that Scott and Oliver described. One might say, as Halloran did, that "it is possible to define the rhetorical tradition, in a somewhat looser way, in terms of the cultural ideal it is built upon. That ideal was perhaps most succinctly stated in Quintilian's description of the perfect orator as 'a good man skilled in speaking.'"[54] Even though Eubanks and Baker recognized the breadth of speech communication and the difficulty in defining the discipline, they expressed a similar view of rhetorical education, writing that such education is "centrally and persistently concerned with human values, here taken to mean universal concepts basic to civil decision and action."[55] Scott himself, even after eschewing the value of definition, wrote that "part of the definition necessary for rhetoric is that it does deal with discourse which has value implications."[56] In all three examples, the common theme of rhetoric is its connection to values, notions of the good, or ethics.

To say that rhetoric is always concerned with issues of ethics or values does not in itself require, however, that one endow either rhetoric or ethics with any essential substance. Rather, it simply recognizes that the communication in which we engage is always bound up with questions of how one chooses to live. Thus, rhetoricians were still largely at a loss for any grounds upon which they might claim the right to make moral judgments of orators. Even if rhetoric was to be "a great energizer of judgment decisions," as Eubanks and Baker wrote, rhetoricians believed that this role required that rhetoric draw its grounding from some axiological system.[57] As such, not only was rhetoric to be a field intimately connected with the philosophical study of ethics, but it also desired to be at the core of the application and testing grounds of such ethics.

Chastising analytic and scientific inquiries for seeming to abandon such questions, rhetorical studies took up the mantle of ethical inquiry. In displacing the authority of scientific inquiry and disavowing analytic philosophical traditions, rhetoricians could claim the highest authority in the study of ethics. As Wieman wrote in 1961, rhetoric was well poised to claim its "distinctive function and highest vocation" to be "to expand indefinitely the range and depth of what can be appreciated as good and distinguished as evil."[58] While moving away from scientific methods and toward a greater concern with philosophical studies, rhetoric did so not as a handmaiden to philosophy—as it had largely approached the sciences—but as a sibling that at times could claim a higher authority on questions of value and ethics than its fellow humanities. Wallace argued in 1963 that rhetoric, over all other fields, could claim to be properly concerned with the appearance and use of value judgments.[59] Yet, rhetoric only faced a greater crisis of legitimacy in making these claims, as definitions of rhetoric failed to provide grounds for ethical or moral judgments.

This crisis of legitimacy was perhaps best handled by the attempts to ground communication ethics in concepts of dialogue and mutuality. By relying upon a certain existential view of the event of communication, scholars such as Poulakos and Wieman attempted to ground their ethical systems in dialogic perspectives. For some, such as John Hardwig, there was a practical imperative that grounded the ethical legitimacy of dialogue. With the term "dialogue," Hardwig attempted to name a form of communication that "aims at truth" through a "give-and-take." Like the previous proponents of discussion and some of the proponents of dialogue, he distinguished dialogic communication from "mere persuasion" or those forms of communication that aim at "agreement achieved by means of speeches." The practical advantage that he credited to dialogue over persuasion shared much with the advantages claimed by the scientific models of discussion. Since speech-making and other forms of one-way persuasion were considered egoistic and were subject to "the appeal to individual intuition," Hardwig hoped that dialogue would hold the possibility of operating on a more reliable rationality—a rationality that "is a public, shared, collective achievement." For Hardwig, each individual mind suffers from subjective corruption, such that "no one, however mature, educated, and 'competent,' has within himself the capabilities to act rationally. On the contrary, the individual needs the cooperation of others *in every particular* moral inquiry that is to progress toward objectivity and rationality."[60] As such, the give-and-take of dialogue claimed a moral legitimacy for Hardwig because it was the path through which one might sustain the only possible rational life. Hardwig's view, however, relied upon both rationality and the capacity of groups to interact optimally, which made it vulnerable to many of the problems shared with the reason-centered and scientific grounds of earlier communication ethics. In many ways, his view was a hybrid between what would become the far more common conception of dialogism and the reason-based ethics that were viewed with increasing skepticism in the discipline.

Dialogism gained a more unique dimension and greater strength through a philosophical inquiry into the structure of communication between persons. W. Homer Turner expressed a common premise among many communication scholars that still has great force today: "Effective communication happens when the sender understands the receiver's frame of reference and communicates in terms of that."[61] While this view was articulated for decades as a practical matter in the persuasion of audiences, dialogism made such an understanding a moral duty in communication. Poulakos noted that from a dialogic view of communication, there are always three elements involved in the dialogue: "the Self, the Other, and the Between." Dialogism was the art of bridging the Between to create some linkage or sharing of the Self with the Other without giving predetermined content to that connection. Poulakos described dialogue as "a mode of existence manifested in the intersubjective activity between two partners, who, in their quest for meaning in life, stand before each other prepared to meet the uniqueness of their situation and follow it wherever it may lead."[62] Note that explicitly denied by Poulakos's dialogic mode is the idea of one person leading the other to a predetermined conclusion. Of course, this view required a similar notion of "give-and-take" or mutuality as other views of dialogue and discussion, but it grounded this requirement not in practical advantages but in the moment of communication—in those elements that make interaction possible. Rather than start with the question of the essence of the beings involved in communicating (the nature of the human), Poulakos started by asking what was the nature of the event of communication.

For Poulakos, as for most advocates of dialogism in the 1960s and 1970s, the privileged part of the dialogic triumvirate was the concept of the Between. The desire to bridge the distance between Self and Other or to focus on the shared or intersubjective of communication led Poulakos to describe the Between as "the force which binds all the particles of an organism together and permits us to consider such an organism alive."[63] The Between—the bond or sharing—is a relationship without which dialogue cannot exist, Poulakos argued. In this view, mutuality is the highest value and imposes the heaviest moral obligation upon the participants in a dialogue.

Thus, the ethic of dialogism was an ethic of mutuality. For advocates of dialogism, the question of whether an act of communication was or was not ethical was based in no small part on "the discovery of the means of symbolism which lead to the greatest mutual understanding and control."[64] This mutuality was not only a sharing of power or control between the participants but a sharing of understanding, a mutuality of comprehension. For Poulakos, this meant that each is open to the other and that interlocutors allow their awareness of each other to "impress on them deeper and affect them decidedly."[65] Sharing, bridging, or fusing together two separate individuals—the Self and the Other—was the event that made speech metaphysically significant.[66] Such speech was significant not merely for the sharing of opinions but for the sharing of perspectives, where each interlocutor comes to understand and incorporate the viewpoint of the other.

Oliver expressed a similar view when discussing the ethics and efficacy of communication across culture, race, or religion. For Oliver, as for Poulakos, Walter, and Wieman, the key to proper communication was found precisely in the between—in what could be shared or was possessed in common. Oliver wrote that anywhere in the world, communication would flourish "under conditions in which the communicants make themselves aware of a community of interests and manifest a communion reflecting mutual affection and respect." The in-common or point of communion could always be reduced, failing other sources of commonality, to an advocacy of humanism—a faith in the fundamental and obvious essence of humanity. Oliver argued that any differences between individuals would "fade into insignificance when a man is viewed as a vital and vibrant human being and is treated as such."[67] Faith could always be placed in the "basic humanity we all have in common" to melt away any differences between individuals.[68]

However, we should note that all the faith in the between and in commonality, as well as all the desire for openness, could not preclude the necessity of disagreement. Wieman and Walter were emphatic that "appreciative understanding of the unique individuality of the other does *not* mean approval of all he thinks, feels, and does."[69] Similarly, Scott argued that, in addition to being willing to change one's mind and to cooperate, one also needs to be willing to speak one's mind and to disagree.[70] The commonness and communion of the between was tempered for communication scholars by the fact that communication itself was spurred by what was not in-common. In fact, rather than being the path to mutual understanding, communication seemed most often to arise from and thrive in those moments in which there was a recognition of difference. Dialogue required the Self and the Other, but it emerged because of something quite the opposite of mutuality or sharing.

Poulakos, perhaps better than any other scholar of the period, tried to grapple with this problem of mutuality. The ideal situation for Poulakos was when "the Self attempt[s] to meet the Other in his uniqueness and peculiarity, and come[s] to terms with him. Coming to terms with the Other becomes actuality when the Other is recognized, accepted, and confirmed as he is." The difficulty arises from the fact that the origin of the relationship between the Self and the Other is precisely not mutual or shared. Rather, Poulakos writes, "it is the Other that allows there to be a Self."[71] The Other holds the privileged position, coming before the Self, giving the possibility of selfhood to the Self, and thus always exceeding the Self in the relationship as well as placing a certain demand upon the Self that the Self cannot reciprocally impose.

Poulakos was quite clear about the disparity in the relationship between Self and Other, writing that "only because there is otherness can [a Self] attempt to establish himself by distinguishing his being from that of the others." Thus, the obligation imposed by the relationship with the Other, the responsibility that one has to that which gives to the Self the very possibility of selfhood, is not in the Between, the sharing or mutuality. These are all elements that come *after* the instantiation of the Self, that are accidental to the existence of Self and Other. From Poulakos's explication of the event of dialogue, we find that what grounds the Self is not the sharing or the Between that is common to the Self and the Other but the difference, the distance, the unshared that separates the Self from the Other. It is the otherness of the Other that Poulakos's explanation credits with creating the possibility of being. If Poulakos is to be taken at his word in his explanation of the debt that the Self owes to the Other, then no commonality can precede otherness, for prior to the approach of the Other, there can be no Self who might establish the in-common. Similarly, Poulakos undermined the focus on the Between when he recognized that the very possibility for the Self and the very possibility of communication are grounded in the fact that "for each of the participants of dialogue the Other is essentially different from himself."[72] This *essential* otherness is prerequisite to the Between.

Wieman and Walter, while by no means as detailed on this issue as Poulakos, made similar claims that deny the possibility of privileging mutuality and commonality in dialogue. For example, they wrote that "it is the *others* that generate our mind and self." While their view was perhaps more psychological than philosophical, they likewise placed the Other in the privileged position of giving selfhood to the self—a relationship that denies the mutuality of self and Other that they sought to establish. For Wieman and Walter, "not only is the 'mind' developed by association with others, but only [by] taking the attitude of another person toward himself does man form a concept of 'self.'"[73] It is only because the Other comes before the self, only because the Other approaches the self, that there can be the possibility of a self. Just as Poulakos revealed this fundamental asymmetry in the relationship of Self and Other, the more psychological views of Wieman and Walter reflected this denial of mutuality as well. This tension within the advocacy of dialogism is a symptom of what the advocates of dialogue had left uninterrogated in the tradition of the discipline. In privileging the between and in establishing mutuality or sharing as the highest value in dialogue, scholars such as Poulakos, Walter, and Wieman expressed the common view among rhetoric and communication scholars that the subject and object of communication is the transmission or sharing of thoughts, feelings, and ideas.

A smaller but still significant number of communication scholars in the 1950s, 1960s, and 1970s were not inclined to focus on the method of communication, whether democratic, dialogic, or otherwise, but instead based their ethical and moral concerns on the quality of the thoughts and ideas expressed or shared. In such a view, the most common standard to be used for the moral evaluation of communication was the truth of the statements made. Truth here first and foremost referred not to the honesty of the speaker but to the congruence between the statement and what is objectively real or true. A fundamental faith in the moral rightness of "Reality" meant that statements consistent with reality not only would carry the day but also would be morally and pragmatically preferable to those that could not claim such consistency.

Rhetoric and communication scholars concerned with ethics have advocated the centrality of truth for many decades. It was neither new nor controversial when Dennis Day wrote in 1966 that "if personal conviction on a particular subject has a preponderance of truth in its favor it will prevail over other views even when all views are fully presented."[74] Similarly, Lawrence noted in 1963 that "there is one quality above all others that has marked the work of the world's greatest public speakers. That quality is truth."[75] Indeed, truth was often held to be the only acceptable content for ethical and effective rhetoric. If rhetoric managed some level of efficacy without truth, then it would be called demagoguery and would have subverted or suppressed the truth through means that made its fair presentation impossible. Charles Lomas argued that the very definition of demagoguery was the employment of "traditional tools of rhetoric with complete indifference to truth."[76] Truth, then, was vulnerable to being distorted or even wholly erased and required ethics to protect it from potentially more efficacious modes of persuasion.

There is already a certain ethic of truth and reality in Lomas's argument, but that ethic was made explicit by speech communication scholars such as Hillbruner and J. Martin Klotsche. Not only were truth and reality the most effective materials of rhetoric, but in holding all preferred choices within the realm of truth and reality, these would also become the standards for moral action. Hillbruner advocated three fundamental criteria for measuring the morality of a speech and guiding the rhetorical critic in his or her criticisms of others' communication: "Seek the truth, tell the truth, and expose lies."[77] The moral worth of an act of communication was thus based upon the truth of the content in that communication. For Klotsche, this was the highest of all values, for from truth comes the only possibility for human freedom.[78] Ethical guidelines in communication, from this perspective, were first and foremost grounded in the moral rightness of objective truth. Even more important, however, was that the rhetorical critic was expected to come to the act of criticism with truth in hand. The critic was then empowered to pass moral judgment upon an act of communication for its congruence to that truth or lack thereof. It is largely out of this school of ethics that the political projects of "debunking" the falsehoods and misperceptions of persuasive campaigns operate. An entire genre of studies in rhetoric and communication was born that took up the crusade of stripping away what critics believed to be lies, deceptions, misdirections, and subterfuge to show the truth and reality that was being obscured by unscrupulous rhetoric. These debunkers made the congruence with truth and reality a vibrant academic, ethical, and political enterprise.

However, truth- and reality-based approaches faced a number of difficulties, even when done as a debunking toward political ends. In the 1960s and 1970s, these difficulties were already challenging the utility of truth and reality as ethical standards from two directions: a questioning of the value of truth in communication and a questioning of the possibility of sufficiently knowing truth. As Oliver pointed out in 1961, the value of truth to a speaker is at best nothing more than a bulwark against major errors rather than a guarantee of efficacy or morality.[79] Indeed, if truth were ever to be known and defined, Oliver argued, there would be no need for rhetoric or even discussion; there would be "no room for compromise," as the truth of the matter would make the goal to be arrived at "immutable."[80] If one considers that the goal of communication was largely understood to be making dissimilar minds more similar by bridging the differences or creating intersubjective junctures, then communication was predicated precisely upon the notion not of truth but of the variability of views. The adherence to a strict view of truth was antithetical not just to dialogue but to the growing study of communication, and especially of rhetoric. Upholding truth and reality as the central ethical or political standard was argued to be, simply, anti-rhetorical.

In place of knowable, objective truth came a view of truth as a product of human interactions and relations. From this view, rather than truth governing the operation of rhetoric, rhetoric was instead the force that gave the truth-value to truths. Truth, then, was a contingent phenomenon. As Scott put it, "It is in time; it can be the result of a process of interaction at a given moment."[81] In renouncing an objective view of truth, many rhetoricians during the 1960s and 1970s argued that reality and truth were created by human action, or, as Brummett put it, "People make their own reality. . . . We must participate in making reality." From Brummett's view, the study of rhetoric focused on a sharing or bridging between self and Other. However, rather than attempting to bring all into line with the truth, such sharing was achieved by individuals advocating and negotiating alternate realities.[82] Both Scott and Brummett advanced arguments for a view of truth and reality as contingent or constructed events. Much was made of this movement during the 1960s and 1970s, and rhetoric as a field relied upon this view at least as much as it was ever beholden to an objectivist view of truth. However, a contingent or constructed truth or reality could not meet the standards for ethical judgment that moralists hoped to establish. In seeking to be able to claim legitimacy for engaging in the moral appraisal of others' acts of communication, critic-moralists required a grounding more stable and legitimate than could be afforded by any contingent or constructed reality. Thus, many rhetorical critics, and particularly those who saw their duty to include passing moral or political judgment, could not fully embrace rhetorical constructivism.

However, we should not mistake the contingency or constructedness of truth and reality that Scott and Brummett described for a willy-nilly attitude toward ethics. Quite on the contrary, most communication scholars of the 1960s and 1970s who advocated views of truth as contingent or constructed wrote significantly on questions of ethics. What emerged from scholars such as Brummett, Scott, and others was a view of ethics as contingent, limited, and variable. That communication ethics would continue to be of interest in the discipline was undoubted. Indeed, at exactly the moment when all possible grounds for stable systems of ethics were disintegrating, the writing on ethics was exploding. The richest portion of this explosion was perhaps precisely in those works that followed the contingency view of truth through to its ethical implications.

The fear of a failing faith in any appeals to objective truths or absolute values was well expressed in 1963 when Myrvin F. Christopherson wrote, "Man cannot find the answer to his problems in an abstract absolute system of thought which theorizes from outside of existence. Thought is only useful when it gets at the problem of the existing individual in the social setting."[83] Part of what Christopherson was expressing was the rising dissatisfaction with mental health explanations for ethical and moral failings. The very possibility of moral judgment had been undermined by the prevalence of social scientific and psychotherapeutic understandings of human behavior. As Mark Klyn noted in 1964, "evil" was no longer a viable concept after the dominance of the social scientific explanations of human behavior. Thus, part of the appeal of the explosion of communication ethics literature to scholars such as Christopherson, Klyn, and others was that it avoided the discourse of the "sick," which had by 1964 been applied "to any culprit from Hitler to the street-corner delinquent."[84] This movement of the social sciences and psychology away from discourses of ethics and toward mental illness, adjustment, and deviancy was already obviously starting in the 1930s and 1940s, but by the 1960s and 1970s the separation had become thorough enough that rhetoric could take up ethics as a core question and even as a definitive part of the field.

However, the appreciation for the contingency of ethics left rhetorical critics in a difficult position. Still compelled to pass moral judgment, they found it difficult to provide any solid ground upon which they might base those judgments. Moralist-critics thus had to confront the contingency of ethics as either a problem to be solved by establishing some absolute or universal system of values or as an addendum or caveat to their critiques. Rogge admonished critics to recognize that "the standards vary as factors in the speech situation vary, that they vary as the necessity for the implementation of the persuader's proposal varies, that they vary as his degree of leadership varies." Since the conditions and standards varied so greatly between speakers and situations, Rogge argued, the critic cannot evaluate the ethics of an act of communication "by checking any timeless, universal set of standards."[85] Scott similarly argued that even if critics have recourse to "some universal ideas in which they are willing to affirm their faith," nonetheless, such ideas are made contingent by the requirement that they engage the specific situation at hand. Thus, even universal ideas "will not give rise to products which are certain."[86] Yet, neither of these views seemed to preclude moralist-critics from passing moral judgment on the communication acts of others. Rather, the critic merely was required to ground his or her judgment in the unique obligations created by the specific situation in which the communication occurred.

Such a foundation, however, was far more conducive to an ethic focused on aiding the individual in choosing how to live his or her life than to a moral system that might allow one to pass judgment on the choices of others. While there was great weight in the belief that, as B. J. Diggs put it, human society requires "common standards, rules, or practices, commonly taught and mutually understood," both the prevalence of social scientific understandings of human behavior and the crumbling philosophical foundations of moral judgments left communication ethics scholars with the recognition that, as Campbell wrote, "men are abandoned because there is no *a priori* truth nor predetermined human nature which can be used as an excuse or justification for action."[87] There was, then, something of a double bind. A certain shared system of norms of behavior was required for human society, but there was an increasing doubt that such norms could be found in any nature, metaphysic, or essence.

This crumbling of moral systems did not diminish responsibility. Quite to the contrary, communication ethics scholars expressed a far greater sense of responsibility when not appealing to timeless or universal grounds for ethics. As Campbell explained, when there is no a priori truth or absolute human nature to which one might appeal for certainty in one's choices, then "the individual is totally responsible for himself, and men are collectively responsible for the societies in which they live."[88] The life of every person is bound up in questions of ethics, and every choice in living is one that fundamentally requires that the individual recognize that this act cannot be given moral certitude. As Scott put it, "We must face decision without the comfortable certainty that God is on our side, knowing that in some ways all causes will be wrong."[89] As stable first premises were made dubious, the responsibility of an individual for his or her choices was only heightened by the fact that the choosing could never appeal to some external truth or righteousness for its morality. Instead, the individual was the site and locus of the event of choice, bearing absolute and total responsibility for that choice and whatever it wrought with no guide or safe harbor that could vouch for that choice.

Consequently, communication ethics scholarship in the 1950s, 1960s, and 1970s brought into sharp focus the fuzziness of ethics. It was precisely in the instability of every ground for moral judgment that ethical questions again became possible. When rhetoric emerged as a discipline unto itself, it required methods and perspectives that would unyoke it from the social scientific and psychotherapeutic models of communication that had dominated the previous decades. Ethics gave the study of rhetoric such an opportunity by offering it status as a philosophical discipline. In failing to find any stable or universal ground for ethics, rhetoricians realized the indeterminacy not only of ethics but also of rhetoric. The inability to define rhetoric as a field and speech communication as a discipline reflected the strength and power of rhetoric and gave both rhetoric and speech communication opportunities to mature. It was these indeterminacies and instabilities that led rhetoricians to philosophical studies, and it was the philosophical approach that allowed them to establish a field of study distinct from the speech sciences.

At the same time, the indeterminacy of the discipline brought forward an explosion of ethical inquiry that enlivened communication ethics. Rather than reaching a truth about the nature of morality or a consensus on an ethical system, by the late 1970s most communication ethics scholars were simply committed, as Campbell put it, to "be constantly engaged in a process of revealing . . . the human power to act in each specific instance."[90] In other words, the question of ethics became a question concerning the ways one can choose to live one's life or regarding what possibilities for being are available to a person today. These are the ethical questions that continued to invigorate and challenge rhetorical studies throughout the last decades of the twentieth century.

5 The Ethics of Objectivism and Relativism

Given the importance and breadth of subject matter in rhetorical studies, perhaps it seems strange to find a strong conservative force within the field of rhetoric and the discipline of speech communication during the last quarter of the twentieth century. The conservation of the discipline, in terms both of preserving the discipline and of creating for it a core and corresponding boundaries, was expressed most clearly in the continuation of the quest to provide definition and cohesion. While ethics maintained a position within the discipline, and though many speech communication scholars continued to advance arguments on ethics not unlike those found in the 1960s and early 1970s, during the last two decades of the twentieth century rhetorical critics and theorists found themselves in the position of specifically advancing and defending various ontologies, epistemologies, and political projects. Inseparable from the ethics of rhetoric that emerged in the discipline, the politics of rhetorical studies in many ways became the legitimating authority by which theories and ethical positions were judged.

From the late 1970s through the 1990s, the discipline of speech communication, and especially rhetoric, continued to maintain a strong interest in ethical questions. After the significant growth during the 1960s and early 1970s, and with rhetoric's increasing tendency to grapple with philosophical questions, speech communication attempted to assert itself through the remainder of the twentieth century as "the most important subject taught in the latter part of the twentieth century. . . . Communication is the ultimate people-making discipline."[1] In addition to speech communication scholars' continued claims about the importance of their work, rhetoricians increasingly viewed their work as "an interdisciplinary enterprise" and expected rhetoric to maintain this status into the foreseeable future.[2] Thus, rhetoric specifically and speech communication more generally claimed a scope of study that could cross any disciplinary boundary and a significance that was fundamental to any human endeavor.

This chapter traces this movement in the discipline through ontology and toward varied political positions from the late 1970s through the 1990s. The continuation of the problem of definition marks the starting point for this discussion, but during this period, the definitional problem itself led into and became embroiled with the philosophical enterprises of rhetoric and communication. The movement of rhetoric toward the study of epistemology and ontology was striking into the very question of what communication is and what it means to study rhetoric. As a prime example of these arguments, this chapter turns to the objectivist criticisms of existential philosophers and then to the relativists' responses. What might be most interesting about these arguments is not their reliance upon philosophical work in ontology and epistemology to establish their differences but rather their frequent use of the criteria of political practicality to assess each position. Also, the concepts of agency and will that pervade both perspectives display some core assumptions about the study of rhetoric in this period that cut across theoretical lines. This chapter concludes with the writings of a handful of rhetorical critics and theorists who called into question the shared assumptions about agency and politics that pervaded much of late-twentieth-century rhetorical theory.

The Recurring Problem of Definition

In many ways, the desire for a coherent philosophy of rhetoric or communication can be traced to a desire to define the discipline of speech communication. While the 1960s and early 1970s saw within the discipline a simultaneous desire for and resistance to definition, by at least the 1980s it seemed that even those who had resisted definition were converted. For example, as early as 1977, Robert Scott began arguing that the concept of communication needed a more restrictive definition: "Distinctions are necessary for research and scholarship to proceed. If we are to study communication, then something must *not* be communication. If all human experience has some aspect about it that should be designated communicative, then there must be other aspects that should not be so designated."[3] Part of what Scott yielded to were the shifting structures and standards of American universities in the period, where the ability to define what one did and to articulate the distinctiveness and uniqueness of its boundaries was a vital administrative obligation.

This problem of definition was of great concern to a large number of scholars in the discipline of speech communication. With a growing gap between increasingly quantitative, experiment-oriented social scientists and more philosophically and humanistically inclined rhetoricians, national conferences were often punctuated by speeches bemoaning the "lack of a clear vision" and extolling the search for "the central issue or organizing principle" that would allow scholars to "make sense" of the discipline.[4] The seeming impossibility of creating an overarching definition that could contain social scientific studies, rhetoric, performance, and so on was only further amplified by the difficulty of defining each of these subfields of speech communication.

The most traditional conceptions of rhetorical studies certainly continued to hold sway in that field, but the simplest view of rhetoric, as "the invention of messages for the sake of gaining adherence to a speaker's point of view," was used more as a counterpoint or as exigence for redefinition than it was actually advanced as the proper definition itself.[5] This tendency to define the field of rhetoric through a history from which one sought to break away, or against which a scholar might rebel, was common among scholars in the late twentieth century. Rhetorical studies, and especially rhetorical criticism, was a site of contested definition, a site where arguments ranged from the narrow view that scholars ought to examine "individual works of art leading to enhanced understanding and appreciation or to normative critical judgments" to the broader view of rhetorical criticism as "pronouncing a judgment upon the persuasive effects of almost anything."[6] These definitions were not merely descriptions, just as no historical study is a purely objective account of what occurred, but also were prescriptive, claiming what rightly should and should not count as rhetoric.

The question concerning which texts or phenomena ought properly to fall under the scrutiny of the rhetorical critic was likewise an argument that continued throughout the period. Just as was the case throughout the twentieth century, scholars in the last two decades acknowledged platform oratory as no longer the primary means of conducting politics. As Michael Calvin McGee put it, "The public's business is now being done more via direct mail, television spots, documentaries, mass entertainment, and 'quotable quotes' on the evening news than through the more traditional media."[7] Perceiving a continued preoccupation with platform oratory in the study of rhetoric, such scholars as McGee and Kari Whittenberger-Keith advocated that the field should broaden its scope "to include popular as well as more traditional scholarly artifacts, in order to truly understand the rhetorical functions of discourse in American society."[8] Similar to calls made by communication scholars since the beginnings of American speech studies, Whittenberger-Keith was arguing for the inclusion not only of popular media but also of "everyday" as well as "private" events of communication. Kent A. Ono and John M. Sloop issued a similar call for research into "vernacular discourse," which they contended had been largely ignored by the discipline. Ono and

Sloop's advocacy calls attention to the fact that by the 1990s, rhetoric and other humanistic modes of engaging communication studies had largely surrendered the central role of dialogue and discussion between individuals or in small groups to the social scientists. In so doing, because social scientists in communication studies were not methodologically well equipped (nor epistemologically well inclined) to ask questions about the ethical or political qualities of communication events, rhetoricians at the end of the twentieth century had to reopen a domain of communication practices that had been recognized for at least scores of decades as perhaps the most ethically and politically important: the conversation and dialogue.

These calls to study everyday, private, and vernacular discourses were claims not only that a proper examination of communication requires a broader perspective but also that the political and ethical obligations of academics established what Ono and Sloop called a "specific need, given historical power relations, to study communities that have been systematically ignored."[9] Similarly, Kendall R. Phillips bemoaned the tendency for rhetorical scholars in the discipline of speech communication to study predominantly mainstream political oratory and texts. By focusing on this public sphere, Phillips argued, rhetorical critics "obscure the complexity and diversity of contemporary discourse by excluding the marginal and resistant by bracketing the differences that motivate dissent."[10] The definitions of both the field of rhetoric and the discipline of speech communication were thus political (and perhaps ethical) questions. They were bound up with the broader discussion of the ethics and politics of speech that cut across the different strands of rhetoric and communication during the time.

Questions of ethics were as prominent in speech communication in this period as in any prior, even if most vociferous in the rhetorical literature. Communication scholars commonly bemoaned a lack of ethics, morals, or values. Ralph Eubanks wrote that he perceived the world of the late 1970s as one of "'cultural derangement,' moral uncertainty, and intellectual skepticism."[11] Walter R. Fisher similarly argued that American society had "lost a sense of wisdom. To regain it, we need to reaffirm the place of value as a component of knowledge."[12] Throughout the history of the spoken word, there is a nearly incessant claim that, at this moment, civilization is somehow in a unique state of moral decline.

As in previous periods, ameliorating this failing in values, wisdom, or ethics was the special province of speech communication, but now also especially of rhetorical studies. As Kenneth E. Andersen put it, "Those of us with academic and professional expertise in communication should be seen as having responsibilities beyond those of the ordinary member of the polis."[13] Studies of ethics, and particularly of communication ethics, were not merely one element of the discipline of speech communication and the field of rhetoric; rather, they were positioned by Ronald Arnett as "the practical heart of the disciplinary field." This is not to say that these scholars believed communication and rhetorical studies would offer the moral panacea that would save the failing values of society—most agreed with Arnett's warning that "Speech Communication cannot with confidence offer *the* right answers."[14] The capacity of speech communication to provide safe passage through the rocky straits of ethical and political dilemmas here differed and was more subdued than in the early-twentieth-century writing of the speech sciences and mental hygienists but was no less energetic in its attention to ethical issues and its significance in the contribution to developing ethical theories.

Regardless of the attenuation of rhetoric's claim to ethical importance, in many ways a desire to engage in the process of moralizing was still woven into the communication ethics literature. Arnett identified communication ethics with the willingness and courage to "question another's decision."[15] Similarly, Andersen argued that communication ethics scholars ought to "provide a sufficient understanding of the communication process so people can validly warn/condemn others when the means are corrosive."[16] Jim A. Kuypers wrote that the need for values was to be found in our need "to hold individual members of society accountable/responsible for their actions/utterances."[17] Ethics were as much tools for the judgment of others and the protection of society as for informing an individual's way of living. Communication was, after all, still quite dangerous. The possibility of demagogues and the specter of Hitler required that rhetoric provide some bulwark against the worst kinds of rhetorical excesses and the capacity for the potent power of persuasion to be put to nefarious ends.

The importance of moralizing was not only prominent in the communication ethics literature but also served a key function in rhetorical criticism. While the perception by rhetorical critics was that "ethical evaluations are infrequently made," such a view described what scholars found unacceptable about the practice of criticism.[18] Many scholars believed that the act of criticism included the burden to pass moral judgment upon the works at hand. These rhetorical scholars did not, however, see this as a continuation of the tradition of rhetorical studies but as a break from it. Craig R. Smith and Howard Streifford in the mid-1970s expressed the view of many rhetorical scholars when they wrote that it was "only recently" that rhetoricians had begun "to suggest that a systematic study of values is essential to sound rhetorical theorizing and criticism."[19] Such studies of value systems were not advanced primarily in order to understand a rhetor's capacity to utilize appeals to values with a given audience. They served instead to fulfill the duty of the rhetorical critic to find and assess the particular values expressed in a rhetorical artifact. Thus, the rhetorical critic was considered as operating under a specific obligation, as James F. Klumpp and Thomas A. Hollihan wrote, "to become morally engaged."[20] In addition to rendering moral judgments, this also meant that the critic was charged with the duty of discerning or constructing ethical systems and moral theories. Criticism embraced not merely determining which rhetorical acts conformed to and expressed values that society ought to uphold and which did not but also theorizing about the nature of those values.

In this role, rhetoricians could claim that their field was the one through which one might discern moral truths. Rhetoric could be not only a place where morality was demonstrated or practiced but also a path for inquiry into moral truth. As Christopher Lyle Johnstone put it, "Moral truth is grasped through the process of practical judging; rhetoric aims at bringing about such judging, and thus at articulating the grounds of moral truth."[21] James M. Tallmon made a similar case for rhetoric's unique claim to ethical and moral knowledge, based on the relationship between rhetoric and the practical judgment of particular cases: "Questions of ethics involve particular cases, which, in turn, involve moral dilemmas. Moral dilemmas can be defined by and bound to real circumstances, real people, and real actions in real time and real space. Such contingencies have traditionally been the special province of rhetorical reasoning."[22] Rhetoric and rhetoricians would thus not only operate under the obligation to consider ethical questions but also find themselves uniquely qualified to answer those questions. Rhetorical criticism and theory were positioned so as to be inextricable from the study of ethics.

Rhetoric's capacity to create, to perpetuate, or to alter moral and ethical systems further fueled the perception of rhetorical criticism and theory as inherently moralistic endeavors. If communication was the process of person-making, it was only logical that it should also be the human activity most significant in the formation of social values. Celeste Michelle Condit referred to this function as "the rhetorical construction of morality."[23] Klumpp and Hollihan, for example, wrote that "the moral imperative demands that the critic recognize that a society remakes its values in responding to problems and opportunities through rhetorical choice."[24] Thus, rhetoric had the capacity both to discover ethical qualities through rhetorical argument and exchange as well as to create and instill ethics through rhetorical exhortation. Whether objectivist or relativist, whether realist or constructivist, rhetoric was the trunk of the ethical tree from which one could trace out its roots or from which its limbs and fruits could grow.

Rhetoric as a Philosophical Enterprise

Rhetoric could thus claim to displace philosophy as the field of study most competent to conduct ethical inquiry. Philosophers, as Calvin O. Schrag put it, were viewed by many rhetoricians as "logic choppers and revelers in pure theory who chase after fugitive epistemological givens and dredge up ponderous thoughts about being and non-being." It was rhetoric, not philosophy, that would generate insight into ethics. Philosophy was viewed as losing relevance to the lived experience of ethics, while rhetoric, Schrag wrote, "at least keeps its pulse on the everyday affairs of the *polis*."[25] The study of rhetoric, positioning itself where philosophy and science had failed, Scott wrote, would be not only "a practical capacity to find means to ends on specific occasions" but, far more important, "a human potentiality to understand the human condition."[26] Perhaps nowhere was this view more clearly expressed than in Frank J. Macke's 1991 article on the evolution of the discipline of speech communication. The very heart of philosophy as the study of being was displaced: "It is through the study of speech (as *parole*), more than philosophy, that students can be led to an awareness of what it means to be a person, how a human being is constituted and how fragile and nomadic—and nameless—life actually is."[27] If the central obsession of philosophy had been the study of being (ontology), rhetoric now laid claim to a more practical, more utile, and more meaningful insight into how beings actually work, what it means to be in the world right now, rather than to the abstract principle of being as a category of existence, an essence, or a theoretical status.

While rhetoricians in the 1960s and 1970s had leaned heavily on philosophers for the grounds of their ethical claims, in the 1980s and 1990s rhetoric was called to stand on its own, to develop its own philosophies, and to treat philosophical texts not as sacred or expert but as arguments to be taken apart and put back together again. In this new role, Paul R. Falzer called upon speech communication scholars to "abandon the geological image with its underlaborer conception of philosophy and bring to an end their discipline's parasitic dependence."[28] Similarly, communication ethics scholars like Arnett warned against placing the discipline "at the mercy of expert opinion" and advocated instead that "argument, debate, and public discourse over what is and is not ethical must continue."[29] Speech communication, rhetoric, and communication ethics claimed a status independent of and equal to philosophy, psychology, or any of the other disciplines and fields upon which they had relied and from which they would continue to draw. It was at this point that speech communication could assert itself as a fully mature discipline and rhetoric as a unique field of new academic research.

The discourse in the discipline did not cease to engage the works of philosophers or psychologists. On the contrary, communication scholars were all the more energetic in their adaptation and application of philosophical texts. However, the function of these texts changed between the 1970s and the 1990s as speech communication repositioned itself, as John Stewart wrote in 1991, "not only as an ontologically derived or secondary phenomena but also as a primary one."[30] Speech communication scholars of all stripes, but especially those in rhetoric and communication ethics, asserted themselves as primary scholars connected with but in no way dependent upon or subordinate to philosophy or psychology.

Given this new relationship to the disciplines that had previously served as the foundations upon which views of communication ethics had been built, rhetoricians and communication ethicists found themselves in the new role of asking fundamental questions about what makes ethics possible. As Eubanks put it in 1980, "The communication ethicist must at last confront the question: What creates moral obligation, or duty, in a symbolic transaction?"[31] Concerned previously with how a particular philosophical view might be deployed or applied to a communication event, scholars were now asked to grapple with such questions as "What ethics?" and, far more difficult, "Why ethics?" Confronted with the need to provide some basis from which to engage in ethical judgment, or at minimum some grounds upon which to claim even the possibility of asking ethical questions, rhetoricians took up studies of epistemology and ontology.

To some extent, this move to epistemological and ontological inquiry had its beginnings in the 1960s and 1970s with the importation of existentialism into speech communication. In the 1980s and 1990s, the furor over the epistemic view of rhetoric was dwarfed by a related debate over the status of "postmodern," "post-structural," and "critical theory" conceptions of communication. A substantial number of communication scholars began both to draw upon and to grapple with such conceptions—taking them not only from philosophy but also from psychology, sociology, media studies, political theory, literary studies, and a host of other areas. Those who engaged these new conceptions argued, as did Stewart, that they "are concerned with issues central to this discipline's research and teaching. They are not simply engaged in esoteric, idiosyncratic, or mystical speculations about arcane philosophical constructs, but are working out genuinely innovative understandings of reason, inquiry, language, and speech communication."[32] This critical distinction not only required research to be practical if it was to be valued in the field of rhetoric but distinguished the field from the pejorative label of philosophy understood as disconnected metaphysical musings.

However, rhetoric and speech communication scholars did not all meet this new literature openly. Indeed, as Douglas E. Thomas noted, the discipline's response was characterized by a tendency to depict postmodernism and post-structuralism "in ways that border on caricature and [that] portray very serious and important scholarship in a trivial way."[33] Edward Schiappa similarly noted that some scholars in the discipline, when confronted with postmodern thinkers, tended to "reduce a complex body of theoretical and critical literature to a stereotype—a stereotype that ought to be resisted."[34] Many of these texts worked out of or through unfamiliar academic traditions, such as German idealism and French literature and poetry. They likewise often contained experiments in style that made the constructions unwieldy, included esoteric or even entirely new terminology, and were usually translated from German, French, or Italian. The result was that the primary texts of postmodern and post-structural thinkers, even in excellent translations, required significantly more attention and work from the reader than was common of American humanities scholarship of the time.

Some in rhetoric simply turned away from the task of theorizing or philosophizing about human communication and chose instead to continue their critical practices without concern for the questions that arose about the grounds for such practices. Some scholars produced short aphorisms or dismissive anecdotes in order to exorcise any concern for the grounds of their work. One such anecdote that is commonly retold is the story of Lloyd Bitzer attempting to substantiate the existence of a knowable, expressible, objective, empirical reality while arguing with an individual who had expressed sympathies with postmodern and post-structural views. Bitzer, as the story goes, attempted a demonstrative argument for such a reality by slamming a book down on the table and asserting, "The book is on the table!"[35] While rhetorically forceful, Bitzer's performance did nothing then, and its retelling still does nothing today, to actually engage the arguments about postmodernism and post-structuralism. If anything, the forcefulness and plainness of the act expressed a blunt refusal to consider and respond to these positions.

As Della Pollock and J. Robert Cox noted, there arose a frequent and at times fervent "refusal to *engage the arguments of critical theory critically,* to come to terms with the ideologically-embedded nature of one's own claims."[36] It was not merely that many scholars went on about the business of rhetorical criticism and ethical theorizing as if nothing had happened in the discipline since the 1970s but also that many of these scholars seemed to reject rabidly the propriety of the questions being posed by communication scholars—which properly were more an extension of the theorizing that started with the infusion of existentialism in the 1950s and 1960s than they were "new."

On the other hand, some scholars participated in the ontological and epistemological debates within the discipline. Perhaps the most significant debate that raged throughout the 1980s and into the 1990s in this field occurred between those who supported an objectivist view and those who advanced a subjectivist view of reality. Cutting across both epistemology and ontology, these two schools of thought not only clashed at the theoretical level but also were enmeshed in arguments about the ethics and politics of communication. Indicting the existential, postmodern, and post-structural views by advocating an existing and at least partially knowable objective reality became a career unto itself for some scholars.

In part, as Pollock and Cox noted, it was a sense that these new philosophies had stripped communication scholars of "the lost Eden of 'common sense'" and a desire to recover stable notions of "the True, the Good, and the Beautiful" that drove some in speech communication to advocate that reality not only objectively exists but that its objective existence is accessible to human knowers.[37] Indeed, for Robert C. Rowland and a significant number of others in rhetoric and speech communication, notions of truth, goodness, and beauty could not be separated from a feeling that the very possibility of "principled argument" relies upon a "real world" against which one might "test arguments."[38] The perceived danger of a world in which all knowledge is reduced to the status of belief was not only an inability to gauge the truth, goodness, or beauty of argument but also, as Earl Croasmun and Richard A. Cherwitz wrote, an inability to base actions on conscious choices.[39] The conflation of existential, postmodern, and post-structural views under the labels "relativism" or "consensus theory" allowed detractors to dismiss such positions en masse for being ethically detrimental views of reality and knowledge, as well as for being politically dangerous. Ono and Sloop described the fear well, noting the common criticism that "the principle danger in taking a 'postmodern' stance that there are no sure truths is inaction. . . . One is left with an uneasy and skeptical outlook that encourages distrust of all positions."[40] We should not, however, mischaracterize all responses to postmodern and post-structural theory as either simple refusal or gross reductionism. There were a number of arguments and clear objections advanced by objectivist rhetorical scholars that did critically engage these emerging approaches to rhetorical scholarship.

The Objectivist Reaction

In response to the "relativistic" rhetorical theorists, scholars such as Croasmun and Cherwitz advanced a distinction between reality and knowledge that would permit them to claim objective grounds for judgment and action.[41] In their view, objective reality could be described as "nonhumanly generated 'recalcitrance' to linguistic creativity."[42] For example, Celeste Condit Railsback argued that "the physiological process of starvation, because of the physiological consequences it entails, exerts an objective force upon human language structures which tends to make 'food' (or its variants) a positive term."[43] It is this "recalcitrance," as empirical and objective reality, that must serve, according to Croasmun and Cherwitz, as the grounds for truth far more than any individual or social belief.[44] Setting aside the significant and obvious problems with the example of food as a positive term, the base argument here has a clear reference to the common experience of the world resisting one's will. The fact that one experiences resistance from objects in the world when one seeks to exercise one's will upon them gives clear evidence that some reality exists outside of perception.

Of course, one of the problems of objective reality, for rhetoricians, involved not only whether or not it existed but how we might come to know it. In some sense, if it was to serve the role of criterion, reality would have to be knowable. Cherwitz and James W. Hikins argued that, at least to some extent, this reality is presented to us in experience "directly." The world exists independently of any perception of it and serves as the fundamental test not only of what is and what is not but also of the relationships among things. Cherwitz and Hikins claimed that relations are not "shaped *by* perspectives," because the objectively existing relations "form the basis *of* human perspectives."[45] They advanced the position that, rather than human perception shaping reality, some kind of objective reality was the basis of human perceptions, giving those perceptions their basic shape and content. In response to the idea that reality or truth was negotiated between individuals—that is, through their relationships—Cherwitz and Hikins argued that this type of intersubjectivist view of reality could operate only if there were already an objective and prior reality that encompassed both the self and other(s) in the relationship as well as the relationship itself. We might end up with some differences in our interpretations as we deploy these perceptions, but the base form of the perceptions was not subjective.

The objective "recalcitrance" that grounded communication and choice for Cherwitz, Condit, Croasmun, Hikins, and Rowland was also a political necessity for some rhetorical scholars who had taken up projects of political emancipation or liberation. For example, Dana Cloud, while recognizing the persuasive force that rhetorical constructions can have, argued that these "cannot be regarded as being as real as the dead and wounded people. This acknowledgment is necessary if we are to be able to privilege politically the voices and realities of people who are, in some real way, oppressed."[46] Cloud and others—either implicitly or explicitly—endorsed the view of reality expressed by Cherwitz, Condit, Croasmun, Hikins, and Rowland, but not because of a particular view of ontology or epistemology. Rather, Cloud did so because any alternative view of reality was politically unacceptable. To permit reality to be anything but objectively determined, from Cloud's perspective, would be to denigrate many peoples' experiences of severe and immediate oppression.

For others, the grounds for positing an objectively existing reality and human access to it were found in the perceived nature of rhetorical acts. Cherwitz and Thomas J. Darwin argued that it would be logically impossible to engage in an act of advocacy if one were skeptical about the objective existence of reality, because "advocacy itself is a nonskeptical act."[47] The existence of rhetoric as advocacy thus seemed to Cherwitz and Darwin to contradict the ideas that reality was relative and that knowledge of objective reality was not possible. Croasmun and Cherwitz similarly argued that the fact that audiences use their distinctions between perception and reality as criteria for the veracity and ethicality of rhetoric likewise attests to the existence of an objective and independent reality that is accessible by the human knower.[48] Here the evidence for an objective reality was grounded in the fact that people's actions demonstrate a belief that such a reality exists.

For the specific study of communication ethics, the most important type of reality was the existence and value of a shared essential nature of all human beings. As Eubanks put it, "The truth most important for us to recognize is that the moral law, constituted in the 'dual demands' of the right and the good, derives from man's essential nature as a valuing creature."[49] In short, if there was an objectively real essence of what it means to be human, then this might serve as the grounds for moral judgment of human action. Eubanks followed in the humanist and neo-Aristotelian traditions of rhetorical ethics, believing that the correspondence of an existent thing to its ideal nature could be the measure of what was good, ethical, valuable, or right. An objectively existing human essence grounded the communication ethics not only of Eubanks but also of Christopher Johnstone and Chaim Perelman. In an effort to transcend the political and cultural limits of the ethics common to democratists and other views, Johnstone argued that "the one thing that all human beings have in common" is "our human substance."[50] The objective reality of a human essence was to provide a way that communication ethics might find a ground that transcends any locality of place or time. Faith in both the existence and the value of a universal human essence thus provided some speech communication scholars with a claim to objective criteria for ethical communication.

Perelman argued that the grounds for communication ethics were properly found in the nature of what is "shared by all humanity," that is to say, in "universal principles of law and morals" such as reason, truth, liberty, justice, and respect for human dignity.[51] Moral law, thus, is objectively real for these communication ethicists since, as Eubanks wrote, it "is man's own essential nature appearing as commanding authority."[52] Communication, in this view, and indeed any human action, is to be judged morally by its degree of correspondence with and support for the presupposed essential nature of the human being. As Johnstone put it, "The fulfillment of human nature emerges from these discussions as the moral 'given' in the search for a sound ethic for communication."[53] Thus, all one had to do was determine the essential nature of humanness and use this as the rule for right action, but again one must have a method to know the true reality of human nature.

The method by which a knower might apprehend objective reality, whether that be an objective physical world or a universal human essence, was not only through direct experience of sensory data but also through a dialectical testing of hypotheses in rhetorical contestation. In this way, rhetoricians who were invested in objective views of reality positioned rhetoric as the proper dialectical method of testing hypotheses about the substance of reality. Since rhetoric took under its purview all those communication events in which there might be argument, rhetoricians considered the process of dialectical argumentation their domain. Thus, the establishment of dialectical argument as the means by which objective truths might be discovered established rhetoric as the means for grasping reality. What is and is not true, from the view of Croasmun and Cherwitz and many other objectivist rhetoricians, was thus best discovered "in the dialectical process of inquiry—the interaction of opposing views."[54] Whatever position could carry the day in a balanced and reasoned exchange was the one most likely to correspond to the true nature of the human.

Communication ethics based on a universal human nature shared this tendency with advocates of other forms of objectivism. According to Johnstone, the fundamental nature of the rhetorical act is not merely "a disclosure of one's practical reasonings" but, far more important, "a submission of those reasonings to the scrutiny of others." Most rhetoricians and communication ethicists who placed their faith in an essential human nature agreed that, as Johnstone put it, "the greater the extent to which a practical proposition withstands the critical scrutiny of other minds, the greater the probability that it is true."[55] This capacity for rhetoric to explore the truth was thus the means not only by which reality might best be known but also by which the criteria for ethical communication should be established. If rhetoric is fallible as a method and our knowledge of the objective truth is always incomplete, this epistemological problem only magnifies the importance of the constant use of proper rhetorical techniques to best approximate the universal essence or the objective truths that ought to guide ethical communication. Thus, human nature perspectives represent an objectivist ethic, in at least the more limited sense that they hold to an objectively existing human essence or nature that should guide communication ethics.

The Relativist Rebuttal

In contrast to the objectivist view of reality, ethics, and rhetoric, a number of scholars drawing on earlier existential and epistemic rhetorics began advocating what they and their detractors would both label "relativistic" views of rhetoric. The relativists began with one simple assertion, a response to the objectivists' desire for knowledge of an objective reality, perhaps most clearly expressed by Scott in 1990 when he wrote that "the twentieth century answer to the seventeenth century question 'How can one be certain?' is that one cannot."[56] The belief that one can have even approximate access to objective reality was supplanted by a skepticism in which every belief would have to be coupled with a certain degree of doubt. Similarly, Scott responded to the search for objective certainty for grounding emancipatory political projects with a warning that it was "the certainty of some commanding Truth taken as axiomatic" that most often legitimized "the justification of injury to others, especially when that injury is wide scale finding expression in social and economic dominance or violence."[57] If one did believe one's actions were based on an objectively real moral rule, then one could justify a wide range of actions without the need for personal responsibility for those actions, as each was merely following out the orders commanded by nature and reality. Under such a model, ethics become merely the choice of whether or not one follows the rules, but one bears no responsibility for the rules themselves, as they are posited to exist objectively. Thus, the objectivist position was characterized not only as theoretically unsound but also as ethically and politically dangerous.

Even rhetorical objectivists such as Eubanks recognized that rhetoric has not only the capacity to express and represent but also "the potential of doing things to the lives of others."[58] Relativists such as Barry Brummett took this view a step further to argue that, rather than a reality, a truth, or a human essence existing prior to and apart from human knowledge, it is precisely "rhetorical communication, or reason-giving discourse designed to influence people symbolically," that is the "active ingredient in cultures which generates and legitimates ethical values, other values, and even reality itself."[59] This is not to say that rhetoric distorts or alters some essential nature, nor even to claim that rhetoric is a poor facsimile of what is "really real." Rather, Brummet, like Michael McGuire, held that *rhetoric in any condition serves the general function of contributing to what counts as knowledge in a society. . . .* Rhetoric is an agent for the social construction of reality."[60] Rather than a priori, universal, or objective truths, the relativist view of rhetoric and ethics saw all truths—whether about the nature of reality, the essence of the human, or the moral quality of an act—as, Brummett wrote, "fundamentally negotiable . . . perforce changeable and subject to discussion."[61] Contrary to the objectivist view of rhetoric finding the reality of the world through dialectical exchange, the relativists posed that rhetoric was engaged in a process of creating these realities and of marshalling belief to enforce their status as truth. Acts of communication, thus, did not have their ethical value because they represented or failed to represent objective reality or human essence; rather, the ethical import of rhetoric originated in its capacity to create reality and to shape the ethical codes by which individuals live. The question was not how to bring the manifest world into accord with the objective ideals but what kind of world we ought to create.

Under the label of relativism or, alternatively, of consensus theory, scholars came to lump together a host of divergent schools of thought. Brummett's ethical relativism, Scott's epistemic rhetoric, existentialist philosophies of communication, and the views of communication influenced by postmodern and post-structural writers were all considered as varying forms of relativism. For example, Cloud argued that post-structuralism was best labeled "relativist" because it depicted reality as "a set of texts, or a discursive formation, rhetorically created and altered."[62] It was by reducing these diverse and divergent schools of thought to relativism that the central arguments over objective reality and human nature continued to be the focal points for rhetorical theorizing at this time.

According to relativists, rhetoric was of central importance in establishing value and reality, because its influence upon people was greater than "education, socialization, or simply being-together."[63] As Sonja K. Foss and Ann Gill put it in their defense of Michel Foucault's post-structural philosophy, relativist rhetorical theory was not merely "the studies of lives and times (history), what is real and good (philosophy), and how individuals think (psychology) because it focuses on rhetoric not as the everyday discourse of our lives but as the global creator of all other thought."[64] Rhetoric, from the relativist position, was the governing discipline, the one that could explain the possibility and the formation of any truth claim made by any other discipline.

Political Foundations for Rhetorical Theories

As noted previously, one of the most ardent criticisms of this view was that it provided no grounds upon which one might base choices—ethical or otherwise. Relativists and consensus theorists responded by pointing out that the problem was as much one of the criteria for choice as it was one of the view of reality. Jeffery Bineham refuted Hikins by pointing out that anxieties about relativism and consensus theory are really due to feelings that certainty is prerequisite to decision.[65] In response to this same problem, Thomas argued that "realizing that all reality is textual does not force one to conclude that there is no means of privileging one interpretation over another. Rather, the realization that all reality is textual forces us to re-evaluate the ways in which we privilege systems of interpretation."[66] Similarly, Brummett held that relativists are not denied the opportunity for choice or action, but they are required to extend arguments to others as rhetorical acts—as arguments rather than as condemnations, judgments, or accusations.[67] From this perspective, the criterion for action was not certainty but rather necessity. One has no choice but to act and to make judgments, and in any such event one must be willing to accept what Scott called "some degree of discomfort."[68] While lacking the moral certitude that empowered the ethical and political condemnations made by objectivists, the relativists did embrace the necessity of decision and choice as a part of the condition of existence. That one lacked stable grounds for such choices only imposed a higher degree of caution and personal responsibility for those choices. One no longer was merely responsible for following a moral law but had to take responsibility for the necessary construction, unavoidable biases, and inevitable fallibility of any law, rule, or guideline that might shape one's choices.

This argument over the criteria for action and the ability of the relativist to decide between alternatives spurred a fierce political argument among rhetoricians in departments of communication. Many committed to liberatory and counter-hegemonic political projects, such as Cloud, argued that from the relativist position, it is not possible to "adjudicate the truth or falsity of discourse, or to speculate about whose interests are served by a particular set of texts."[69] Not only the status of knowledge as relative but also the status of reality as indeterminate or contingent seemed politically paralyzing to some speech communication scholars. Evan Blythin argued that the view of reality "as always in a state of flux and uncertainty" would lead one into "a kind of existential despair not appropriate to decision-making."[70] What was at stake in this argument was the question of whose work would be considered politically relevant. Working within a discipline that had long been concerned with politics, rhetoricians were now explicitly judging arguments, theories, and philosophies by their political potential as much as by their internal coherence or their scholarly merit.

What was significantly different about the arguments from the late 1970s through the 1990s, compared to much of what had come before, was that some rhetoricians and other speech communication scholars were now viewing their scholarly research and publications as fundamentally political acts. Whereas the discipline of speech communication had always been politicized, by the 1980s the predominant view of rhetoricians had come to be that, as Schiappa put it, "there is an unmistakable political dimension to every act of theory, criticism, and teaching that we perform."[71] As Thomas K. Nakayama and Robert L. Krizek argued, whether it was rhetorical theory, rhetorical criticism, communication ethics, or even social scientific research, scholarship was often recognized as "'politically created' within constitutive sociohierarchical power relations."[72] As politically potent work, scholarship thus bore certain responsibilities beyond veracity, intellectual contribution, or professionalism. A scholar was now considered to be politically responsible for his or her work, as well as being what Klumpp and Hollihan called "a moral participant, cognizant of the power and responsibility that accompanies full critical participation in his/her society."[73] This meant not only that scholars had a political responsibility in the conduct of their profession but that the political impacts of any theory were valid reasons for the adoption or dismissal of that position.

Scholars who ignored, eschewed, or denied their political and moral responsibilities were accused of supporting what Hollihan described as "the mystery that preserves the social order." They were, in short, complicit in continuing the social and political ills against which many rhetorical theorists and critics positioned their work. Hollihan argued that if the critic would actively take up the potential for his or her scholarship to have moral or political import, then scholars could work to "illuminate the implications of mystification, peel back the mystery, and thus raise the issues that can lead to social change."[74] On the other hand, when Michael Leff attempted to advocate a form of criticism or theory that might not advance a political cause, he was criticized by Barbara Warnick for potentially mystifying and celebrating "the discourse of power."[75] The moralistic judgment that was common to rhetorical criticism was turned inward to judge rhetorical theory and scholarship itself.

The common belief in the politicality of scholarship focused rhetorical scholars' attention on questions concerning which rhetorical theories and methods were most appropriate for achieving emancipatory political purposes. Thus, the arguments made against the relativist positions were often claims of political superiority. For example, John Murphy's criticism of critical rhetoric argued that the "preoccupation with change in discursive formation, public vocabularies, performative traditions, or whatever label one wishes to use, can occlude the struggles of those . . . who put their lives at risk as they struggle for change in material circumstances."[76] Put more vehemently by Cloud, the defense of "practical truth, bodily reality, and material oppression" as more than merely discursive is crucial if one wishes to recognize that people do in fact go hungry and die in war.[77] In both these cases there lurks the objectively real world that exists independent of our perception and demands of our rhetoric a truth, an accuracy of depiction, if it is to be ethically and politically sound.

Objectivist rhetoricians also critiqued relativist and postmodern rhetorics for failing to provide a clearly defined political goal or project. Whatever social or political change might come from relativistic theories, Philip Wander argued, it could not be considered progressive: "To be progressive, change must progress toward something. That something, oriented around traditional humanist notions of human potential, is grounded in the emancipation of human potential."[78] Maurice Charland made the indictment all the clearer when he criticized rhetoricians influenced by the writings of Foucault for offering "no *telos* except for constant critique." Without such a guiding end point, Charland argued, "*praxis* is halted because we have no reason to intervene one way or another."[79] A truly political project must ground itself, according to these critics, in a culminating, ideal state of government, consciousness, relations, or being. The objectivist ethic demanded a politics that worked toward making present an ideal grounded in some claim to moral righteousness. Such moral righteousness and political idealism likewise demanded some kind of reality, such as human nature, to give it a foundation and status as truth.

In response to these criticisms, rhetoric scholars influenced by postmodern and post-structural writings argued that they did indeed have constructive political projects and perhaps even a *telos* that guided their scholarship. Ronald F. Wendt expressed this position well in 1996: "Those who envision modernism and postmodernism as complementary and interrelated (labeled 'affirmative postmodernists' by Rosenau, 1992) will recognize progression toward goals (and the resultant politics) even within postmodernism (see Schrag, 1992). Postmodernism (and textual poaching) in this sense is not free of agendas or progression, but both the goals themselves and the tactics for reaching these goals will look quite different from modern rational approaches."[80] Rather than call into question the value of a *telos* or of a programmatic political project, Wendt here echoed most other critical rhetoricians arguing that they either had a superior strategy or a superior political vision. If the objectivists accused them of having no politics or goals, it was only because their goals and politics were so radically different in their very form. However, in attempting to rebut Cloud and Murphy, some post-structural and postmodern rhetorical scholars tried to make their politics look more recognizable to objectivists. Ono and Sloop noted that even the "skeptical critic necessarily and often unconsciously commits to a *telos* despite her attempts to resist the ever-present threat of dogmatism." Thus, in their readings and deployments of the writings of postmodern and post-structural thinkers, especially in the case of Foucault, they claimed to hold "the same type of *telos*" that rhetoricians generally found politically necessary.[81] From the combination of the postmodern and post-structural works with the teleological political projects of liberation, critical rhetorician Raymie E. McKerrow argued that their projects contained not only a specific end vision for the future but also a specific instrument for realizing that vision.[82] Indeed, the means and the goal were broadly interconnected for critical rhetoricians as critique itself took on a strong political meaning.

The goal and political *telos* of many critical rhetoric scholars was defined at least in part by critical rhetoric's oppositional stance. The form of critique advanced by McKerrow and other critical rhetoricians gained its force and legitimacy by having "as its object something which it is 'against.'"[83] In many ways, this is not substantially different from the ideological view expressed by Wander. Indeed, the very definition of Wander's ideological rhetorical studies centered on recognizing "the existence of powerful vested interests benefiting from and consistently urging policies and technologies that threaten life on this planet," then combining this recognition with a motivation to fight against these "vested interests" and to "search for alternatives."[84] Ideological and critical rhetorics, while grounded in different ontological and epistemological positions regarding objectivity and relativity, wound up at nearly the same political point. Both took stances against existing political and economic forces for the purpose of realizing their individual visions of a better future. That is to say, both engaged in political projects of liberation or emancipation.

Barbara Biesecker noted this tendency for postmodern and post-structural thinking to be used merely as support for or as building blocks of political and academic projects that were already acceptable within the discipline. While scholars found in post-structural thought "a critical lexicon . . . establishing a crucial point of contact between us and others in the humanities," Biesecker wrote, the deployment of that lexicon nonetheless allowed rhetoricians "to study the art of persuasion in roughly the same old way."[85] Nowhere was this truer than in the discipline's interactions with the work of Foucault. Even after Foucault had written several essays explicitly and unequivocally critiquing humanism, the humanist underpinnings of the discipline's politics made it quite easy for Carole Blair and Martha Cooper to read Foucault as "certainly sympathetic to the general character of the humanist perspective."[86] Some of the objectivist political rhetoricians, such as Charland, would claim that "Foucault's project becomes integrated into a rewritten canon of invention for the critic committed to undermining structures of power."[87] Foucault is just one case of how relativistic, existential, postmodern, and post-structural views, though finding their way into the discipline throughout the 1970s, 1980s, and 1990s, were in many ways being assimilated into mainstream projects more than they were generating additional ways of thinking about rhetoric or politics.

However, there were noticeable moments of slippage, when there emerged the possibility of a politics that was fundamentally different from humanist projects. For example, the notion of a project or *telos* in critical rhetoric seems at times to represent more a moment of reflection than an end goal or even an ideal. McKerrow wrote that, whereas some political projects seek as their end goal the establishment of a certain stable and ideal power relation, "a critical rhetor would experience no such contentment. There is an ever-present tension between one's life at a moment in time, with a set of power relations relatively intact, and the possibility of constant challenge which would revise that set."[88] The goal, from this vantage point, is not to escape from the influences or dynamics of power, nor to establish some ideal set of power relations, but to seek out the possibilities that might be present but not yet utilized within existing power relations. As McKerrow put it, "Power, thus conceived, is not repressive, but productive—it is an active[,] potentially positive force which creates social relations and sustains them through the appropriation of a discourse that 'models' the relations through its expression."[89] Productive power relations, not repressing but repeating and sustaining particular relations, are not hegemonic forces of pure exclusion and control. Rather, power's productivity, repetition, and sustaining force are full of holes, gaps, inconsistencies, and opportunities. Nakayama noted that a relation of power, whether conceived of as productive or repressive, "is never complete, and sometimes a different voice will emerge, a voice that someone may not have heard before. In these instances there is a moment of shock, strangeness, perhaps even humor."[90] Here politics were articulated as a mode of engagement, a way of living, an ethos, rather than as a struggle to make the world into the manifestation of an ideal. This other kind of politics had goals, but only as waypoints and trajectories that would change over the course of living and choosing, like paths charted by the stars over an open sea, a sea without shores or harbors but where everything is in constant motion.

Rather than being a political project opposing one ideal order against the deficient existing order, this view of politics focused on resistances already found between the lines of discourse—in what Biesecker called "those virtual breaks or structures of excess opened up by practices performed within the already established lines of making sense."[91] The potential for resistance, in this space already opening and operating within discourses and relations, was radically different from the view that an ideologically corrupt world needs to be made to conform to the ideal vision of human organization or essence. The ideological projects were focused on being *against* a particular hierarchy. Most chose a particular "ism" on which to pin all the world's ills—capitalism, militarism, sexism, racism, and the like. The futility of this position was well expressed by Scott: "Although it may be convenient to single out some hierarchy, refining it, making it more regular, more all encompassing, than we probably formerly experienced it, we are simultaneously in a tangle of hierarchies—do the intertwining of the roles growing out of gender, races, classes, sexual preferences, professions, nationalities, regions, families make a neat spectrum or do they lead to contradictions and confusions, dead-ends and doubling-backs, sortings out to suit the moment? We find it difficult to rebel completely; shaking off the shackles of one hierarchy, willy nilly, we are likely to be thoroughly conventional in terms of another."[92] This futility was simultaneously the very productivity that made another type of politics possible. The politics that Biesecker, McKerrow, and Nakayama outlined took advantage of precisely these contradictions, confusions, dead ends, and doubling-backs. Such politics could not seek to establish a new and more complete order or structure, because any such order would be incomplete, transient, and itself always full of holes, contradictions, and dead ends. It was a politics that could not focus on the refinement and isolation of one master hierarchy, one trope of repression or oppression, in hopes of merely inverting or annihilating the hierarchy. Instead, it was a politics of the interstice, operating in the between, the gaps, the holes, the confusions, the contradictions, the dead ends, and the doubling-backs.

Thus, simultaneous to the movement of rhetoric displacing philosophy as the site for the exploration of moral truths and to the articulation of a clear objectivist theory of rhetoric was the relativism and subjectivism that would challenge many of the core dispositions of the rationalist and neo-Aristotelian traditions but would also repeat many of those same themes. Each side not only took up ontological and epistemological arguments in their debates but adjudicated the acceptability of their theories significantly by their political and ethical implications. The importance of a positive political *telos* and end goal for one's political commitments became widely accepted criteria for good rhetorical theory. Yet, a few voices were, at the same time, expressing the possibility of a politics that would ground its legitimacy in an exploration of the openings, spacings, and interstices of communities and relations rather than in the instantiation of a new end state of institutions or identities. In this contest, humanism found another avenue for return, in a more simple but very strong notion of innate will or agency in the human being. Thus, we might ask now how the notion of will found in the relativist positions and the assumptions about community that pervaded late-twentieth-century communication studies brought a new form of humanism to the discipline that was especially recalcitrant.

6 The Recalcitrance of Humanism

The nature of the human mind and the capacity and qualities of human agents were persistent issues for speech and rhetoric scholars, but in the last decades of the twentieth century, the specific focus on the issue of will and the very possibility of being an agent in the world gained a special fascination. Will, as the basic constitutive event of most ethics and the necessary component of most views of political commitment, was perhaps the single most important principle of late-twentieth-century communication studies, even while its articulation was largely indirect. Communication as the encounter of will thus found two juxtaposed purposes: sharing and distancing. In assumptions about community and identity, this juxtaposition of communion and alterity presented two very different models of politics. While humanism's persistent reappearance and determined commitment to bringing people together continued to hold the central position in rhetoric and communication, a new level of nuance, ethical importance, and political potency arose in the exploration of anti-humanist theories and their corresponding political dispositions and strategies.

This chapter takes on the final three themes in this historical study: agency, language, and community. In many ways, these represent the major questions or driving problems for communication ethics and rhetorical studies at the beginning of the twenty-first century. In looking at the end of the twentieth century, this chapter starts with a study of how communication and rhetoric scholars took up the questions of will and agency. In discussions of will and agency, we find a blurring of the distinction between rhetorical theory, ethics, and politics. Will and agency not only became essential to all three of these areas of inquiry but were also understood as prerequisite or foundational problems for any attempt to think about humans living together. Yet, the complexity and diversity of the approaches to agency at the end of the twentieth century cut against earlier drives to unify thought under the banner of humanism. The second theme of this chapter is the other foundational problematic of human relation: language and representation. Communication and rhetoric scholars at the end of the twentieth century faced, in a way far more explicit than in previous periods, the question of language's limits and the role of language in the structure of ethics and human relations. From these two questions, one of agency and one of language, we come to community. The problem of community breaks into the twenty-first century as the central problem for ethics and politics and simultaneously reinforces earlier political and ethical theories of communion and sharing while also inverting those values through the development of principles of incommensurability and otherness. As such, community takes on a diversity of meanings that span the ethical and political registers.

The Willful Human Agent

Perhaps the most common way that humanism continually returned in speech communication was through the presumption of an innate free will as a basic part of human existence. The objectivist rhetoricians, as well as a large portion of the relativists, relied upon the idea of an individual human will as an intentional agent. While the objectivists gave the human will a greater degree of specific substance or form, most of the relativists were no less dependent on the existence of an autonomous human will that, while constrained by socialization, was nonetheless an original source of thought and action. That is to say, while objectivist and essentialist views of humanity argued that specific characteristics of will—a particular form of reason, a structure of language, and so on—are universal to humanness, relativists equally relied upon a notion of innate human will, even if they refused to give it a specific form.

The most obvious way that rhetorical studies had long relied on such a view of human agency was in its dependence upon the trope of intention in the interpretation of texts. Working from the writings of Michel Foucault, Dilip Parameshwar Gaonkar noted that the "egological temptation" in rhetorical studies "seeks to establish the sovereignty of the founding subject. It prompts us to discover behind what is said the intention of those who said it."[1] Traditional rhetorical critics, such as Michael Leff, argued that rhetoric, as the study of persuasion, is composed of two primary dimensions: the intentional and the extensional. "The intentional dimension has to do with the purpose of the rhetor as he or she composes discourse designed to persuade an audience. The extensional dimension has to do with the persuasive effect, the actual impact of discourse on an audience."[2] The study of rhetoric could choose to privilege one side or the other, with some combination of the two, but the intentional will was broadly pervasive even in the relativist theories.

More politically inclined rhetoricians, reflecting on the political nature of their own work, would complicate the notion of the intentional author, but only by adding more intentional individuals to the picture. For example, Barbara Warnick commented that "in any instance of rhetorical criticism there are two sources (the original rhetor and the critic)."[3] Regardless of whether what was being discussed was an objectivist or relativist view of truth and ethics, the vast majority of scholars began with the assumption, as Robert Scott put it, that "intentional beings" created rhetoric and were at the core of rhetorical studies. Thus, the single most common understanding of communication throughout the 1980s and 1990s was, as Scott wrote, that "the world of communication is the world of interacting intentions."[4] Not only did such a view make rhetoric reliant upon intentionality, but it placed the intending will at the very center of rhetorical inquiry.

The interpretation of rhetorical texts, regardless of what else it might include, still frequently focused on the intent of the author. Providing meaning for a text, according to W. Ross Winterowd, relied on the critic's capacity to "supply an intention for it."[5] With infrequent deviation, the discipline was governed by the view that, as Donald G. Ellis wrote, "the best way to discover the 'meaning' of a message is to turn to the speaker's or writer's intentions."[6] Only in rare cases, such as in some of the writings of Gaonkar, Barbara Biesecker, and Douglas Thomas, was the idea advanced that one might engage in rhetorical studies without committing the "intentional fallacy." The inability of the discipline—including most relativist rhetoricians—to escape the egological temptation or intentional fallacy, Thomas argued, was a fundamental barrier to rhetoricians embracing "the tenets of poststructuralism or postmodernism."[7] Or, to phrase it from the flip side of the argument, Ellis called upon speech communication scholars to move away from post-structural accounts of communication because such accounts deny the authority of intention, which was a central, defining tenet of rhetoric.[8]

This belief in the conscious, willing agent—the one who intends and then acts on those intentions—was not only central to rhetoricians' interpretive approaches but also, and perhaps more important, core to almost all theories of communication ethics. Even if intent was not to be the measure of an act, it was at minimum the individual's initiation of communication—his or her decision to engage in communication—that obligated that individual, as Kenneth Andersen wrote, to "accept the responsibility associated with that act."[9] It was action, or the enactment of willful choice, that Richard Crable argued "implies an ethical question."[10] Ethics were located in and reliant upon the willful human agent who acted, made choices, intended, and sought to actualize those intents.

Accordingly, the purpose of moralistic critique and ethical training was, in large part, to cultivate what Christopher Johnstone called "habits and dispositions that will sustain the capacity for intelligent choice."[11] In short, the willful human agent, in making choices and taking actions, constructed for himself or herself an ethical identity and engaged in dialogues with others that might also create their ethical identities. The agent, as an intending subject, was also self-constituting, mutually engaged with other intending subjects. In our communication, we are constituting our ethical identities, developing our ethical habits collectively, through an interaction of intentional wills. Thus, rhetorical pedagogy as well as criticism could be charged with providing the proper moral rules by which such choices could be made responsibly. Intentional wills needed to be trained to promote ethical habits and dispositions, and rhetoric was the ideal place for such training. After all, rhetoric was the means by which intending agents would influence each other's ethical dispositions.

However, this notion of the willful agent or intending subject did not go wholly uninterrogated. The investigation of the intending subject by rhetoric scholars in the 1980s and 1990s returned to the central debate between humanist/objectivist and postmodernist/relativist rhetoricians. Neither would deny that there is, in fact, a willful agent, an intending subject, imbued with agency and will. Rather, they would argue about whether such a subject has determining characteristics besides innate agency. While communication scholars influenced by postmodern and post-structural writings would claim that "human identity ('the self') can be more fruitfully viewed as situated and emergent, not predetermined," the implications of this claim usually had far more to do with role-taking behavior than with the status of will or agency per se.[12] In their reading of Foucault as a humanist, for example, Carole Blair and Martha Cooper argued that his concept of the "'dispersion' of the human subject was based upon his recognition that humans are able to play a multiplicity of different roles in and through discourse."[13] Gaonkar, while acknowledging a concept of the intending subject as an effect rather than as a prime cause, nonetheless can be read to echo a view of dispersion similar to that of Blair and Cooper's: "The 'discoursing' subject is dispersed in a plurality of roles, positions, and functions."[14] Thus, the view of the human as the intending subject and willful agent was still strong among the relativist rhetoricians, even those influenced by postmodern and post-structural writings. In this account of the subject as a role player, the individual has not only the capacity for choices about actions but also the capacity to choose who he or she is. As Cooper put it, "A certain persona, or role, must be assumed, or constituted, by the subject."[15] The individual agent, at bare minimum, is empowered to make some limited selection of what role he or she will play and, by some readings, is capable of constituting or creating roles for himself or herself.

This view of human agency is not radically different from the view of some moderate or even staunch objectivists in rhetorical studies. In short, some relativists assumed that there is some form of absolute and a priori human will or agency that empowers the individual to create or choose social roles. The autonomy of this subject is thus limited or constrained only by what Kent Ono and John Sloop called "the rest of the social system."[16] The core issue became whether or not there are certain other universal characteristic features of the human subject—besides agency and will—that might properly guide rational choice, ethical decision-making, perception of reality, and the like. We do not need to downplay the significance of this issue to note the importance of the similarity between the humanists/objectivists and postmodernists/relativists. It was certainly no small thing for rhetoricians like Calvin Schrag to advance a view of rationality—one of the sacred universals of neo-Aristotelian and humanist rhetorics—"as an achievement of communicative praxis rather than as a preexistent logos that antedates and governs it."[17] Rationality, reason, *logos*, and the related notions of correct thinking and deliberation were not only central to most rhetorical ethics but foundational to the dialectical method of rhetorical inquiry that objectivists advocated. To claim, as John Stewart did, that such processes have a "non-rational, pre-reflective base" was to deny the vast majority of objectivism's legitimacy.[18] Nonetheless, for many late-twentieth-century rhetoric scholars, this denial could coexist quite peacefully with a simultaneous acceptance of the idea that the "I" as a willful agent, an intending subject, was absolute, prior to any particularities, and universal. One merely needed to strip that "I" of any determining features other than will or agency, and liberatory or emancipatory politics could find a home in the relativist and postmodern rhetorical theories.

In communication ethics, the faith in an a priori, willful agent or intending subject was clearly expressed in the relationship between the self and the other in the event of consciousness. In perhaps the most thoroughly developed essay on objectivist rhetorical theory, Richard Cherwitz and James Hikins laid out an understanding of the emergence of consciousness as a relationship between self and other. Consciousness, they argued, is a "natural event which occurs when and only when an entity comes to stand in a particular relationship to other entities within a context of particulars." These entities and their relationship are not contingent or relative phenomena, at least not at their most basic, ontological level. Rather, Cherwitz and Hikins claimed that even if "entities in the universe are what they are solely because of the relationships in which they stand to other entities," those relationships themselves, and hence also the ontological status of the entities, are objectively determined.[19] Even if meaning exists only in relation to other things, if that relation is objectively determined, then the relative meaning is also objectively determined.

Most relativists, while perhaps less certain about the originative or objective status of the relationships, did posit consciousness or at minimum the subjective will of the individual as absolute. For them, it was the intentional choices of the two subjective wills that would build the relationships that would determine the possibilities and limits of each other's being and thinking. The other person, in this view, is a subjective consciousness who has a unique perspective on the world. The conflicts between self and other thus occur because of two different (but not incommensurable) perspectives—two wills that approach one another from different ways of seeing the world.

The humanists/objectivists and the postmodernists/relativists thus converged in featuring the ethical relationship between self and other, though the differences in their reasons are not insignificant. The objectivist, like the relativist, maintained that each person has a different view of reality—a different perspective. Some views may more accurately correspond to the objectively existing truth than others, but the most accurate depiction of true reality will come out through the dialectical clash between opposing views. There is a practical necessity to being able to consider the other's perspective as logically and as fairly as possible. Johnstone noted this as a fundamental part of the structure of ethical advocacy: "When we honestly submit to others the conclusions and justifications that are consequent upon our practical reasoning, we implicitly recognize the possibility of our own error."[20] Similarly, Scott wrote that "the most certain-sounding-styled sentence is uncertain if addressed to another rhetorically. If agreement is sought, only the other can complete the declaration."[21] Whether seen from the objectivist or relativist justification, rhetoric was intrinsically a test of one's ideas, and it sought validation from others. Indeed, consensus-theory relativism was perhaps even more dependent on intersubjective agreement for truth claims than the objectivist dialectic model of rhetoric.

Language and Representation

The ethical component of interactions between self and other came not only in the interaction's capacity to establish and test truth claims (whether objective or relative truth) but also in the acknowledgment and recognition of the other by the self. Both objectivists and relativists placed high value on the capacity to understand or take the perspective of an interlocutor. Celeste Condit argued that "the ability to take the perspective of the other is a basic requisite of morality and the contents of perspective-taking are human needs, desires, values, and ideas."[22] Likewise, relativists, and especially those influenced by existential writers, argued that the recognition and understanding of the other are critical to ethical communication. However, such recognitions could not be grounded in assumptions about an objective human essence.

Regardless of such significant differences, both views relied upon the capacity of communication to affect recognition and understanding of another's perspective—the ability of a self to come to see as the other sees. As such, both depended on a conception of language as a system for transferring messages. In other words, the function of language as primarily (if not solely) a means of sharing meanings was a prerequisite assumption of both the objectivist dialectic and the relativist perspective-taking. Perhaps no single assumption has more consistently operated in American speech communication than the notion of language as a tool of transmission. John H. Powers noted in his 1995 attempt to give coherence to the discipline that "the most central tier of human communication theory and research—the tier from which all of our other interests appear to radiate—concerns the inherent nature of messages themselves."[23] Powers went so far as to call the concept of message "the single core concept that most clearly differentiates any *communication*-centered discipline from all other intellectual pursuits."[24] Even what Stewart called the "many inconsistencies and half-truths" that "ordinary language philosophers" from at least the nineteenth century forward have identified with representational views of language did not substantially mitigate the tendency for "virtually all speech communication research and teaching" to rely upon "the assumption that language is fundamentally a system of symbols."[25] Some version, whether explicitly stated or more indirectly assumed, of the sharing and transmitting model of communication is perhaps the single most common premise in the study of rhetoric and communication.

This representational view of language did not require communication scholars to take the most naive view of language as a purely transparent and neutral tool. Rather, language might be conceived as an imperfect representation or as containing certain political biases within its system of representation. For example, Condit noted that because "discourse takes place in a language structure, that structure provides objective limitations on the truths that may be stated."[26] The language spoken and the way of speaking are politicized, but the question of representation remains largely uninterrogated. Saying that learning to write and "speak in 'proper' English" hides some voices while developing others did not require Thomas Nakayama to abandon the idea that language is a system of representing and transmitting meaning. It simply required that he consider representation as being potentially incomplete, inaccurate, or inauthentic.[27] Indeed, language could distort one's very capacity to externalize one's self, to share, to open oneself so that another could see one's point of view or encounter the distance in perspectives. Even small events of communication could be given great weight in how they might affect such transmissions or sharings.

Rhetoricians and communication scholars were quick to catch on to the political and ethical importance of even simple language acts. Raymie McKerrow isolated perhaps the most common political language issue for communication scholars when he wrote that "one can't put too fine an edge on the power or process of naming."[28] It was precisely because language's primary function was considered to be representation that naming became so important. The symbol was expected to represent the thing fairly and honestly, or, at minimum, the way in which the symbol represented the thing was to be a primary feature of the politics of language. This view of language, as corruptible representation, meant that emancipatory and liberatory political projects could engage speech communication in part by unmasking the namings or representations by which meaning was made politically disadvantageous to particular individuals or groups while favoring others. This was simultaneously a recognition that we are always constituted within a web of language and a belief that a progressive politics of language could be simply a matter of providing better political representation or better political meanings from within a given system of representation and signification. Much like the "debunking" work that attempted to correct falsehoods with truths, the politics here sought to replace distorting or biased terminology with those names and labels believed to be more accurate by their convergence to a social or political ideal.

There were very few exceptions to this understanding of language in the rhetoric literature of the 1980s and 1990s. Perhaps the most detailed criticism of this view was undertaken in Stewart's defense of postmodern communication theory. Stewart stated plainly that "language is not fundamentally or only a system of signs and/or symbols."[29] Working from the belief that language's representational character is corruptible or incomplete, Stewart argued that "because language cannot be characterized as simply an instrument or tool that humans deploy, it cannot be the case that humans simply 'use' it to 'encode cognitions.'" The function and force of language, if it were not a trustworthy system of representation, might be located in an event that is prior to representation—a function that language serves without relying upon the transmission or representation of a message, much less upon the intent of a rhetor. For Stewart, "language (communication) is not representation but presentation; it is not symbolic but constitutive."[30] The event of language does not give representation to a thought but presents the self to an other; it does not symbolize meaning but rather constitutes the very possibility of saying "I." As Frank Macke wrote, communication "is not important to rhetoric as a vehicle for self-centered expression, but as a window to understanding the Other as rupture, as difference, as a 'nameless voice.'"[31] Here, understanding of the Other has nothing to do with sharing, commonality, perspective-taking, or recognition. Rather, it is understanding the Other *as other*, as difference *qua* difference, rather than as a difference to be organized, associated with, transcended, or interrupted by some bridging or joining principle. Here, what is first and foremost communicated in any communication is the fact that you and I are not one. This is not a sharing or a commonality but the sheer simple fact that we are otherwise to one another. Only after that evocation of alterity is any thought of sharing possible.

Community and Communication Ethics

To interrupt the priority of sharing and transmitting meaning was not simply to make another theoretical move or to think about communication in another way. Such an interruption of the priority of communion in speech communication dislodged the entire ethical and political doctrine that had dominated the discipline since its inception. From a politics of dialectic, democratic governance, and the requisite clash of wills, the de-privileging of language as representation required an entirely different way of thinking about the functions of politics and ethics. The site of that reconfiguration in speech communication was found not around the discussions of the "polis" nor even of "praxis"—two terms whose networks of usage in the discipline were too tightly woven to provide the snags essential to a rethinking of politics. Instead, it was in the much looser and less disciplined term of "community" that a politics of the interstice developed.

To say that the term "community" was looser and less disciplined than many other terms is not to say that the concept of community was not commonly discussed and, to some extent, was not central to communication ethics and rhetorical theory. It is instead to say that community, unlike terms such as "politics," "polis," and "praxis," was substantially less theorized. In the invocation of community, communication scholars rarely sought to develop either foundations or causes for the *communitas*, instead taking its purpose and existence as a given. One of the most common assumptions about community in the discipline was its reliance upon sameness and communion.

141

Whether approached from a relativist or objectivist vantage, as Scott put it, "commitment to the norms of the community" was the almost universally unquestioned prerequisite to the existence of community.[32] Chaim Perelman similarly argued that "without common devotion" to shared values, "there is no political or religious community. It is this devotion which unites the members of such a community."[33] Commonality—the sharing of values, goals, or visions—was the governing metaphor of community underlying the notions of politics and ethics that have historically been dominant in the discipline of speech communication and the field of rhetoric. Whether those values are expressions of universal or essential human goods or are derived from logical axioms or are generated through the social construction of reality, these commonalities are privileged as the foundation of the possibility of being-together.

When such a conception of community is assumed, it becomes easy to argue that what is common or shared has a certain moral force. Moralism, as the urge to pass moral judgment upon others, gained force from ethics and politics that were grounded in notions of sameness and commonality, regardless of the source of the in-common. For example, though arguing that all such commonalities are rhetorically constructed, Barry Brummett also claimed that "among people who were raised within the same community, ethical standards can be applied to the actions of others because participation in a community entails acceptance of its standards."[34] The privileging of commonality was no less critical to objectivists such as Perelman, who argued that "the values common to all members of the community must be considered more fundamental than those which tend to separate it."[35] Thus, regardless of which side of the relativist/objectivist debate one might advance, community and the ethics and politics of being in community tended to focus communication scholars on the value of sameness or similitude.

Interrupting this valuation of sameness, however, was an increasing tendency to represent the social fabric of community as fragmented and unstable. Stewart noted that postmodern and post-structural thought within and outside the discipline of speech communication was embracing "fallibility rather than certainty, historical and cultural variability rather than invariance, and the fragmentary rather than the totality."[36] While the fallibility/certainty distinction was largely embroiled in the relativism/objectivism debate, the issues of totality and invariance were also important in discussions of politics and community. John Murphy's characterization of culture as "a heterogeneous mishmash of performative traditions" could be found not only in critical and postmodern rhetorics but also in advocates of teleological emancipatory political projects.[37]

This move toward a view of social life and communication as fragmented and heterogeneous also posed a new challenge to critics of rhetoric. If community and communication were becoming fragmented, then not only might standards also become fragmented and partial but so too the objects under analysis by rhetorical critics themselves. Yet, the ways that such fragmentation impeded the construction of a "whole and harmonious text," as Michael McGee described, was not so much a barrier to the idea of criticism, or even of community, as it was an obstacle that willful rhetors and critics would overcome by building coherent discourses out of "scraps and pieces of evidence."[38] The focus of rhetorical criticism and the politics of rhetoric, under this fragmentarian view, was pushed away from a broad view of community consensus. However, rather than taking the fragmentation of community as offering the possibility of a politic and an ethic of fragmentation, most communication scholars mended this fragmentation through the will of the rhetor/critic who would piece together a text until it was sufficiently unified to be subjected to relatively traditional modes of criticism. Alternatively, the rhetor/critic might simply narrow the scope of community to something substantially more localized, as Mary S. Strine noted critical theorists had often done, in hopes of escaping the fragmentation of larger community structures.[39] Hence, fragmentation was assimilated into rhetorical theory and communication ethics without the interruption of communion or commonality. Nor did fragmentation significantly affect community as a political and ethical standard. Rather, it only demanded that communities be smaller and more localized.

Far more difficult to integrate into the existing politics of sameness was the conception of communities as highly unstable or variable. Even if the rhetor/critic could construct a coherent community from the disparate fragments of culture or could narrow the critical lens until a more coherent community came into view, that community, according to Ono and Sloop, would always be in transition, "never fixed, never essentializable."[40] When the heterogeneity of space or of persons is combined with the heterogeneity of time—the variation and instability of any community—all consensus becomes suspect. As Murphy noted in his criticism of critical rhetoric, the combination of fragmentation and variance would render untenable not only universalist or essentialist notions of reason, identity, ethics, and politics but also any intersubjective notions grounded upon concepts such as community knowledge or norms.[41]

Biesecker called this the "gift of deconstruction": an obligation "to resist universalizing gestures, enabling us to open up a space wherein it becomes possible for us to discern the considerable heterogeneity of the social sphere."[42]

Likewise, this is one reason that consensus-based theories of knowledge, which largely ruled the relativist views of rhetoric, became less tenable. Since the consensus-based theories of knowledge, ethics, and community all relied upon community consensus or norms against which a communicative act might be judged, these theories, as Stewart argued, required "a considerable degree of both discreteness and stability" in both the community and the communicative act.[43] If the things being compared are unstable or indiscrete, then comparison will be at minimum unreliable, if not impossible. Hence, the use of community norms or community consensus as standards for determining veracity or ethicality lost much of its coherence.

Perhaps nowhere were the stakes of these different visions of community more powerfully expressed than in discussions of race and gender in the 1980s and 1990s. During these last two decades of the twentieth century, a number of communication scholars sympathetic to postmodern or post-structural accounts began to inquire about the role of race and gender in communication and about the role of communication in our understandings of race and gender. While much of the antiracism and antisexism literature of the 1960s and 1970s had followed a logic of sameness, identification, and unity—usually emphasizing universal humanism—the logic of scholars such as Robert Krizek, Thomas Nakayama, Janice Norton, R. Anthony Slagle, and Julia T. Wood focused on otherness and the politics of the interstice.

These scholars noted that community consensus, community norms, and common experience historically represented, as Wood put it, "only values, perspectives, and experiences of those who enjoy positions of dominance in the culture."[44] The emancipatory political projects that were undertaken by many rhetorical scholars, both relativists and objectivists, tended to lump individuals into "historically oppressed groups" and then to analyze and critique discourse on the basis of the rhetor/critic's understanding of the particular category or group. For example, Slagle noted "the tendency of liberationists to impose a unitary identity upon gay men, lesbians, and bisexuals." The result of this focus on discrete and definable "co-cultures," "oppressed groups," or "dominated communities" in liberatory and emancipatory political projects was that "those who do not fit the mold constructed by the leaders of the movements" were fundamentally alienated from what was claimed as their own liberation.[45] While at times these insights were hailed as unique and new, we should also note certain filiations of thought with the writings of William Utterback, Parke Burgess, and Kenneth Burke in previous decades, while likewise recognizing the critical differences in the arguments and approach. The argument in the 1990s certainly developed along a different trajectory, but the recognition that even liberatory and emancipatory appeals to common beliefs or shared higher values were bound up with exercises of power and force had been argued for a long time prior.

In place of liberation through commonality or sameness, Nakayama and Krizek posed the idea of a resistance in the interstice. This was not to say that contradiction is sufficient to disassemble white privilege or other forms of domination, for often it is precisely through its contradictions, they wrote, that a discursive formation "is able to maneuver through and around challenges to its space."[46] Rather, it was to say that there exists the possibility of a politics that resides in the incompleteness of power, in its holes, dead ends, and doubling-backs. These politics made use of the contradictions, to be certain, but not with the goal of liberating an ideal vision of the free human inside every person; after all, such a vision, for these scholars, was only the instantiation of a particular relation of power as natural or universal. Rather, it was a seeking to think between established lines of making sense, without a project, without a *telos*, except for the desire to explore other ways of relating to one another.

Such a notion of politics in speech communication and in rhetoric could only function, however, if one was willing to interrogate the concept of language as primarily a form of sharing meaning. The very idea of perspective-taking was antithetical to the politics of Krizek, Nakayama, Norton, Slagle, and Wood. Language, communication, even the most open listening to others, Wood wrote, "does not yield concrete knowledge of their lives, nor does it entitle us to appropriate their experiences."[47] However, it might whisper the rupture of notions of identity and essence that overwrite the uniqueness of self and other.

Such careful listening might lead one to hear the absolutely incommensurable and unbridgeable otherness of another person. Such a listening, such a conception of communication, was central to the politics of the interstice that had only begun to emerge in rhetoric and in speech communication at the end of the twentieth century. In tracing out such a relationship, Norton called first and foremost not for a political project, nor even for a concept of ethics, but for a reconsideration of language and subjectivity. She invited scholars to "take seriously the possibility of surrendering the Burkeian tradition of thinking identification as their 'master' trope in favor of thinking a theory of rhetoric that takes sexual *difference* seriously, thus interrupting a discourse of the same and letting the eventfulness of rhetoric move the thinking of human subjectivity onto a new trajectory."[48] Here, then, was a development in rhetoric that would return to some of the early problems of dialogism but also push on that long-repeated theme of sharing and fusion that has governed thinking of communication.

Thus, at the close of the twentieth century was the opening of a third way, neither objectivist nor relativist and decidedly not humanist. The struggles in this new space, however, were not entirely new to the field of rhetoric or the discipline of speech communication. Instead, new vocabularies and new literatures were exploring ways to address questions that had persistently reappeared throughout the twentieth century and continue in the scholarship today. The current scene of scholarship in rhetoric and communication studies still grapples with many of these same issues, working its way through and into vocabularies and ways of thinking that bring us back to questions that have been persistent in the history of the discipline. Much of our past, even those first decades of the twentieth century, is still with us today, for good or ill. As we inescapably return to these questions as well as pursue new lines of research and modes of inquiry, we can hold that past close to us and refer to the opportunities and detours it might make present today.

Conclusion: History, Community, and Alterity Ethics

After a century of efforts to establish ethical codes, values systems, and moral rules that might guide communication, we have generated more questions and uncovered more gaps and have today a vast diversity of opportunities for thinking about communication and about how one can choose to live one's life. In the past hundred years, every attempt to lay out an ethic that might safely guide communication has also created some tension, some unanswered question, or some inconsistency that has brought us back to questions of ethics once again. In each movement toward a stable ethical model, snags have opened the model to a proliferation of alternatives and contradictions. Even while the discipline was passing an ethical credo for communication in the 1990s, the very possibility of such a credo was called into question by communication ethicists studying contemporary communication philosophies. For example, in 2000 and 2001, Michael J. Hyde and Jeffrey W. Murray laid out some of the basic ideas from Emmanuel Levinas that cast doubt on any credo, set of rules, or even stable guidelines for communication ethics.[1]

The regularities, tensions, and inconsistencies that have emerged in discussions of ethics, agency, and politics have produced difficulties with the view that communication comprises simply a transfer of meaning, problems in defining the discipline, challenges to essentialist views of humanity, and critiques of liberatory ideological politics. Today, these all give the discipline multiple opportunities for ways of thinking, including some that do not return to sameness, fusion, or identification as their grounding metaphors. In many ways, the tensions and the regularities have reinforced one another. Regularities produced gaps, snags, and inconsistencies that were spaces for other thoughts, while tensions and contradictions mobilized and energized the regularities of the discipline by providing impetus for their continued advocacy. For example, the eruption of existentialism on the scene in the 1950s and 1960s was vital to the mobilization of scholars who provided greater theorization and justification for rationalist and humanist rhetorical theories. These tensions often cut across the subdisciples and specializations in speech communication and rhetorical studies. As such, they offer opportunities not only to communication ethics but also to communication pedagogy, political communication, and rhetorical theory and criticism.

History in Tension

Let us look back on the twentieth century to focus our attention on the tensions that have provided communication studies with their richness, as well as on the regularities that have sometimes been left unexamined. By activating selected elements of the history of the discipline, we can begin to explore how scholars today are grappling with some of the possibilities for communication, agency, ethics, and politics that interrupt a dependence upon a human essence, an established political project, a normative rationality, or even an innate human agency. By paying close attention to the interstices, the ruptures, the doubling-backs, we might set out how these movements today are connected to the history of the discipline. Rather than understanding contemporary rhetorical theories as alien intruders or external correctives, we can connect these works as articulations of something that the study of communication has always hinted at: the possibility of a communication that does not rely upon fusion and unity.

During the past hundred years and long before that, the most common way in which scholars described communication was as a system of transferring or sharing meaning. The meaning to be shared or transferred is what the orator desires to share—that is to say, what the speaker intends to transfer. From J. Berg Esenwein in the earliest part of the 1900s to Michael Leff in the 1990s, the capacity to share what one wishes with the mind of another was the most common measure of successful communication.[2] Following this view, training in speech communication most often has focused on how a speaker most effectively brings audiences to share his or her views, understand his or her information, or take a desired perspective. Even as rhetoric increasingly turned away from efficiency and efficacy as the governing principles of theory and criticism, as Omar Swartz has documented, pedagogy in communication has most frequently returned to these values.[3] In so doing, the goals of intending, transferring, and sharing have continued to dominate rhetoric and speech communication.

Yet, intentional and representational views of communication have never been the sole voice of the discipline. Problems with such views of communication have been persistent throughout the past hundred years. In the first decades of the twentieth century, psychological theories of the unconscious made intention both more difficult to discern and far less influential in the study of communication behaviors. Mental hygiene meant that those who were not properly mentally adjusted would communicate their maladjustment—quite unintentionally—in every moment of speaking. For the mental hygienists in the 1920s and 1930s, communication revealed not the intended message of the speaker so much as the character or quality of that speaker as a person. Psychological theorists also argued that intent could not govern how an audience would react to or understand what a speaker might say. Thus, in most cases, the psychological makeup of the audience could significantly alter the reception and understanding of communication. Additionally, since communication not only reflected but also affected an individual's character, it might be a means to adjust individuals to society. Through training in speech, the mind was not so much expressed as it was brought into line with the standards established for healthy mental life. In such cases, communication was less the transfer of intended meaning than it was a psychotherapeutic tool. Far more important to the teacher/therapist than understanding what the student or patient intends to say is listening to how it is said and discerning what this might reveal. In these early-twentieth-century psychological theories of communication, transfer of intended meaning was neither the central function of communication nor even a proper description of how communication occurs.

In the 1950s, 1960s, and 1970s, existential philosophy added its own set of questions to the view of communication as the transfer of intended meaning. Communication scholars such as Karlyn Campbell and William Hesseltine argued that the author does not own, control, or give meaning to a text.[4] Once a sentence is spoken, once a page is written, it leaves the author and is irrecoverably severed from the author, regardless of whether the author's name will circulate alongside that statement. Not only will the psychology of the audience interpret the statement in a way that deviates from what the author intended, but the statement will begin to circulate, to connect to other statements, to disconnect from statements. In so doing, it will exceed any uses to which the author desired that it might be put. Words will reshape themselves in different times, contexts, and media. Phrases will take on new significance, or their significance for the author may be lost on the reader or the auditor. Even the author's name itself, as it circulates as a part of a text, may take on different implications, lose its previous context or connection to other names and phrases, or find new context and connections. Rhetoric is itself animate.

In the latter part of the century, critical and postmodern rhetorical scholars expanded and responded to the existential and ideological theories. Not only did many rhetoric scholars deny the capacity of the author to control the meaning of a statement, but some also questioned the function of language as a system of representation. Scholars such as John Stewart and Frank Macke wrote about something other than representation, something in language or in the act of communicating that hints at a communication that is prior to anything like representation.[5] This is the moment of the approach of an "Other," the moment at which it seems that something like communication might be possible, or perhaps must be possible. In communication, even before language, there is the moment in which one is forced to recognize—forced to realize—that there is another person here before one. As the French philosopher Jean-Luc Nancy wrote in 1991, "Communication is the constitutive fact of an exposition to the outside that defines singularity."[6] Communication is what constitutes one's being exposed to things outside of oneself, and it is in this exposure that the idea of being a singular person is possible, that I can come to think and say "I." This is a communication that does not require anything in particular to be intended and is not merely a transfer of meaning. However, there is something like a meaning, a sharing of the event or the moment of otherness. Levinas called this "a relationship with a singularity located outside the theme of the speech, a singularity that is not thematized by the speech but is approached."[7] What he has described is how communication is always first an encounter with a singular Other (this other person before me now) without that Other being yet contained by language; he or she is simply a singular Other here before me that I acknowledge in some way. This is not to say that we do not have some content, words, or thing that is "said" in communication but that an important part of what we offer up in communication does not become shared or in-common. Nancy demonstrated that in communication, "only the limit is common and the limit is not a place, but the sharing of places, their spacing. There is no common place."[8] The very first fact of communication is not the creation or existence of a between, a common bond, but that simple fact that you and I are not one and can never be completely one.

Indeed, all communication and the continuation of all communication is predicated upon this premise, as can be seen even in the inquiry into some dialogic ethicists' dream of knowing and understanding the standpoint of an interlocutor. The first evocation of communication is found not in words nor in any system of signs or symbols but in the event of communicating. In communication is the evocation of the "I" that can emerge only in response to the approach of a specific Other who is before one. We find in our history not only a challenge to the view of communication as the transfer of meaning but also the possibility of ethics and politics that do not rely on a representational view of language and need not privilege either the recovery of human essence or the communion of minds.

Of course, the practices found in twentieth-century rhetorical studies also demonstrate that whether one starts from a psychological, an existential, or a post-structural account of communication, confining the study of communication or even of rhetoric to public oratory is not feasible. Both historically and theoretically, the study of public address and grand oratory was never the dominant focus of speech scholarship. The consideration of everyday communication, vernacular discourses, and mass media as objects of study can be seen in the earliest decades of the twentieth century. Throughout the history of communication and rhetorical studies, while many have focused on platform oratory and "beltway politics" (that is, politics focused on formal governmental action and the actions of government officials), others in the discipline have studied the everyday, have questioned the centrality of platform oratory to communication pedagogy and rhetorical theory, and even have challenged the restriction of politics to overt rhetorics of governance.

It should thus be no surprise that the discipline has found it so difficult to define its boundaries or even to establish central precepts. While the desire for definition has been constant and insatiable, efforts at definition have been often equivocal and generally unsatisfying. One can certainly create a workable enough definition for political purposes, but the inductive move from selected examples to general principles is by nature incomplete—it must erase some of the particulars from the examples in order to create the generality. Likewise, the diverse and transient nature of the discipline, regardless of what regularities we might point out, make such inductions inaccurate from their inception. This is not to argue that there is no value in such generalizations. At their worst, they still may be necessary strategic depictions of the discipline for administrators within the contemporary academy. At their best, attempts at definition may aid in the identification and consideration of assumptions or premises that were previously unexamined.

The great danger in attempts to define the discipline is that one might take the general result of such an induction and apply it deductively in determining the inclusion or exclusion of certain types of scholarship. This effect—the disciplining force of defining a discipline—undermines what scholars throughout the twentieth century have lauded as communication studies' greatest strength: their diversity of approaches and philosophies. During the 1960s and 1970s, William G. Carleton, Anthony Hillbruner, Robert Oliver, and Robert Scott all noted this danger in the attempts to define the discipline.[9] That danger and the wariness it has generated were no less present in the 1930s or in the 1990s, even if the commentary on the topic was perhaps not as focused.

The impossibility of a complete or stable definition of speech communication and rhetorical studies is demonstrated by the constant and unyielding attempts to define the discipline. Yet, there is also an ethical and political dimension to this definition, as it mirrors the desire to define communities by a unitary identity that late-twentieth-century scholars such as Anthony Slagle, Thomas Nakayama, and Robert Krizek have noted as so detrimental to many individuals' attempts to find a practicable space for living.[10]

Rather than setting out boundaries for the discipline or defining its core elements, one can note regularities within the discipline and the regularity of their interruption. Perhaps one of the most notable regularities within the study of communication in the twentieth century was the belief that speech, communication, and rhetoric can all be understood, at least in part, as the simultaneous study of being, ethics, and politics. Put another way, in seeking to study communication, scholars in the twentieth century repeatedly attempted to articulate some grounding principles or detailed philosophy that would account for the being communicating, the ethics of communication, and the politics of communication.

The "I" as Responsibility

Most commonly, communication scholars have grounded communication, ethics, and politics in a vision of the essential or ideal nature of the human being. In the earliest decades, this was most often based on psychological theories of human nature and psycho-philosophical views of the essence of the human mind. In later periods, while social sciences provided premises for views of human nature, scholars such as Christopher Johnstone and Chaim Perelman turned toward more philosophical foundations for the essence of humanity.[11] The faith in the essence of the human repeated itself, though not without challenges, throughout the past hundred years. It operated first as a belief in the existence of a substantive and a priori essence of the human individual that is universally shared among all persons. This essential nature of the human was given normative value such that what is most human became the criteria for what is good, right, and true. Thus, a humanistic faith posited that in order to know the values or truth of communication, one must know the substantive essence that is universally and most distinctively human.

This humanism common in rhetoric affected how the field understood not only itself but also other academic fields. During the 1960s and 1970s, many of the communication scholars working with existentialist texts infused their readings with humanistic overtones. Like John Poulakos, scholars deeply invested in a humanistic tradition found it quite easy to read existentialism—particularly Sartre—as an affirmation of some essential human nature or, at a minimum, a true and "real" self.[12] Similarly, communication studies in the 1980s and 1990s most often encountered continental philosophies either as unacceptable rejections of humanism or as forms of relativism and role-taking that would permit an essential form of agency to retain in every human.[13] At the same time, the insistence upon humanism was prodded by the possibility of a communication that is not grounded on any shared substance, much less on anything universal.

A few scholars in communication studies, such as Henry Wieman and Douglas Ehninger, articulated the possibility of viewing the individual as being produced through communication.[14] In their writings, there was not first being and then communicating. Neither could one properly say that there was first communicating and then being. Rather, they might say that communicating *is* being, or that being *is* communicating: being-communicating. In the event of communication, and in taking up communication again and again, being emerges. Objectivists like Richard Cherwitz, James Hikins, and others noted that one cannot become an individual except in a particular relation to other individuals.[15] However, contrary to the view of these objectivists, such relations may not require any objective determinations. Yet, they also may not be subjectively determined by the human will. The relations one has with others may be neither the result of an objective order of determinations nor within the subjective control of the individual. Rather, our history offers us the possibility of thinking of a relation that occurs only in the incessant murmur of a communication that comes before any particular ordering or determination of relationships. This might be called a relation that is the sheer being-in-relation, without relying upon that relation to take a particular form.

The existence of relations that are neither objectively determined nor subjectively chosen counters both the objectivist reliance on a priori order and the relativist reliance upon human will or agency as the ground of relations and ethics. Instead, at the beginning of the twenty-first century, rhetoric and communication scholars are beginning to consider the possibility of relations that are incessant but not static, are requisite but accidental, and are grounded first and foremost in an experience of otherness. As philosophical thinking continues to develop within and transform the field of rhetorical studies, we are called upon, as we have been since at least the 1950s, to engage our foundational questions and to grapple with the very meaning and possibility of communication, of being in relation.

Relations are incessant in that being-in-relation is a requisite element of being. This is not merely to state that we rely upon others to give us a sense of self or to position identity, which may be quite reasonable. More important, the very possibility of a self requires the approach of an Other from which the self might differentiate. The "I" emerges because an Other draws the "I" into being. What is incessant is not the particular structure of the relationship that one might have with a specific Other but the existence of being-in-relation without requiring that relation to take a specific form. That is to say, the existence of relation is a condition of being. This is not to say that a relation can occur or be experienced without some concrete Other that is experienced in a particular relation, but rather that the particulars of that relation are not the requirement for being. Relation is first a making-other of the self and the Other, before the alterity of the two can be organized into a specific structure of relationship. It is this first element of relation, the sheer being-in-relation, that is the necessary element of being. While some particularities that organize relations are required for one to experience relation, the specific particularities of any encounter are not in themselves the necessary form of being-in-relation.

Eighteenth-century German idealist Immanuel Kant argued that the experience of any object can be said to be dependent on its being in relation, since the experience must occur in time and space, and both time and space are purely phenomena of relation.[16] If one says that something exists in a particular space, such existence is only experienced as a relationship to other things in other locations (for example, "The book is *on* the table" expresses a spatial relationship between the book and the table). To be in space is possible only as a being in spatial relationships. Likewise with time: when one says that something exists in time, it is in relation to other things in time (for example, "The book *is* on the table" implies a specific temporal relationship between the book, the table, and the speaker). The problem with the example of the book and the table is that it expresses an unnecessary relationship. Surely the book can be said to exist without being on the table. What the book cannot do is exist without being in relation to other things in time and space. The prerequisite for the existence of the book is not to be found in the particularities of this specific relationship between the book and the table but in the fact that some manifest relationship between the book and other objects in time and space must exist, whatever specific form they might take. Of course, there must be some particular relationship in order for the book to exist, but the form or qualities of the particular relationship are not required. Necessarily prior to the determination of any specific relationship, an object must be in a relation of alterity to other objects. Only then can the particularities of the relationship be established by organizing a multiplicity of objects into systems or structures of particular relationships, such as proximity, similarity, or even sameness. In other words, absent the fact of sheer relationality, experience of concrete particular relations is not possible.

Like the book and the table, the "I" is only possible as being-in-relation to an Other. However, it is not any specific or particular relationship that brings the "I" into being but rather the sheer fact that there is any relation at all. Before there can be any specific kind of relationship between the "I" and an Other, there must first be the event of the eruption of the "I." The "I" erupts onto the scene in the moment of being called into relation with an Other, regardless of the form such a relation might take. In being called into relation, there is first the announcement of the exteriority of the "I" and the Other—their separation from one another is what makes any particular relation's manifestation possible. To say that this relationality—this event of relation to otherness—is incessant is to say that it cannot be done away with or dismissed into the past. Being-as-relation never ceases. It cannot be replaced with being-as-substance. However, it is also not static. Because this first relation is not a sharing or communion or even a particular differentiation but is first the approach of an Other that separates the "I" out as Other, there is no unyielding structure or substratum to being-in-relation. The requisite relationality that calls the "I" into being contains no specific determination except the alterity of the "I" and the Other and the requirement that they manifest in some undetermined concrete relationship.

A static self emerges only if one takes a particular form or content of a relationship to be the grounding of the self. Just as the book certainly must exist in relation to other objects without requiring a particular relationship, so too does the self exist in relation to others without that relation requiring a particular shape. Contrary to Hikins's objectively determined relationships or Poulakos's specific type of humanist relationships as the grounds of the self, the self is dependent upon the event of relation without a specific substance or form being required of that relation. Relation occurs in concrete particulars, but any given particulars are not themselves requisite to being-in-relation. They are only necessary addenda to the first relation of alterity that makes all other relationships possible. Thus, relations change, shift, fall away, emerge, and shatter but never cease. Relations are incessant but not static.

One might still consider such relations to be the result of a subjective will, but this would mistake the possibility of agency for the determination of existence. It is certainly true that individuals have agency—that is to say, we do make choices and take actions. At times, we certainly choose to engage in particular types of relationships and not in others. However, what we do not have any choice about is the necessity of being in relation and the chance emergence of relationships. If being is not understood as a universal or timeless form but as relation or as relationality, then being is not so much a thing that might exist as it is an event of existing. That is to say, as a relation, being is more an event than a thing. If "being" is a verb—to be—then it is a happening rather than an object ("being" as a noun), which most accurately describes what we find in communication. Just as the physical community of existence is a community in a relation of mutual determination, like the book and the table giving each other their possibility for existence through their position in space and time, so too is a community of persons bound up by the necessity of each person being in sheer relationality, such as you and I are necessarily related, though the content or structure of that relation may be malleable or even indeterminable.

Thus, an event of being does not choose whether or not to be in relation to other events in time and space. Rather, every event of being is already required to be in relation to every other event of being in time and space for its possibility. However, it is not required to be in any particular relationship, merely in a relation to every Other, a relation that is not uniform. No specific relationship is required for an event of being but merely a relation of otherness—the experience of singularity—though this can be manifested only in some concrete experience of an Other. As such, being-in-relation is dependent neither upon any objective determination nor upon any subjective choice but merely upon the simple fact of relation—that is, upon the prerequisite otherness that must distinguish one from an Other before any particular determinations of their relationships might be created or before any will is possible.

Such a relation, then, is not found in what one might say is shared among, similar between, or agreed upon by a self and an Other, or in even how they are different or where they disagree. Rather, it emerges first and foremost in the alterity of the "I" and the Other. Such separation is not so much in the particulars of their character or personhood that might differentiate them as it is in the simple fact that they are not one, the fact that they can be other to one another. Just as the existence of the book or the table has no real need of any specific particulars about the book or the table, so too does the relationship between an "I" and an Other require nothing except that they exist in some relation, which again requires that they are other to one another. That is to say, the relation that grounds the event of being is not a relationship that might be understood as a particular differentiation or specific difference between the one and the Other but comes instead from a relation of otherness or alterity. As Levinas wrote, my neighbor does not concern me because he or she would be recognized as belonging to the same genus but rather because he or she "is precisely *other*."[17] Relation *qua* relation,

relation that does not require a particular form or substance, recognizes that the possibility of a particular relationship requires the establishment of two things other to one another that might only then be placed in relation. It is only because the event of being is an event of otherness that any particular relationship can then become possible.

The Faint Call of Reciprocity

Such an understanding of communication and of being makes the possibility of a communication ethic grounded in mutual and reciprocal relations difficult. Much of twentieth-century communication ethics focused on how interlocutors might be able to take the perspective of the Other in communication. Both objectivist and relativist communication ethics considered an understanding of the viewpoint of the Other central to ethical communication. Similarly, most of the advocates of discussion and dialogism spanning the century argued for a focus on what was shared between the discussants, emphasizing the intersubjective, the between, and communion.

Contrary to many of these advocates' own conclusions, the articulation of dialogism, especially in the 1970s and later, made it difficult to continue to consider the relationship as reciprocal. As Poulakos argued, the Other is what makes it possible for there to be a self; the Other is the only source of the capacity for there to be an "I." Poulakos's own argument requires that one privilege the Other in communication, contrary to his conclusion that the ethical importance is found in the between. It is only because of this Other before one that the articulation of the "I" is possible. This Other is what has evoked the opportunity for agency, the opportunity for response. As such, this Other has given to one, in this particular moment, one's event of being as an agent. One's very agency—one's basic capacity to say "I"—is owed to this Other in this moment.

Here we can see the difficulties that theorists and scholars of communication and rhetoric have been struggling with for a very long time. In the desire to find a more stable and safe foundation upon which to build ethical systems and political projects, scholars have continually found, in psychology, philosophy, and rhetorical theory, that every solid basis sits atop these incessantly shifting indeterminacies. However, rather than disabling ethics or disempowering scholars, these problems, which have been repeatedly posed and pondered over the last hundred years, have invigorated the discipline. Sensing the unstable foundations upon which communication ethics had been established, Ralph Eubanks in 1980 asked what creates any moral obligation.[18] In short, why bother with ethics at all? But Campbell had already answered this question ten years earlier: it is because we have no choice but to be thrown into this world with others and yet without any objective guidance for our actions.[19] As Campbell noted, it is exactly the lack of any objective grounds for ethics that makes ethics such an important area of study and that establishes the high level of responsibility that each person must take for his or her actions.

Questions of ethics in communication are simply unavoidable. There is no possibility to escape the realm of responsibility in one's events of communication. The self is neither by nature nor by divine gift an individual agent that acts in the world but rather comes to such a capacity by virtue of being-communicating in relation to each individual Other before one. The self is an effect—of relation, of language, of chance event—emerging in response to the experience of otherness. This emergence is not a progressive development but a continual reemergence. This view of agency and selfhood has been whispered within the discipline of communication studies for a long time now. From such a perspective, one might consider that all the things that one does and that one can do happen only by virtue of response. Thus, responsibility is not an accident, it does not emerge as posterior to individual freedom, and it is not incurred as a result of a specific commitment being made. Instead, as Levinas has argued, responsibility precedes all these things and precedes any element of the individual responsible.[20] It is only in the ability to respond that one has agency. The ability for response is the very definition and constitution of agency, of being an "I," and hence the very possibility of choice and action is constituted in its most fundamental way of nothing except for responsibility. One's response-ability is owed to the Other. Poulakos's own argument articulates such an understanding, even if he eschews the conclusion. Hikins's argument can likewise lead one here, if it is separated from the belief in the objective form of relationships. So can the arguments of many existentialist and postmodern communication scholars, whether they might follow this path or not. Unlike the Kantian or neo-Kantian objective relations that posit a governing rule that we must obey or the humanist standard of an ideal human essence that we ought to seek to realize, responsibility is the acknowledgment that every appeal to a rule or an essence is a choice I have made that I must be wholly responsible for; that every choice I make, whether I rely upon a credo or a guideline, is my choice; and only I am the one who can bear its burden. In fact, the responses I choose are the whole of the meaning of who and what I am: there is nothing that makes me up except for this responsibility, this absolute and irrevocable fact that I can be an "I" only because I must respond; I am thrown into this world and constituted by choices for which there can be no sure answer. The fact that I cannot know and yet must decide is the very definition of agency, for if I knew, I would have absolutely no use for decision or choosing.

From any of these views, one's very capacity to say "I" is already owed to the Other. It is already an effect of having been approached in an event of communication, a communication that precedes any particular speech or writing. This is not to say that the speaking mouth does not utter words that we take to signify meaning or to facilitate sharing but that speaking is not so much a transmission or communion as it is, as Nancy wrote, "a beating of a singular site against other singular sites."[21] This is a beating not with clubs or fists but like chests pressed close together with the hearts each keeping their own time and feeling, in some small way, the fact that there is another. The first fact of communication is the embrace.

In the necessity of relations, I am already indebted to this Other, this particular one before me, but also to all the others as well. This is the requirement that the event of being always be an event of relation and that relationality never occurs merely as one-to-one but rather that one always begins in community. If ethics is about the choices that one makes in living, the rules with which one might fit oneself out, and the art of being-in-relation, then ethics cannot be separated from community. Being as the event of being, as being-communicating, is the communication of a sheer being rather than the communicating of the particulars of a being or an ideal vision of Being. Being-communicating is the practice of living as relation; it is the opening of a site for the call of ethics that precedes any political system, shared substance, or common bond. This might be the only sharing truly possible in communication, the sharing of what Nancy called "the interval" or "the scant being of the interval." This is not an abstract concept or noumenal ideal, he wrote, but rather it is "our whole reality, our most concrete, most existing, most 'in the world' reality."[22]

Ethics of Speech

Understanding one's ethical obligations in this way makes dubious our attempts to resolve the tension between ethics and efficacy. Throughout the twentieth century, communication scholars have grappled with the incompatibility between almost every view of communication ethics and the most effective means of persuasion. Trying to resolve this tension through the conflation of ethics and efficacy has repeatedly failed. There is simply too much counterevidence, both historically and in our daily lives, to believe that ethical communication is the most persuasive. Rather, if one's desire is to create as many adherents to one's own views as possible, ethics are at best a minimal concern and more likely is an impediment to be overcome by rhetorical skill.

From the first decade of the 1900s through the 1990s, being socially responsible, mentally healthy, morally pure, or ethically sound in one way or another has contradicted what we believe about effective persuasion. In the first half of the twentieth century, the need to balance dominance with passivity in mental health was opposed to the need for high levels of dominance in persuasion. Likewise, discussion and dialogue from the 1930s through today require that one be open to changing one's own views and that one approach others as having some significant chance of being more correct than oneself. Neither position is particularly conducive to compliance-gaining. Not even reason can escape this dilemma, as more than one scholar since at least the 1940s has pointed out that reason functions just as well in threats and coercion as it does in other forms of persuasion. Additionally, the effectiveness of strictly rational argument as a persuasive strategy is at best dubious. Only the invocation of additional moral rules to protect reason can support reason's possibility of outweighing the persuasive force of "unreasoned" argument.

Simply, one cannot resolve the persuasion versus ethics dilemma except to recognize that communication that seeks to bring an audience or interlocutor to a foregone conclusion contradicts the vast majority of the communication ethics scholarship generated in the twentieth century. Part of the problem, of course, is that the very definition of effectiveness and efficacy has been governed by persuasion and compliance-gaining. If one wishes to engage in persuasion and to retain something of communication ethics, one might turn away from advocacy and toward the loose flow of a conversation or the exploration of a concept. Such communication is as much a wandering as it is persuasion, and it takes as its goal not the establishment of law or belief so much as the value of the event of communication. This would be a revaluation of communication or a redefinition of what we might mean when we speak of effectiveness.

Political projects based upon ideal visions of human liberation or on the ordering of society into an ideal structure must either disavow the practice of communication as a loose conversation or else surrender the primacy of achieving their ideal visions. In their goal to advance ideological and humanist political projects, such communication scholars as Maurice Charland and Philip Wander required a form of communication that brings an audience to the conclusion already determined by the rhetor, moving the audience to the rhetor's predetermined ends.[23] For all such teleological political projects, the problem, in no small part, is that their vision of community is based upon a universal human essence or a universal political ideal. Indeed, any communication that demands conclusion or even consensus, in some ways, will contradict the debt that one owes to the Other in communication.

This is not to say that one must eschew decision or action. Rather, one is always deciding and acting. Passivity is divided from activity only in the belief that the will is originative and that response can be withheld. In understanding will as reactive, as emerging only as response, one finds action to be grounded in the choosing of response. As such, one cannot decline from choice and hence is always already choosing, deciding, and responding. Being-communicating is the responsive will acting in uncertainty with the proper hesitation that is appropriate in thoughtful action. It is an acting that recognizes that every choice is dangerous, that there are no safe harbors for decision-making. Because of this it leads, as Michel Foucault wrote, not to paralysis or apathy but instead to a recognition that "we always have something to do . . . to a hyper- and pessimistic activism."[24] It is an acting that is immediately reflected upon. It is an acting that places no more value on precedent or consistency of action than on opening the question again. This is acting as opening rather than as closure. After all, as Giorgio Agamben noted, if we knew our essence or our *telos*, then there would be no need for choice, will, or freedom, and "no ethical experience would be possible—there would be only tasks to be done."[25] Whereas the views of communication and ethics that were most common in the twentieth century sought agreement, which would then lead to action and hence to completion, this other view of communication that has been gently repeated in the discipline for a hundred years refuses agreement and embraces the necessity and inevitability of action but never accepts completion.

This is a communication that can never be party to a *telos* or an *archē* that one might seek to achieve or recover. Likewise, this is neither a science of being nor being as a work to be finished. Rather, it is communication as the event of being; it is the art of being-communicating. In contrast to developing a unified set of predictive theories about being or communication, or to viewing being as a work to be completed, conceiving of being as an art, a way, or a *techne* cannot be separated from the concept of practice. Science is the act of will that can claim for itself an origin in its theorist. It is the movement of desire in the desire for meaning. A work as completion, as what has been or can be finished, such as a poem or a painting, will eventually be finally done and over, but an art is neither will nor work. An art is a practice, that in its status as teachable and as always changing is never owned, and because it is not a product or finished work but rather the practice of the art, it has no completion of its own. Art is the gesture that "withdraws from presentation the values of 'self' (on the side of the origin) and 'presence' (on the side of the end)."[26] It is neither the attempt to uncover the "really true" self of humanist essence or divine endowment, nor is it trying to make the ideal become present in the world as occurs in teleological political projects. Instead, an art of rhetoric is a style of practice, a way of being in the world, that is nothing but a continual practice that can never be completed and is always open to mutation.

The status of art as incomplete and without ownership establishes its dynamism and idiosyncrasy. An art can never be conducted uniformly, regardless of the regularity of its manifest occurrence. One cannot discipline an art of rhetoric that conceptualizes itself as the practice of rhetoric in order to make all of rhetoric's manifestations uniform. An art is always in the process of mutation, and in each gesture it differs from every other gesture, regardless of, or perhaps precisely because of, the regularity that makes it an art. The gestures of the rhetorics of Martin Luther King or Gorgias or Eleanor Roosevelt differ from each other and differ in themselves. An art is "fragmentary or fractal: the realm of essenceless existence."[27] Only from the view of science might we attempt to organize and discipline the fragmentary art of rhetoric into a system, into genres, or into a whole. Yet, no matter how successful science might be in its goal to theorize the rhetorical, rhetoric in its manifestation as gesture and as art will always exceed it. The art of rhetoric has never had a single form, nor has it ever stabilized. Even in Greece and Rome, there were multiple arts of rhetoric, and the art a teacher taught always mutated in its teaching, its learning, and its practice.

The Politics of Communication

The question that many contemporary communication scholars might ask of such a view of communication is how it can be politically effective. Political efficacy has been, for many in speech communication, a governing criterion for what views of rhetoric are and are not acceptable. If one takes the term "politics" to operate in the way that scholars such as Charland and Wander used it, then the answer is already apparent. Because the politics of these scholars were based upon a particular belief in an established political project or ideal political end, most often connected to the recovery of a true human nature or of what is most common and virtuous about humanity as a whole, a politics that refuses any *arché* or *telos* could not satisfy them. From such a perspective, no ontology or epistemology can be satisfactory if it does not serve the established liberatory political project.

Similar to communication scholars of the early twentieth century, current advocates of teleological political projects and ideal human visions provide grounds upon which to argue that we ought to indoctrinate others into those political projects. Today, Wander is no less an advocate of sending forth armies to oppose all the cults of wrong than were W. H. MacKellar, C. C. Trillingham, and Alfred Westfall during the 1930s and 1940s.[28] It is easy to sympathize with such views when one daily witnesses the astounding problems that require our immediate attention and action. While we are driven to be politically active and engage a search to change certain political and material conditions, two dangers should be carefully considered. First, from such a position, principles of right, reason, and teleological politics can easily justify the use of the combat-oriented, conquer-at-all-costs rhetoric that was common in speech communication's involvement in World War I and that continues in the advocacy of liberation today. Second, a failure to consider how common practices, assumptions about being and community, and basic systems of discourse recreate and reinforce these conditions of domination may leave the politically minded with no role other than the amelioration of symptoms without any attention to how those symptoms reoccur. As such, the liberatory humanist political projects may achieve some necessary incremental gains in reducing the severity of certain social ills but do so at the cost of reinforcing the basic assumptions and modes of relation that guarantee the reemergence of these problems.

Particularly telling is how many of the authors who work most closely with questions of stark oppression and strategies for confronting oppression critique the teleological communication politics and essentialist views of humanity. While most of the communication scholars advancing ideological and critical rhetorical theories advocate a view of community grounded in commonality, sameness, and sharing, some scholars focused upon questions of race, gender, and sexual orientation argue that the singularity of each being and the instability of both beings and their relations make any notion of community based on sharing or sameness suspect. Listening closely to scholars such as Krizek, Nakayama, Slagle, and many others, one hears a clear and vivid experience of the in-common erasing singularity. These scholars make plain the costs of communication and community grounded in sameness and sharing as they articulate how the very capacity for one to be a self is erased when the sameness that governs a community writes over otherness. Those who do not fit the established understanding of the in-common become exiles within the community—not removed, but captive within a community in which their existence cannot be acknowledged. As Alphonso Lingis wrote, "The community that produces something in common, that establishes truth and that now establishes a technological universe of simulacra, excludes the savages, the mystics, the psychotics—excludes their utterances and their bodies. It excludes them in its own space: tortures."[29] This is the price of communication ethics and politics grounded in commonality, communion, and fusion. All those aliens, those foreign to that dream of the idealized human nature or the perfected political order, those who do not feel the world in the senses that this common community demands, the ones who do not believe in the same gods, those whose thinking embodies wholly different movements, they are held captive inside those communities as aberrant, subhuman, damaged, undeveloped—as the primitives, the maladjusted, the weak, the immoral—and their captivity is a state of constant denial and refusal. This is a community whose very definition and constitution is as a system of perpetual torture, a torture escapable only by the impossible assimilation into the perfected ideals of the community or by suicide, and since no member will be the ideal vision, every member experiences some element of this torture, though to widely varying degrees. As such, the community of the in-common, of the shared, is also the community of alienation and self-loathing.

Even the advocacy of feminist and antiracism theories within rhetorical studies often take the form of advocating the shared substance or shared experience of "The Woman" or "The African American." While valuable in their identification and criticism of patriarchy or white privilege, these critiques often tend to replicate the model of discrimination. In the past twenty years, scholars such as bell hooks and Kimberle Crenshaw have made plain the whiteness of feminist theory and the patriarchy of antiracist movements, a recognition that can be frequently found in today's communication studies literature. In the proliferation of such recognitions of the instability and danger of communities grounded in commonality or shared bonds, there is the possibility of a community that operates at the sheer limit of being-as-relation.

Rather than considering community as a form of contract or an expression of an a priori ideal, the concept of the event of being as being-communicating gives rise to a consideration of community as an event that likewise requires no content or specific form. Levinas demonstrated the first movement of such an art of relating when he wrote that "the collectivity in which I say 'you or we' is not a plural of the I."[30] Community is, first and foremost, simply being-together in any experience of simple coexistence, before any specific reasons or order might be given for being together. This is not to say that community is merely an assemblage of monads, for being is always being-in-relation. Hence, the event of being occurs only in a dynamic community. Just as the table and the book rely upon each other for their individual positions in time and space, so too does every event of being require the event of a community of others. Because the Other gives to one the possibility of saying "I," the self becomes a self only in community with others. Any substance or form that we might give to this community, whether it be a political contract or a looser affiliation, is made possible only in that we begin in relation, in a dynamic relation of mutual effect. Solely because the sheer and scant being-together makes the "I" possible can we then attempt to organize or divide our prior community into political entities. This sheer being-together makes it possible for a community to seek to articulate itself, to ask what its purposes ought to be, to explore its definitions or boundaries.

Disciplinary History

This is not unlike the movement we see in the formation and transformation of the discipline of speech communication across the twentieth century, as the relationality in which scholars found themselves thrown together was really the space of those departments, conferences, and associations that formed organically between 1900 and 1940, establishing purposes or even seeking out definitions only after they had already found themselves in response to each other. Today, the discipline of communication and the field of rhetoric are much broader and less unified than they sometimes are taken to be. What counts as being within the discourse community of rhetoric and communication scholars is not governed by shared belief, values, projects, and the like. What is at stake in what counts as part of the discipline is not trivial, just as the definition of politics is anything but trivial. The stakes are who gets to speak, who gets to count, what options are available for living and relating within our communities. The stakes are no less in any community when a single uniform vision of that community or a single ideal political view comes to position itself as the form of relation. The history of twentieth-century communication studies does offer us another way. Throughout the last hundred years, the priority of fusion and communion have been interrupted by conceptions of communication that open a space for voices that would embrace difference as more than an addendum or obstacle to sameness, voices that speak of otherness rather than of diversity.

How we write histories of this discipline is important. A history can often erase some voices within the discipline by simply excising them, forgetting them, or organizing them into a dialectic that overcomes the tensions they create. As such, any history is a political project with political implications. Likewise, this study is a political intervention. In an attempt to do history in a way that questions the assumption that history reports the facts and in an attempt to use history to open a space for thinking about communication and ethics in other ways, such writing embroils itself not only in the politics of the discipline but likewise in the politics of being-communicating. While traditional histories often pave over interruptions and contradictions with dialectics or synoptic organization, this study has tried to maintain these events in their dispersion while recognizing regularities and challenges. In so doing, it has tried to follow Foucault's advice that the historian attempt to identify problems, unleash them, and reveal them within complex frameworks "to shut the mouths of prophets and legislators: all those who speak *for* others and *above* others."[31] If I have been successful at all, then I hope that I have not produced a comprehensive catalogue of the discipline, and I desire not to have regulated scholarship into a particular set of questions or rules. Moreover, I hope that I have not prophesied what will come but instead that I have put the question of how rhetoric relates to ethics and politics in a new way and have unsettled our memory of this relationship in such a way that more questions and more possibilities emerge. In short, I have simply posited that communication and rhetorical studies are, and always have been, much broader than we often portray.

Perhaps the most ambitious argument to be found in the last hundred years is that the incredible complexity of the discipline itself performs something of the idea of a community that is bound together without any universal ideals or teleological projects. In terms of ethics, the contradictions and variances at any given moment, as well as the changes across time, make the idea of a credo or system of ethics for communication questionable. Instead, we have a call to take up questions of ethics again and again, without any finality to our responses. In the politics of the discipline, again, we find that attempts to make the discipline consistent are not simply reports but are performances of a desire for a coherent past that might justify the present and give safe passage into the future. In no small part due to the rhetorical nature of any historical enterprise, all our histories of the discipline will be more prescriptive than descriptive. They are attempts to make the discipline look or seem one way or another. No less so is this book.

Yet, if this is so, then let us choose models of history and tellings of the discipline that do not excise those most closely working with oppression, let us disavow the creation of restrictive definitions that undermine our capacity to follow many of the opportunities present in our past, let us avoid assimilating theories purely for the sake of making them conform to beltway politics, and let us embrace the possibility of communication ethics and politics that can also challenge humanism. In short, let us tell stories about our past that open it up to us, that give us more opportunities for thinking, writing, communicating, and living.

We find in the last hundred years and in much of the scholarship today the possibility to consider the difficulty and struggle of communication and ethics as opportunities rather than as barriers. As such, in contrast to the dialectical politics that have promised the chimera of continual movement toward the better or the true, our past offers to us the alternative of maintaining a tension that permits a community without fusion and a politics that is not grounded in sameness. This is not a lack of unity, for there is no reason to privilege unity as something that we might lack. Rather, it is to embrace community as a site of otherness; it is the scant community of being-as-relation. From such a history, we owe no allegiance to a uniformity of project, method, or object of study. Instead, as a community of others, we have open to us a space in which the event of being is allowed to manifest itself as the possibility of a communicating that is not focused upon meaning or agreement. We have present in our past the possibility of ethics and politics that are grounded in the impossibility of fusion and the absolute otherness that make the sheer event of being possible.

Notes
Bibliography
Index

Notes

Introduction: Communication, Speech, and History

1. Lanham, *Electronic Word*, 155.
2. Clarke, *Rhetoric at Rome*, 115.
3. Lanham, *Electronic Word*, 155.
4. Burke, *Language*, 16.
5. Scott, "On Viewing," 10.
6. Harvey, "Contemporary French Thought," 214.
7. Arnett, "Status . . . in Speech Journals," 69.
8. Andersen, "History," 5.
9. E.g., Benson, *Speech Communication*; Cohen, *History of Speech Communication*; Kuypers and King, *Twentieth-Century Roots*; Phillips and Wood, *Speech Communication*.
10. Kuypers and King, "Introduction," ix.
11. Keith, *Democracy as Discussion*.
12. Schiappa, "Interdisciplinarity and Social Practice," 142.
13. Andrews, "Rhetoric."
14. Scott, "Necessary Pluralism," 200.
15. Murphy, "Critical Rhetoric," 11.
16. Cohen, *History of Speech Communication*, 157.
17. Woolbert, "Ethics," 66.
18. Holt, "Speaker in Relation to Himself."
19. MacGregor, "Personal Development"; Kersey, "Speech and Life"; Crocker, "Oblique Approach"; Irwin, "Mental Hygiene"; E. Murray, "Speech Training."
20. Gislason, "Relation of the Speaker."
21. Pellegrini, "Public Speaking."
22. Blair, "Contested Histories," 403.
23. Ibid., 417.
24. Schiappa, "Interdisciplinarity and Social Practice," 146.

1. Preparing the Speaker to Stand Tall

1. Esenwein, *How to Attract*, 3.
2. Woolbert, "Problem in Pragmatism," 273.
3. Winans, *Speech Making*, 1.

4. Gislason, "Relation of the Speaker," 44.

5. Mosher, "Debate," 338.

6. Esenwein, *How to Attract*, 5.

7. Gislason, "Relation of the Speaker," 40.

8. Brigance, "American Speech," 15.

9. Ibid., 16.

10. Pellegrini, "Public Speaking," 346.

11. MacKellar, "Cultural Value," 14.

12. Esenwein, *How to Attract*, 149.

13. Woolbert, "Problem in Pragmatism," 264.

14. Ibid., 268.

15. Robinson, "Speech," 368.

16. Williamson, "Democracy," 354.

17. Cohen's use of the debate between Hunt and Woolbert is an excellent example. See Cohen, *History of Speech Communication*, 54–64.

18. Gray, "How Much Are We Dependent," 279.

19. Ibid., 267.

20. Smith, Easton, and Murray, "Integrated Speech Program," 3.

21. See, e.g., Kuypers and King, "Introduction," xii; and Windt, "Everett Lee Hunt," 10–11.

22. Wichelns, "Tendencies," 2.

23. Gray, "How Much Are We Dependent," 278.

24. Esenwein, *How to Attract*, 3.

25. Gislason, "Relation of the Speaker," 41.

26. Kalp, "Some Principles," 296.

27. MacGregor, "Personal Development," 57.

28. Ibid.

29. Winter, "Teacher of Public Speaking," 23.

30. Auer, "Tools of Social Inquiry," 537.

31. For example, see Winans, *Speech Making*, 4.

32. E. Murray, "Fundamental in Speech," 2.

33. Bietry, "Speech Teacher," 10.

34. E. Murray, "Speech Training," 45.

35. Gislason, "Relation of the Speaker," 44.

36. Gray, "How Much Are We Dependent," 263.

37. Program of the 1935 Conference.

38. Morse, "Mental Hygiene," 125.

39. Bryngelson, "Applying Hygienic Principles," 351; Bietry, "Speech Teacher," 14.

40. Stinchfield-Hawk, "Speech Community Service," 11.

41. Kalp, "Some Principles," 298.

42. E. Murray, "Speech Training," 44.

43. O'Neill, "Aims and Standards," 356.

44. E. Murray, "Speech Training," 38–39.

45. Dow, "Personality Traits," 531.

46. E. Murray, "Fundamental in Speech," 2.

47. Gislason, "Relation of the Speaker," 44.

48. MacGregor, "Personal Development," 53.

49. Bietry, "Speech Teacher," 9.
50. E. Murray, "Fundamental in Speech," 3.
51. Farma, 1929 Eastern Public Speaking Conference transcripts, 88–89.
52. Robinson, "Speech," 368.
53. MacGregor, "Personal Development," 49–50.
54. E. Murray, "Fundamental in Speech," 3.
55. Morse, "Mental Hygiene," 129–30.
56. Robinson, "Speech," 376; Bietry, "Speech Teacher," 11.
57. Cable, "Speech," 19.
58. Wales and Zimmerman, "Activity Unit Analysis," 18.
59. E. Murray, "Speech Training," 38.
60. Winter, "Teacher of Public Speaking," 25.
61. Bietry, "Speech Teacher," 9.
62. Robinson, "Speech," 372–73. Emphasis in original.
63. E. Murray, "Speech Training," 40.
64. E. Murray, "Fundamental in Speech," 3.
65. Bietry, "Speech Teacher," 12.
66. E. Murray, "Speech Training," 41.
67. Kalp, "Some Principles," 297.
68. Irwin, "Mental Hygiene," 213.
69. O'Neill, "Aims and Standards," 349–50.
70. Smith, Easton, and Murray, "Integrated Speech Program," 3.
71. Irwin, "Mental Hygiene," 214.
72. Smith, Easton, and Murray, "Integrated Speech Program," 2.
73. Esenwein, *How to Attract*, 5.
74. Krapp, "Central Task," 371.
75. MacGregor, "Personal Development," 49.
76. Ibid., 50.
77. Gray, "How Much Are We Dependent," 261.
78. MacGregor, "Personal Development," 51.
79. California State Department of Education, "Place of Speech," v.
80. Bryngelson, "Speech and Its Hygiene," 86.
81. Esenwein, *How to Attract*, 4.
82. Lambertson, "Hitler, the Orator," 125, 127.
83. Pellegrini, "Public Speaking," 347.
84. Merry, "National Defense," 59.
85. Woolbert, "Ethics," 66.
86. Pellegrini, "Public Speaking," 350.
87. Ibid., 349.
88. Lambertson, "Hitler, the Orator," 128.

2. Rhetoric, Discussion, and Character

1. See Isserman, *Which Side Were You On?*, ch. 1.
2. Kohn, *American Political Prisoners*, 9–10.
3. Nuttal, "Re-evaluation of the Place of Speech," 3.
4. Auer, "Tools of Social Inquiry," 533.
5. Krapp, "Central Task," 371.

6. Ibid.

7. Gray, "How Much Are We Dependent," 264.

8. McGrew, "Speech," 42.

9. Krapp, "Central Task," 371–372.

10. Smith, Easton, and Murray, "Integrated Speech Program," 3.

11. Grey, "Better Communication," 133.

12. Robinson, "Speech," 371–372.

13. Winans, *Speech Making*, 1.

14. Smith, Easton, and Murray, "Integrated Speech Program," 1.

15. Cohen, *History of Speech Communication*, 50–66.

16. Gullan, "War Time," 373.

17. Bietry, "Speech Teacher," 12.

18. Trillingham, "Speech Education," 8.

19. Wichelns, "Tendencies," 3.

20. Greaves, "Speech for the Many," 4.

21. Krapp, "Central Task," 370.

22. Wichelns, "Tendencies," 3.

23. Keith, *Democracy as Discussion*.

24. Wichelns, "Tendencies," 3.

25. Bryant, "Some Problèmes of Scope," 188.

26. Mr. Page, transcribed as a speaker at the Eastern Public Speaking Conference of 1929, Eastern Communication Association Records, accn. 1474, box 3, folders 1–2, p. 148, J. Willard Marriott Library, University of Utah, Salt Lake City.

27. Mosher, "Debate," 333.

28. Pellegrini, "Public Speaking," 348–49.

29. Auer, "Tools of Social Inquiry," 535.

30. Smith, Easton, and Murray, "Integrated Speech Program," 1.

31. McBurney, "Some Contributions," 9.

32. Holm, "War-Time Approach," 12.

33. Konigsberg et al., "Teaching Public Discussion," 13.

34. Auer, "Tools of Social Inquiry," 539.

35. Konigsberg et al., "Teaching Public Discussion," 13.

36. McBurney, "Some Contributions," 11.

37. Ibid., 6.

38. Keith, *Democracy as Discussion*, 98–104.

39. McBurney, "Some Contributions," 11.

40. E. Murray, "Fundamental in Speech," 2.

41. Balduf, "How Departments of Speech Can Cooperate," 271.

42. Konigsberg et al., "Teaching Public Discussion," 13.

43. Balduf, "How Departments of Speech Can Cooperate," 272.

44. Auer, "Tools of Social Inquiry," 536.

45. Konigsberg et al., "Teaching Public Discussion," 13; Dickens, "Discussion," 155.

46. Lambertson, "Hitler, the Orator," 130–31.

47. Wiley, "Rhetoric of American Democracy," 159.

48. Kalp, "Some Principles," 299.

49. Dickens, "Discussion," 155–56.

50. Mosher, "Debate," 334, 339.

51. Ibid., 338.

52. Ibid., 333.

53. E. Murray, "Fundamental in Speech," 1.

54. As quoted in Robinson, "Speech," 368.

55. MacKellar, "Cultural Value," 11.

56. Trillingham, "Speech Education," 8, 7.

57. Hansen, "Speech in a Nation at War," 272.

58. Holm, "War-Time Approach," 11.

59. Trillingham, "Speech Education," 9.

60. Innes, "Function of Discussion and Debate," 60.

61. Woolbert, "Ethics," 71.

62. Church, "Value of Debate," 63.

63. Westfall, "What Speech Teachers May Do," 7.

64. Keith, *Democracy as Discussion*, 251.

65. Trillingham, "Speech Education," 7.

66. A. F. Wilenden as quoted in Auer, "Tools of Social Inquiry," 536–37.

67. Hance, "Public Address," 164.

68. Dickens, "Discussion," 154, 153.

69. Brandenburg, "Quintilian," 27, 28.

70. Trillingham, "Speech Education," 7.

71. E. Murray, "Fundamental in Speech," 1–2.

72. Auer, "Tools of Social Inquiry," 537.

73. Program of the 1930 Conference.

74. MacKellar, "Cultural Value," 15.

75. Hale, "Freedom through Speech," 9.

76. Van Wye, "Speech Training," 371.

77. Emery, "Verbal Warfare"; Merry, "National Defense," 56–57; Stinchfield-Hawk, "Speech Community Service," 10; Van Wye, "Speech Training," 367–68.

78. Program of the 1940 Conference.

79. Brigance and Immel, *Speech for Military Service*, 2.

80. Capp to Leroy Lewis, May 26, 1942, Southern States Communication Association Records, accn. 1661, box 65, no. 742, J. Willard Marriott Library, University of Utah, Salt Lake City.

81. Balduf, "How Departments of Speech Can Cooperate," 272.

82. Merry, "National Defense," 58.

83. Van Wye, "Speech Training," 370.

84. Knower, "Speech Curricula," 148.

85. Merry, "National Defense," 57, 59.

86. Van Wye, "Speech Training," 369.

87. Merry, "National Defense," 58.

88. Grey, "Better Communication," 133.

89. Hansen, "Speech in a Nation at War," 274.

90. Hunt, "Rhetorical Mood," 4.

91. Trillingham, "Speech Education," 8.

92. Kantner, "Social Responsibility," 67.

93. Dow, "Personality Traits," 531.

94. Pellegrini, "Public Speaking," 350.

95. Irwin, "Mental Hygiene," 213.

96. Utterback, "Appeal to Force," 1–3.

97. Lambertson, "Hitler, the Orator," 123.

98. Ibid., 129, 125, 130.

99. Ibid., 127, 123, 130.

100. Ibid., 134, 137, 133, 131, 137–38.

101. Zelko, "Roosevelt's Rhythm," 138–39.

102. Lambertson, "Hitler, the Orator," 130.

103. Brandenburg, "Quintilian," 23.

104. Esenwein, *How to Attract*, 45.

105. Platz, *History of Public Speaking*, 285.

106. Esenwein, *How to Attract*, 94–95.

107. Lyman Abbot as quoted in O'Neill, "Aims and Standards," 359.

108. Bryngelson, "Speech and Its Hygiene," 85.

109. Esenwein, *How to Attract*, 95.

110. MacKellar, "Cultural Value," 10.

111. Robinson, "Speech," 372.

112. As quoted in Hansen, "Speech in a Nation at War," 273.

113. Kantner, "Social Responsibility," 73.

114. Woolbert, "Ethics," 65.

115. C. Ellis, "Good Man," 85.

116. Clark, "These Truths," 448, 447.

117. Wells, "Ethical Problems," 116. Emphasis in original.

118. C. Ellis, "Good Man," 87.

119. Holm, "War-Time Approach," 11.

120. Hale, "Freedom through Speech," 13.

121. "Introducing the Convention Theme."

122. Smith, Easton, and Murray, "Integrated Speech Program," 3.

123. As quoted by Knower, "Speech Curricula," 149.

124. C. Ellis, "Good Man," 89.

125. Brandenburg, "Quintilian," 27.

3. From Speech Science to Rhetoric and Philosophy

1. Held, "Needed," 2.

2. Halloran, "Tradition and Theory," 238.

3. Held, "Needed," 2.

4. Gulley, "New Amorality," 3.

5. Program of the 1953 Conference.

6. Buehler, "Credo," 4. See also a similar view expressed by Turner, "In the Beginning," 198.

7. Schweinsberg-Reichart, "Speech Education," 35.

8. Oliver, "Varied Rhetorics," 214.

9. Brockriede, "Arguers as Lovers," 9.

10. Black, "Second Persona," 113.

11. Eubanks and Baker, "Axiology of Rhetoric," 158, 167.

12. Kantner, "Speech and Education," 17. Emphasis in original.

13. Casmir, "Hitler," 15–16.
14. Ehninger, "Synoptic View," 449.
15. Schweinsberg-Reichart, "Speech Education," 39.
16. Wieman, "Philosophical Significance of Speech," 174.
17. Enholm, "Rhetoric as an Instrument," 226.
18. For examples of early communication ethicists who argued that communication ethics ought to focus on the means rather than on the ends of rhetorical acts, see Nilsen, "Criticism," 177; and Wallace, "Ethical Basis," 3.
19. Eubanks, "Nihilism," 191.
20. Chesebro, "Construct for Assessing Ethics," 104.
21. Lomas, "Rhetoric and Demagoguery," 168, 162.
22. Flynn, "Aristotelian Basis," 179.
23. Bowen, "Dilemma of Values," 19.
24. Gulley, "New Amorality," 8.
25. Bowen, "Dilemma of Values," 20.
26. Casmir, "Hitler," 16.
27. Lomas, "Rhetoric and Demagoguery," 161.
28. Rogge, "Evaluating the Ethics of a Speaker," 420.
29. Hillbruner, "Moral Imperative," 237.
30. Nilsen, "Criticism," 178.
31. Flynt, "Ethics of a Democratic Persuasion," 40.
32. Eubanks and Baker, "Axiology of Rhetoric," 159.
33. Black, "Second Persona," 109.
34. Bock, "Axiology and Rhetorical Criticism," 96.
35. Chesebro, "Construct for Assessing Ethics," 105. Emphasis in original.
36. Andrews, "Reflections," 316.
37. Oliver, "Ethics and Efficiency," 13.
38. For example, see Hesseltine, "Speech and History," 178.
39. Oliver, "Ethics and Efficiency," 12.
40. Wallace, "Substance of Rhetoric," 248, 240.
41. Corder, "Ethical Argument," 352.
42. Baird, "Speech and the 'New' Philosophies," 241.
43. Halloran, "Tradition and Theory," 241.
44. Redfield, "Difficult Duty," 7.
45. Eisenstadt, "Good Speech," 98.
46. Wallace, "Substance of Rhetoric," 244; Bowen, "Dilemma of Values," 20.
47. Bock, "Axiology and Rhetorical Criticism," 94–95.
48. Micken, "Worried Look," 7.
49. Bowen, "Dilemma of Values," 20.
50. Resolution of the Speech Association of the Eastern States, passed 1958, Eastern Communication Association Records, accn. 1474, box 2, folder 9, J. Marriott Library, University of Utah, Salt Lake City.
51. Campbell, "Ontological Foundations," 106.
52. Ibid., 101.
53. Scott, "Some Implications," 272.
54. Walter, "On Views of Rhetoric," 377.
55. Hunt, "Rhetoric as a Humane Study," 116.

56. Halloran, "Tradition and Theory," 239.

57. Hunt, "Rhetoric as a Humane Study," 115.

58. Klyn, "Problem of Evil," 26.

59. Ehninger, "Synoptic View," 451.

60. Flynn, "Aristotelian Basis," 180.

61. Baird, "Speech and the 'New' Philosophies," 244.

62. Wallace, "Substance of Rhetoric," 243.

63. Rieke and Smith, "Dilemma of Ethics," 229.

64. Haiman, "Re-examination," 8.

65. Lomas, "Rhetoric and Demagoguery," 165.

66. Flynt, "Ethics of a Democratic Persuasion," 40. Some confusion in interpreting this quotation is caused by the absence of commas. Whether Flynt argued that appeals to emotions essentially short-circuit critical thinking or that only those certain appeals to emotions that can have such an effect are unethical is made ambiguous by the lack of commas to offset the subordinate clause. Though it is not entirely clear from the whole essay, I have chosen to read the claim as the former rather than the latter, but I have left the quotation unaltered to maintain the ambiguity of the original text. The distinction also may not be critical for my purposes here.

67. Washburn, "Speech Communication," 9.

68. Nilsen, "Free Speech," 243.

69. Haiman, "Re-examination," 6–7.

70. Day, "Ethics of Democratic Debate," 10.

71. Brockriede, "Arguers as Lovers," 4.

72. Lomas, "Rhetoric and Demagoguery," 165. It seems reasonable from context to read Lomas to more properly mean "words that evoke conditioned emotional responses," since he did clearly argue that words could be put to reasoned purposes that did not evoke emotions.

73. Haiman, "Re-examination," 4.

74. Simons, "Patterns of Persuasion," 26.

75. Van de Vate, "Reasoning and Threatening," 178–79.

76. Sillars, "Rhetoric as Act," 279.

77. Haiman, "Re-examination," 7.

78. Freeman, "Ethical Evaluation," 361.

79. Howard, "Speech Education," 24.

80. Burgess, "Crisis Rhetoric," 64.

81. Ibid., 68–69.

82. Burke, "Dramatistic View . . . Part Two," 460.

83. Burgess, "Crisis Rhetoric," 73.

84. Haiman, "Rhetoric of the Streets," 105.

85. Casmir, "Hitler," 9.

86. Christopherson, "Speech and the 'New' Philosophies Revisited," 8.

87. Scott, "On Viewing," 9.

88. Scott and Smith, "Rhetoric of Confrontation," 7–8.

89. Scott, "Fresh Attitude," 135, 136.

90. Clevenger, "Speaker and Society," 96.

91. Campbell, "Ontological Foundations," 99.

92. Mavrodes, "Problem of Evil," 96.

93. Haiman, "Rhetoric of the Streets," 113.

94. Walter, "On Views of Rhetoric," 381, 374.

95. Smith, "Toward a Philosophy of Speech," 4.

96. Walter, "On Views of Rhetoric," 374, 367.

97. E.g., H. Johnstone, "Relevance of Rhetoric" and "Rationality and Rhetoric."

98. H. Johnstone, "Relevance of Rhetoric," 44.

99. Walter, "On Views of Rhetoric," 376.

100. Scott, "Some Implications," 267.

101. Scott, "On Viewing," 16–17.

102. Nilsen, "Criticism," 178.

103. Gronbeck, "From 'Is' to 'Ought,'" 39.

104. Eubanks, "Nihilism," 188.

4. Humanism, Rhetoric, and Existential Ethics

1. Campbell, "Ontological Foundations," 97.

2. Burke, "Postscripts," 211.

3. Eubanks, "Nihilism," 190.

4. Ibid., 195, 188.

5. Flynn, "Aristotelian Basis," 187.

6. Wieman, "Philosophical Significance of Speech," 175.

7. Scott, "Fresh Attitude," 134.

8. Flynn, "Aristotelian Basis," 180.

9. Van de Vate, "Reasoning and Threatening," 178.

10. Poulakos, "Components of Dialogue," 211.

11. Nilsen, "Free Speech," 236.

12. Baker and Eubanks, "Democracy," 75.

13. Lawrence, "Power of Good Speech," 2.

14. Wallace, "Ethical Basis," 5.

15. Rogge, "Evaluating the Ethics of a Speaker," 420, 425.

16. Clevenger, "Speaker and Society," 94.

17. Burgess, "Rhetoric of Black Power," 123.

18. Haiman, "Rhetoric of the Streets," 114.

19. Brummett, "Some Implications," 32.

20. Campbell, "Rhetorical Implications," 161.

21. Eubanks, "Nihilism," 190.

22. Oliver, "Takers All," 31.

23. Eubanks, "Nihilism," 189.

24. Wieman and Walter, "Toward an Analysis of Ethics," 267.

25. Burgess, "Crisis Rhetoric," 62.

26. Eubanks, "Nihilism," 189.

27. Ehninger, "Synoptic View," 452.

28. Enholm, "Rhetoric as an Instrument," 225.

29. Burke, "Dramatistic View . . . Part III," 81.

30. Burke, "Dramatistic View . . . Part Two," 446.

31. Ibid., 449.

32. Gerry Phillipsen at the University of Washington has been working on exactly this project.

33. Halloran, "Tradition and Theory," 234, 235.

34. Scott, "On *Not* Defining 'Rhetoric,'" 81.

35. Smith, "Toward a Philosophy of Speech," 5.

36. Baccus, personal correspondences, Western Speech Communication Association Records, ms. 620, box 3, folder 13, J. Willard Marriott Library, University of Utah, Salt Lake City.

37. Scott, "Some Implications," 274.

38. Kneupper, "Direction," 36.

39. Walter, "On Views of Rhetoric," 375.

40. Kneupper, "Direction," 33.

41. Campbell, "Ontological Foundations," 104.

42. Nilsen, "Criticism," 175.

43. Hesseltine, "Speech and History," 178.

44. Campbell, "Rhetorical Implications," 159.

45. Sillars, "Rhetoric as Act," 279.

46. E.g., Dance, "Centrality of the Spoken Word," 197.

47. Phifer, "New Breed," 7.

48. Hillbruner, "Moral Imperative," 228.

49. Baker and Eubanks, "Democracy," 75.

50. Carleton, "Effective Speech," 13.

51. Campbell, "Ontological Foundations," 106.

52. Scott, "Synoptic View," 439.

53. Oliver, "Varied Rhetorics," 216.

54. Halloran, "Tradition and Theory," 235.

55. Eubanks and Baker, "Axiology of Rhetoric," 157.

56. Scott, "Some Implications," 274.

57. Eubanks and Baker, "Axiology of Rhetoric," 162.

58. Wieman, "Philosophical Significance of Speech," 172.

59. Wallace, "Substance of Rhetoric," 241.

60. Hardwig, "Achievement of Moral Rationality," 183, 181, 171–72.

61. Turner, "In the Beginning," 197.

62. Poulakos, "Components of Dialogue," 199.

63. Ibid., 209.

64. Wieman and Walter, "Toward an Analysis of Ethics," 270.

65. Poulakos, "Components of Dialogue," 209–10.

66. Wieman, "Philosophical Significance of Speech," 171.

67. Oliver, "Communication," 9, 8.

68. Oliver, "Varied Rhetorics," 213.

69. Wieman and Walter, "Toward an Analysis of Ethics," 268. Emphasis in original.

70. Scott, "Philosophy of Discussion," 241, 244.

71. Poulakos, "Components of Dialogue," 206, 205.

72. Ibid., 200, 204.

73. Wieman and Walter, "Toward an Analysis of Ethics," 268. Emphasis in original.

74. Day, "Ethics of Democratic Debate," 8.

75. Lawrence, "Power of Good Speech," 2.

76. Lomas, "Rhetoric and Demagoguery," 161.

77. Hillbruner, "Moral Imperative," 238.

78. Klotsche, "Oral Communication," 3.

79. Oliver, "Conversational Rules," 19.

80. Oliver, "Varied Rhetorics," 218.

81. Scott, "On Viewing," 13.

82. Brummett, "Some Implications," 28, 31.

83. Christopherson, "Speech and the 'New' Philosophies Revisited," 8.

84. Klyn, "Problem of Evil," 26.

85. Rogge, "Evaluating the Ethics of a Speaker," 425, 423.

86. Scott, "On Viewing," 14.

87. Diggs, "Persuasion and Ethics," 369; Campbell, "Rhetorical Implications," 157.

88. Campbell, "Rhetorical Implications," 157.

89. Scott, "Some Implications," 275.

90. Campbell, "Rhetorical Implications," 157.

5. The Ethics of Objectivism and Relativism

1. Hart, "Why Communication?" 101.

2. Scott, "Communication," 258.

3. Ibid.

4. Quotations here are from Ellen Wartella and David Zarefsky as quoted by Powers, "Intellectual Structure," 191.

5. E.g., Deetz, "Reclaiming the Subject Matter," 239.

6. Baskerville, "Must We All Be Rhetorical Critics?" 112.

7. McGee, "Text, Context," 286.

8. Whittenberger-Keith, "Good Person Behaving Well," 42.

9. Ono and Sloop, "Critique of Vernacular Discourse," 20.

10. Phillips, "Spaces of Public Dissension," 245.

11. Eubanks, "Axiological Issues," 13.

12. Fisher, "Toward a Logic of Good Reasons."

13. Andersen, "Communication Ethics," 226.

14. Arnett, "Practical Philosophy," 208, 216.

15. Ibid., 215.

16. Andersen, "Communication Ethics," 227.

17. Kuypers, "*Doxa* and a Critical Rhetoric," 457.

18. Crable, "Ethical Codes," 32.

19. Smith and Streifford, "Axiological Adjunct," 22.

20. Klumpp and Hollihan, "Rhetorical Criticism," 87.

21. C. Johnstone, "Aristotelian Trilogy," 13.

22. Tallmon, "Casuistry," 385.

23. Condit, "Crafting Virtue," 94.

24. Klumpp and Hollihan, "Rhetorical Criticism," 90.

25. Schrag, "Rhetoric Resituated," 167, 168.

26. Scott, "On Viewing . . . Ten Years Later," 266.

27. Macke, "Communication Left Speechless," 140–41.

28. Falzer, "On Behalf of Skeptical Rhetoric," 247.

29. Arnett, "Status . . . in Speech Journals," 55.
30. Stewart, "Speech and Human Being," 71.
31. Eubanks, "Reflections," 303.
32. Stewart, "Postmodern Look," 375.
33. Thomas, "Deconstructive Rationality," 77.
34. Schiappa, "Interdisciplinarity and Social Practice," 144.
35. A number of versions of this story have been told by Bitzer's colleagues and students, which may indicate that this was a common ploy. See, for one example, John Bowers, "Maybe the Fad Has Passed: Postmodernism," Communication, Research, and Theory Network list-serve (CRTNet) post #5831, March 5, 2001, archived at http://lists1.cac.psu.edu/cgi-bin/wa?A2=ind0103&L=crtnet&P=R1727.
36. Pollock and Cox, "Historicizing 'Reason,'" 171.
37. Ibid., 170.
38. Rowland, "Why Rational Argument Needs Defending," 87.
39. Croasmun and Cherwitz, "Beyond Rhetorical Relativism," 6.
40. Ono and Sloop, "Commitment to *Telos*," 50.
41. Croasmun and Cherwitz, "Beyond Rhetorical Relativism," 8.
42. Railsback, "Beyond Rhetorical Relativism," 353.
43. Ibid., 355.
44. Croasmun and Cherwitz, "Beyond Rhetorical Relativism," 7.
45. Cherwitz and Hikins, "Rhetorical Perspectivism," 259.
46. Cloud, "Materiality of Discourse," 157.
47. Cherwitz and Darwin, "Why the 'Epistemic' in Epistemic Rhetoric?" 193.
48. Croasmun and Cherwitz, "Beyond Rhetorical Relativism," 11.
49. Eubanks, "Reflections," 306.
50. C. Johnstone, "Ethics, Wisdom, and the Mission," 179.
51. Perelman, "Rhetoric and Politics," 134.
52. Eubanks, "Axiological Issues," 17.
53. C. Johnstone, "Ethics, Wisdom, and the Mission," 178.
54. Croasmun and Cherwitz, "Beyond Rhetorical Relativism," 14.
55. C. Johnstone, "Aristotelian Trilogy," 16, 13.
56. Scott, "Epistemic Rhetoric and Criticism," 302.
57. Scott, "On Viewing . . . Ten Years Later," 264.
58. Eubanks, "Reflections," 301.
59. Brummett, "Defense of Ethical Relativism," 293.
60. McGuire, "Ethics of Rhetoric," 136–37. Emphasis in original.
61. Brummett, "Defense of Ethical Relativism," 294.
62. Cloud, "Materiality of Discourse," 152.
63. Brummett, "Defense of Ethical Relativism," 288.
64. Foss and Gill, "Foucault's Theory," 398.
65. Bineham, "From Within the Looking Glass," 183.
66. Thomas, "Deconstructive Rationality," 75.
67. Brummett, "Defense of Ethical Relativism," 295.
68. Scott, "On Viewing . . . Ten Years Later," 265.
69. Cloud, "Materiality of Discourse," 153.
70. Blythin, "'Arguers as Lovers,'" 181.
71. Schiappa, "Interdisciplinarity," 145.

72. Nakayama and Krizek, "Whiteness," 304.
73. Klumpp and Hollihan, "Rhetorical Criticism," 94.
74. Hollihan, "Evidencing Moral Claims," 230.
75. Warnick, "Leff in Context," 236.
76. Murphy, "Critical Rhetoric," 13.
77. Cloud, "Materiality of Discourse," 159.
78. Wander, "Third Persona," 205.
79. Charland, "Finding a Horizon," 72.
80. Wendt, "Answers to the Gaze," 269.
81. Ono and Sloop, "Commitment to *Telos*," 53.
82. McKerrow, "Critical Rhetoric: Theory," 109.
83. Ibid., 92.
84. Wander, "Ideological Turn," 18.
85. Biesecker, "Michel Foucault," 351.
86. Blair and Cooper, "Humanist Turn," 151.
87. Charland, "Finding a Horizon," 71.
88. McKerrow, "Critical Rhetoric in a Postmodern World," 78.
89. McKerrow, "Critical Rhetoric: Theory," 99.
90. Nakayama, "Les Voix de L'Autre," 241.
91. Biesecker, "Michel Foucault," 357.
92. Scott, "Necessary Pluralism," 203.

6. The Recalcitrance of Humanism

1. Gaonkar, "Foucault on Discourse," 253.
2. Leff, "Things Made by Words," 223.
3. Warnick, "Leff in Context," 232.
4. Scott, "Communication," 264–65.
5. Winterowd, "Rhetoric of Beneficence," 65.
6. D. Ellis, "Post-structuralism and Language," 221.
7. Thomas, "Deconstructive Rationality," 71.
8. D. Ellis, "Post-structuralism and Language," 221.
9. Andersen, "Communication," 220.
10. Crable, "Ethical Codes," 29.
11. C. Johnstone, "Dewey," 190.
12. Stewart, "Postmodern Look," 369.
13. Blair and Cooper, "Humanist Turn," 154.
14. Gaonkar, "Foucault on Discourse," 257.
15. Cooper, "Rhetorical Criticism," 7.
16. Ono and Sloop, "Commitment to *Telos*," 50.
17. Schrag, "Rhetoric Resituated," 172.
18. Stewart, "Foundations," 190.
19. Cherwitz and Hikins, "Rhetorical Perspectivism," 252.
20. C. Johnstone, "Aristotelian Trilogy," 16.
21. Scott, "Necessary Pluralism," 201.
22. Condit, "Crafting Virtue," 83.
23. Powers, "Intellectual Structure," 193.
24. Ibid., 192.

25. Stewart, "Foundations," 200.

26. Railsback, "Beyond Rhetorical Relativism," 356.

27. Nakayama, "Les Voix de L'Autre," 241.

28. McKerrow, "Critical Rhetoric: Theory," 105.

29. Stewart, "Speech and Human Being," 69.

30. Stewart, "Postmodern Look," 365, 364.

31. Macke, "Communication Left Speechless," 138.

32. Scott, "On Viewing . . . Ten Years Later," 263.

33. Perelman, "Rhetoric and Politics," 131.

34. Brummett, "Defense of Ethical Relativism," 289.

35. Perelman, "Rhetoric and Politics," 131.

36. Stewart, "Postmodern Look," 356.

37. Murphy, "Critical Rhetoric," 11.

38. McGee, "Text, Context," 287, 279.

39. Strine, "Critical Theory," 195–201.

40. Ono and Sloop, "Critique of Vernacular Discourse," 26.

41. Murphy, "Critical Rhetoric," 4.

42. Biesecker, "Rethinking the Rhetorical Situation," 126.

43. Stewart, "Postmodern Look," 370.

44. Wood, "Diversity and Commonality," 378.

45. Slagle, "In Defense of Queer Nation," 86.

46. Nakayama and Krizek, "Whiteness," 302.

47. Wood, "Diversity and Commonality," 375.

48. Norton, "Rhetorical Criticism," 42.

Conclusion: History, Community, and Alterity Ethics

1. Hyde, *Call of Conscience*; J. Murray, "Bakhtinian Answerability."

2. Esenwein, *How to Attract*; Leff, "Things Made by Words."

3. For additional studies of this trend, see Gehrke, "Teaching Argumentation Existentially"; Schiappa, "Interdisciplinarity and Social Practice"; and Swartz, *Conducting Socially Responsible Research* and "Interdisciplinary and Pedagogical Implications."

4. Campbell, "Rhetorical Implications"; Hesseltine, "Speech and History."

5. Stewart, "Postmodern Look"; Macke, "Communication Left Speechless."

6. Nancy, *Inoperative Community*, 29.

7. Levinas, *Collected Philosophical Papers*, 115.

8. Nancy, *Inoperative Community*, 73.

9. Carleton, "Effective Speech"; Hillbruner, "Moral Imperative"; Oliver, "Communication"; Scott, "On *Not* Defining Rhetoric."

10. Nakayama and Krizek, "Whiteness"; Slagle, "In Defense of Queer Nation."

11. C. Johnstone, "Ethics, Wisdom, and the Mission"; Perelman, "Rhetoric and Politics."

12. Poulakos, "Components of Dialogue."

13. For an example of the rejection of Michel Foucault for his anti-humanism, see Fisher, "Narrative Paradigm," 356. For an example of a reading of Foucault as a humanist, see Blair and Cooper, "Humanist Turn."

14. Wieman, "Philosophical Significance of Speech"; Ehninger, "Synoptic View."

15. Cherwitz and Hikins, "Rhetorical Perspectivism."

16. For an extended discussion of Kant's argument for relationality as prerequisite to experience and the implications for communication ethics, see Gehrke, "Turning Kant."

17. Levinas, *Otherwise*, 87.

18. Eubanks, "Reflections."

19. Campbell, "Ontological Foundations."

20. Levinas, *Otherwise*, 114.

21. Nancy, *Inoperative Community*, 31.

22. Nancy, *Birth to Presence*, 318.

23. Charland, "Finding a Horizon"; Wander, "Third Persona."

24. Foucault, "On the Genealogy of Ethics," 231–32.

25. Agamben, *Coming Community*, 42.

26. Nancy, *Sense of the World*, 41.

27. Ibid., 139.

28. MacKellar, "Cultural Value"; Trillingham, "Speech Education"; Westfall, "What Speech Teachers May Do."

29. Lingis, *Community*, 13.

30. Levinas, *Totality and Infinity*, 39.

31. Foucault, *Remarks on Marx*, 159.

Bibliography

Agamben, Giorgio. *The Coming Community*. Translated by Michael Hardt. Minneapolis: University of Minnesota Press, 1993.

Andersen, Kenneth E. "Communication Ethics: The Non-Participant's Role." *Southern Speech Communication Journal* 49 (1984): 219–28.

———. "A History of Communication Ethics." In *Conversations on Communication Ethics*, edited by Karen Joy Greenberg, 3–19. Norwood, N.J.: Ablex, 1991.

Andrews, James R. "Reflections on the National Character in American Rhetoric." *Quarterly Journal of Speech* 57 (1971): 316–24.

———. "The Rhetoric of History: The Constitutional Convention." *Today's Speech* 16, no. 4 (1968): 23–26.

Arnett, Ronald C. "The Practical Philosophy of Communication Ethics and Free Speech as the Foundation for Speech Communication." *Communication Quarterly* 38 (1990): 208–17.

———. "The Status of Communication Ethics Scholarship in Speech Communication Journals from 1915 to 1985." *Central States Speech Journal* 38 (1987): 44–61.

———. "The Status of Communication Ethics Scholarship in Speech Journals from 1915 to 1985." In *Conversations on Communication Ethics*, edited by Karen Joy Greenberg, 55–72. Norwood, N.J.: Ablex, 1991.

Auer, J. Jeffery. "Tools of Social Inquiry: Argumentation, Discussion, and Debate." *Quarterly Journal of Speech* 25 (1939): 533–39.

Baird, A. Craig. "Speech and the 'New' Philosophies." *Central States Speech Journal* 13 (1962): 241–46.

Baker, Virgil L., and Ralph T. Eubanks. "Democracy: Challenge to Rhetorical Education." *Quarterly Journal of Speech* 46 (1960): 72–78.

Balduf, Emery W. "How Departments of Speech Can Cooperate with Government in the War Effort." *Quarterly Journal of Speech* 29 (1943): 271–76.

Baskerville, Barnett. "Must We All Be Rhetorical Critics?" *Quarterly Journal of Speech* 63 (1977): 107–16.

Benson, Thomas, ed. *Speech Communication in the 20th Century*. Carbondale: Southern Illinois University Press, 1985.

Biesecker, Barbara. "Michel Foucault and the Question of Rhetoric." *Philosophy and Rhetoric* 25 (1992): 351–64.

187

———. "Rethinking the Rhetorical Situation from within the Thematic of *Differance*." *Philosophy and Rhetoric* 22 (1989): 110–30.

Bietry, J. Richard. "The Speech Teacher in a Changing Social World." *Western Speech* 3, no. 3 (1939): 9–14.

Bineham, Jeffery. "From within the Looking-Glass: The Ontology of Consensus Theory—Bineham's Rejoinder." *Communication Studies* 40 (1989): 182–88.

Black, Edwin. "The Second Persona." *Quarterly Journal of Speech* 56 (1970): 109–19.

Blair, Carole. "Contested Histories of Rhetoric: The Politics of Preservation, Progress, and Change." *Quarterly Journal of Speech* 78 (1992): 403–28.

Blair, Carole, and Martha Cooper. "The Humanist Turn in Foucault's Rhetoric of Inquiry." *Quarterly Journal of Speech* 73 (1987): 151–71.

Blythin, Evan. "'Arguers as Lovers': A Critical Perspective." *Philosophy and Rhetoric* 12 (1979): 176–86.

Bock, Douglas G. "Axiology and Rhetorical Criticism: Some Dimensions of the Critical Judgment." *Western Speech* 37, no. 2 (1973): 87–96.

Bowen, Harry W. "The Dilemma of Values: A Challenge to Speech Teachers." *Today's Speech* 8, no. 4 (1960): 18–36.

Brandenburg, Earnest. "Quintilian and the Good Orator." *Quarterly Journal of Speech* 34 (1948): 23–29.

Brigance, William Norwood. "American Speech in This Changing Age." *Southern Speech Bulletin* 1, no. 1 (1935): 15–18.

Brigance, William Norwood, and Ray Keeslar Immel. *Speech for Military Service.* New York: F. S. Crofts, 1943.

Brockriede, Wayne. "Arguers as Lovers." *Philosophy and Rhetoric* 5 (1972): 1–11.

Brummett, Barry. "A Defense of Ethical Relativism as Rhetorically Grounded." *Western Journal of Speech Communication* 45 (1981): 286–98.

———. "Some Implications of 'Process' or 'Intersubjectivity': Postmodern Rhetoric." *Philosophy and Rhetoric* 9 (1976): 21–51.

Bryant, Donald C. "Some Problems of Scope and Method in Rhetorical Scholarship." *Quarterly Journal of Speech* 23 (1937): 182–89.

Bryngelson, Bryng. "Applying Hygienic Principles to Speech Problems." *Quarterly Journal of Speech* 29 (1943): 351–54.

———. "Speech and Its Hygiene." *Quarterly Journal of Speech* 28 (1942): 85–86.

Buehler, E. C. "Credo—A Declaration of Faith Concerning Speech Education." *Central States Speech Journal* 12 (1960): 4–5.

Burgess, Parke G. "Crisis Rhetoric: Coercion vs. Force." *Quarterly Journal of Speech* 59 (1973): 61–73.

———. "The Rhetoric of Black Power: A Moral Demand?" *Quarterly Journal of Speech* 54 (1968): 122–33.

Burke, Kenneth. "A Dramatistic View of the Origins of Language: Part Two." *Quarterly Journal of Speech* 38 (1952): 446–60.

———. "A Dramatistic View of the Origins of Language: Part III." *Quarterly Journal of Speech* 39 (1953): 79–92.

———. *Language as Symbolic Action: Essays on Life, Literature, and Method.* Berkeley: University of California Press, 1966.

———. "Postscripts on the Negative." *Quarterly Journal of Speech* 39 (1953): 209–16.

Cable, W. Arthur. "Speech: A Basic Training in the Educational System." In *Revaluation of the Place of Speech in the Educational Process: Papers from the Convention of the Western Association of Teachers of Speech*. Redlands, Calif.: University of Redlands Debate Bureau, 1935.

California State Department of Education. "The Place of Speech in the Educational Process." *Proceedings of the 1934 Western Association of Teachers of Speech Convention*. Western Speech Communication Association Records, ms. 620, box 1. J. Willard Marriott Library, University of Utah, Salt Lake City.

Campbell, Karlyn Kohrs. "The Ontological Foundations of Rhetorical Theory." *Philosophy and Rhetoric* 3 (1970): 97–108.

————. "The Rhetorical Implications of the Axiology of Jean-Paul Sartre." *Western Speech* 35 (1971): 155–61.

Carleton, William G. "Effective Speech in a Democracy." *Southern Speech Journal* 17 (1951): 2–13.

Casmir, Fred L. "The Hitler I Heard." *Quarterly Journal of Speech* 49 (1963): 8–16.

Charland, Maurice. "Finding a Horizon and Telos: The Challenge to Critical Rhetoric." *Quarterly Journal of Speech* 77 (1991): 71–74.

Cherwitz, Richard A., and Thomas J. Darwin. "Why the 'Epistemic' in Epistemic Rhetoric? The Paradox of Rhetoric as Performance." *Text and Performance Quarterly* 15 (1995): 189–205.

Cherwitz, Richard A., and James W. Hikins. "Rhetorical Perspectivism." *Quarterly Journal of Speech* 69 (1983): 249–66.

Chesebro, James W. "A Construct for Assessing Ethics in Communication." *Central States Speech Journal* 20 (1969): 104–14.

Christopherson, Myrvin F. "Speech and the 'New' Philosophies Revisited." *Central States Speech Journal* 14 (1963): 5–11.

Church, Carrie E. "The Value of Debate in Attaining Social and Political Leadership." *Proceedings of the 1934 Western Association of Teachers of Speech Convention*. Western Speech Communication Association Records, ms. 620, box 1. J. Willard Marriott Library, University of Utah, Salt Lake City.

Clark, Robert D. "These Truths We Hold Self-Evident." *Quarterly Journal of Speech* 34 (1948): 445–50.

Clarke, M. L. *Rhetoric at Rome: A Historical Survey*. New York: Routledge, 1996.

Clevenger, Theodore, Jr. "Speaker and Society: The Role of Freedom in a Democratic State." *Southern Speech Journal* 26 (1960): 93–99.

Cloud, Dana. "The Materiality of Discourse as Oxymoron: A Challenge to Critical Rhetoric." *Western Journal of Communication* 58 (1994): 141–63.

Cohen, Herman. *The History of Speech Communication: The Emergence of a Discipline, 1914–1945*. Annandale, Va.: Speech Communication Association, 1994.

Condit, Celeste Michelle. "Crafting Virtue: The Rhetorical Construction of Public Morality." *Quarterly Journal of Speech* 73 (1987): 79–97.

Cooper, Martha. "Rhetorical Criticism and Foucault's Philosophy of Discursive Events." *Central States Speech Journal* 39 (1988): 1–17.

Corder, James W. "Ethical Argument and *Rambler* No. 154." *Quarterly Journal of Speech* 54 (1968): 352–56.

Crable, Richard E. "Ethical Codes, Accountability, and Argumentation." *Quarterly Journal of Speech* 64 (1978): 23–32.

Croasmun, Earl, and Richard A. Cherwitz. "Beyond Rhetorical Relativism." *Quarterly Journal of Speech* 68 (1982): 1–16.

Crocker, Lionel. "An Oblique Approach to Mental Hygiene for Public Speakers." *Southern Speech Journal* 8 (1943): 120–22.

Dance, Frank E. X. "The Centrality of the Spoken Word." *Central States Speech Journal* 23 (1972): 197–201.

Day, Dennis G. "The Ethics of Democratic Debate." *Central States Speech Journal* 17 (1966): 5–14.

Deetz, Stanley. "Reclaiming the Subject Matter as a Guide to Mutual Understanding: Effectiveness and Ethics in Interpersonal Interaction." *Communication Quarterly* 38 (1990): 226–43.

Dickens, Milton. "Discussion, Democracy, Dictatorship." *Quarterly Journal of Speech* 33 (1947): 151–58.

Diggs, B. J. "Persuasion and Ethics." *Quarterly Journal of Speech* 50 (1964): 359–73.

Dow, Clyde W. "The Personality Traits of Effective Speakers." *Quarterly Journal of Speech* 27 (1941): 525–32.

Eastern Communication Association Records. J. Willard Marriott Library, University of Utah, Salt Lake City.

Ehninger, Douglas. "A Synoptic View of Systems of Western Rhetoric." *Quarterly Journal of Speech* 61 (1975): 448–53.

Eisenstadt, Arthur A. "Good Speech—Educational Bulwark to Democracy." *Southern Speech Journal* 25 (1959): 96–100.

Ellis, Carroll Brooks. "A Good Man Speaking Well." *Southern Speech Journal* 11 (1946): 85–89.

Ellis, Donald G. "Post-structuralism and Language: Non-sense." *Communication Monographs* 58 (1991): 213–24.

Emery, Walter B. "Verbal Warfare." *Quarterly Journal of Speech* 30 (1944): 154–57.

Enholm, Donald K. "Rhetoric as an Instrument for Understanding and Improving Human Relations." *Southern Speech Communication Journal* 41 (1976): 223–36.

Esenwein, J. Berg. *How to Attract and Hold an Audience: A Practical Treatise on the Nature, Preparation, and Delivery of Public Discourse.* New York: Hinds, Noble, and Eldredge, 1902.

Eubanks, Ralph T. "Axiological Issues in Rhetorical Inquiry." *Southern Speech Communication Journal* 44 (1978): 11–24.

———. "Nihilism and the Problem of Worthy Rhetoric." *Southern Speech Journal* 33 (1968): 187–99.

———. "Reflections on the Moral Dimension of Communication." *Southern Speech Communication Journal* 45 (1980): 297–312.

Eubanks, Ralph T., and Virgil L. Baker. "Toward an Axiology of Rhetoric." *Quarterly Journal of Speech* 48 (1962): 157–68.

Falzer, Paul R. "On Behalf of Skeptical Rhetoric." *Philosophy and Rhetoric* 24 (1991): 238–54.

Farma, William. 1929 Eastern Public Speaking Conference transcripts. Eastern Communication Association Records, accn. 1474, box 3, folders 1–2. J. Willard Marriott Library, University of Utah, Salt Lake City.

Fisher, Walter R. "The Narrative Paradigm: An Elaboration." *Communication Monographs* 52 (1985): 347–67.

———. "Toward a Logic of Good Reasons." *Quarterly Journal of Speech* 64 (1978): 376–84.

Flynn, Lawrence J. "The Aristotelian Basis for the Ethics of Speaking." *Speech Teacher* 6 (1957): 179–87.

Flynt, Wayne. "The Ethics of a Democratic Persuasion and the Birmingham Crisis." *Southern Speech Journal* 35 (1969): 40–53.

Foss, Sonja K., and Ann Gill. "Michel Foucault's Theory of Rhetoric as Epistemic." *Western Journal of Speech Communication* 51 (1987): 384–401.

Foucault, Michel. "On the Genealogy of Ethics." In *Michel Foucault: Beyond Structuralism and Hermeneutics*, 2nd ed., edited by Hubert L. Dreyfus and Paul Rabinow, 229–52. Chicago: University of Chicago Press, 1983.

———. *Remarks on Marx*. Translated by R. James Goldstein and James Cascaito. New York: Semiotext(e), 1991.

Freeman, Patricia Lynn. "An Ethical Evaluation of the Persuasive Strategies of Glenn W. Turner of Turner Enterprises." *Southern Speech Communication Journal* 38 (1973): 347–61.

Gaonkar, Dilip Parameshwar. "Foucault on Discourse: Methods and Temptations." *Journal of the American Forensic Association* 18 (1982): 246–57.

Gehrke, Pat J. "Teaching Argumentation Existentially: Argumentation Pedagogy and Theories of Rhetoric as Epistemic." *Argumentation and Advocacy* 35 (1998): 76–86.

———. "Turning Kant Against the Priority of Autonomy: Communication Ethics and the Duty to Community." *Philosophy and Rhetoric* 35 (2002): 1–21.

Gislason, H. B. "The Relation of the Speaker to His Audience." *Quarterly Journal of Public Speaking* 2 (1916): 39–45.

Gray, Giles Wilkeson. "How Much Are We Dependent upon the Ancient Greeks or Romans?" *Quarterly Journal of Speech Education* 9 (1923): 258–80.

Greaves, Halbert. "Speech for the Many." *Western Speech* 2, no. 2 (1938): 1–4.

Grey, Lennox. "Toward a Better Communication in 1944, and After." *Quarterly Journal of Speech* 30 (1944): 131–36.

Gronbeck, Bruce E. "From 'Is' to 'Ought': Alternative Strategies." *Central States Speech Journal* 19 (1968): 31–39.

Gullan, Marjorie. "War Time Is Education Time." *Quarterly Journal of Speech* 27 (1941): 371–76.

Gulley, Halbert E. "The New Amorality in American Communication." *Today's Speech* 18, no. 1 (1970): 3–8.

Haiman, Franklyn S. "A Re-examination of the Ethics of Persuasion." *Central States Speech Journal* 3, no. 2 (1952): 4–9.

———. "The Rhetoric of the Streets: Some Legal and Ethical Considerations." *Quarterly Journal of Speech* 53 (1967): 99–115.

Hale, Lester L. "Freedom through Speech." *Southern Speech Journal* 14 (1948): 9–15.

Halloran, S. M. "Tradition and Theory in Rhetoric." *Quarterly Journal of Speech* 62 (1976): 234–41.

Hance, Kenneth G. "Public Address in a Democracy at War." *Quarterly Journal of Speech* 30 (1944): 158–64.

Hansen, John D. "Speech in a Nation at War." *Quarterly Journal of Speech* 28 (1942): 271–74.

Hardwig, John. "The Achievement of Moral Rationality." *Philosophy and Rhetoric* 6 (1973): 171–85.

Hart, Roderick P. "Why Communication? Why Education? Toward a Politics of Teaching." *Communication Education* 42 (1993): 97–106.

Harvey, Irene. "Contemporary French Thought and the Art of Rhetoric." *Philosophy and Rhetoric* 18 (1985): 199–215.

Held, McDonald W. "Needed—A Value System." *Southern Speech Journal* 26 (1960): 1–9.

Hesseltine, William B. "Speech and History." *Central States Speech Journal* 12 (1961): 176–81.

Hillbruner, Anthony. "The Moral Imperative of Criticism." *Southern Speech Communication Journal* 40 (1975): 228–47.

Hollihan, Thomas A. "Evidencing Moral Claims: The Activist Rhetorical Critic's First Task." *Western Journal of Communication* 58 (1994): 229–34.

Holm, James N. "A War-Time Approach to Public Speaking." *Quarterly Journal of Speech* 29 (1943): 10–13.

Holt, Mrs. Charles M. "The Speaker in Relation to Himself." *Quarterly Journal of Speech* 1 (1915): 276–83.

Howard, Hal. "Speech Education in a Political World." *Today's Speech* 14, no. 1 (1966): 24–25.

Hunt, Everett. "The Rhetorical Mood of World War II." *Quarterly Journal of Speech* 29 (1943): 1–5.

———. "Rhetoric as a Humane Study." *Quarterly Journal of Speech* 41 (1955): 114–17.

Hyde, Michael J. *The Call of Conscience: Heidegger and Levinas, Rhetoric and the Euthanasia Debate.* Columbia: University of South Carolina Press, 2001.

Innes, James. "The Function of Discussion and Debate." *Debater's Magazine* 1, no. 3 (1945). Eastern Communication Association Records, accn. 1474, box 25, folder 1. J. Willard Marriott Library, University of Utah, Salt Lake City.

"Introducing the Convention Theme." *Proceedings of the 1933 Western Association of Teachers of Speech Convention.* Western Speech Communication Association Records, ms. 620, box 1. J. Willard Marriott Library, University of Utah, Salt Lake City.

Irwin, R. L. "Mental Hygiene in the Teaching of Fundamentals." *Quarterly Journal of Speech* 28 (1942): 212–15.

Isserman, Maurice. *Which Side Were You On? The American Communist Party during the Second World War.* Urbana: University of Illinois Press, 1993.

Johnstone, Christopher Lyle. "An Aristotelian Trilogy: Ethics, Rhetoric, Politics, and the Search for Moral Truth." *Philosophy and Rhetoric* 13 (1980): 1–24.

———. "Dewey, Ethics, and Rhetoric: Toward a Contemporary Conception of Practical Wisdom." *Philosophy and Rhetoric* 16 (1983): 185–207.

———. "Ethics, Wisdom, and the Mission of Contemporary Rhetoric: The Realization of Human Being." *Central States Speech Journal* 32 (1981): 177–88.

Johnstone, Henry W. "Rationality and Rhetoric in Philosophy." *Quarterly Journal of Speech* 59 (1973): 381–89.

———. "The Relevance of Rhetoric to Philosophy and Philosophy to Rhetoric." *Quarterly Journal of Speech* 52 (1966): 41–46.

Kalp, Earl S. "Some Principles of Speech Education." *Quarterly Journal of Speech* 23 (1937): 296–99.

Kantner, Claude E. "Social Responsibility in Speech Education." *Southern Speech Journal* 14 (1948): 67–73.

———. "Speech and Education in a Democracy." *Southern Speech Journal* 17 (1951): 14–22.

Keith, William M. *Democracy as Discussion: Civic Education and the American Forum Movement*. Lanham, Md.: Lexington Books, 2007.

Kersey, Vierling. "Speech and Life." *Western Speech* 1, no. 1 (1937): 1.

Klotsche, J. Martin. "Oral Communication in Today's World." *Central States Speech Journal* 3, no. 1 (1951): 1–4.

Klumpp, James F., and Thomas A. Hollihan. "Rhetorical Criticism as Moral Action." *Quarterly Journal of Speech* 75 (1989): 84–96.

Klyn, Mark S. "The Problem of Evil: A Further Study and Response." *Western Speech* 28 (1964): 22–27.

Kneupper, Charles W. "Direction for Contemporary Rhetorical Theory." *Today's Speech* 22, no. 3 (1974): 31–38.

Knower, Franklin H. "Speech Curricula and Activities in Wartime." *Quarterly Journal of Speech* 29 (1943): 146–51.

Kohn, Stephen Martin. *American Political Prisoners: Prosecutions under the Espionage and Sedition Acts*. Westport, Conn.: Greenwood, 1994.

Konigsberg, Evelyn, Elizabeth A. Douris, Charles F. Edgecomb, Phyllis M. Haffman, and Muriel G. Leahy. "Teaching Public Discussion during the War." *Quarterly Journal of Speech* 29 (1943): 13–18.

Krapp, George P. "The Central Task in Teaching Speech." *Quarterly Journal of Speech* 18 (1932): 370–80.

Kuypers, Jim A. "*Doxa* and a Critical Rhetoric: Accounting for the Rhetorical Agent through Prudence." *Communication Quarterly* 44 (1996): 452–62.

Kuypers, Jim A., and Andrew King. "Introduction." In *Twentieth-Century Roots of Rhetorical Studies*, edited by Jim A. Kuypers and Andrew King, ix–xx. Westport, Conn.: Praeger, 2001.

———, eds. *Twentieth-Century Roots of Rhetorical Studies*. Westport, Conn.: Praeger, 2001.

Lambertson, F. W. "Hitler, the Orator: A Study in Mob Psychology." *Quarterly Journal of Speech* 28 (1942): 123–31.

Lanham, Richard A. *The Electronic Word: Democracy, Technology, and the Arts*. Chicago: University of Chicago Press, 1995.

Lawrence, David L. "The Power of Good Speech." *Today's Speech* 11, no. 1 (1963): 2–3.

Leff, Michael. "Things Made by Words: Reflections on Textual Criticism." *Quarterly Journal of Speech* 78 (1992): 223–31.

Levinas, Emmanuel. *Collected Philosophical Papers*. Translated by Alphonso Lingis. Dordrecht, Netherlands: M. Nijhoff, 1986.

———. *Otherwise Than Being or Beyond Essence*. Translated by Alphonso Lingis. Boston: Kluwer Academic Publishers, 1991.

———. *Totality and Infinity: An Essay on Exteriority*. Translated by Alphonso Lingis. Pittsburgh: Duquesne University Press, 1969.

Lingis, Alphonso. *The Community of Those Who Have Nothing in Common*. Bloomington: University of Indiana Press, 1994.

Lomas, Charles W. "Rhetoric and Demagoguery." *Western Speech* 25 (1961): 160–68.

MacGregor, Virginia Claire. "Personal Development in Beginning Speech Training." *Quarterly Journal of Speech* 20 (1934): 47–57.

Macke, Frank J. "Communication Left Speechless: A Critical Examination of the Evolution of Speech Communication as an Academic Discipline." *Communication Education* 40 (1991): 125–43.

MacKellar, W. H. "The Cultural Value of Speech Curricula." *Southern Speech Bulletin* 2, no. 2 (1937): 10–15.

Mavrodes, George I. "The Problem of Evil as a Rhetorical Problem." *Philosophy and Rhetoric* 1 (1968): 91–102.

McBurney, James H. "Some Contributions of Classical Dialectic and Rhetoric to a Philosophy of Discussion." *Quarterly Journal of Speech* 23 (1937): 1–13.

McGee, Michael Calvin. "Text, Context, and the Fragmentation of Contemporary Culture." *Western Journal of Speech Communication* 54 (1990): 274–89.

McGrew, J. Fred. "Speech: A Wider Vision." In *Revaluation of the Place of Speech in the Educational Process: Papers from the Convention of the Western Association of Teachers of Speech*. Redlands, Calif.: University of Redlands Debate Bureau, 1935.

McGuire, Michael. "The Ethics of Rhetoric: The Morality of Knowledge." *Southern Speech Communication Journal* 45 (1980): 133–48.

McKerrow, Raymie E. "Critical Rhetoric in a Postmodern World." *Quarterly Journal of Speech* 77 (1991): 75–78.

———. "Critical Rhetoric: Theory and Praxis." *Communication Monographs* 56 (1989): 91–111.

Merry, Glenn W. "National Defense and Public Speaking." *Quarterly Journal of Speech Education* 4 (1918): 53–60.

Micken, Ralph A. "A Worried Look at the New Rhetoric." *Today's Speech* 12, no. 3 (1964): 6–7.

Miller, Joseph W. "Winston Churchill, Spokesman for Democracy." *Quarterly Journal of Speech* 28 (1942): 131–38.

Morse, Wayne. "Mental Hygiene in Teaching Speech." 1929 Eastern Public Speaking Conference transcripts. Eastern Communication Association Records, accn. 1474, box 3, folders 1–2. J. Willard Marriott Library, University of Utah, Salt Lake City.

Mosher, Joseph A. "Debate and the World We Live In." *Quarterly Journal of Speech Education* 10 (1924): 332–39.

Murphy, John M. "Critical Rhetoric as Political Discourse." *Argumentation and Advocacy* 32 (1995): 1–15.

Murray, Elwood. "Speech Training as a Mental Hygiene Method." *Quarterly Journal of Speech* 20 (1934): 37–47.

———. "What Is Fundamental in Speech?" *Southern Speech Bulletin* 4, no. 2 (1938): 1–4.

Murray, Jeffrey W. "Bakhtinian Answerability and Levinasian Responsibility." *Southern Communication Journal* 65 (2000): 133–150.

Nakayama, Thomas K. "Les Voix de L'Autre." *Western Journal of Communication* 61 (1997): 235–42.

Nakayama, Thomas K., and Robert L. Krizek. "Whiteness: A Strategic Rhetoric." *Quarterly Journal of Speech* 81 (1995): 291–319.

Nancy, Jean-Luc. *The Birth to Presence.* Translated by Brian Holmes. Stanford, Calif.: Stanford University Press, 1993.

———. *The Inoperative Community.* Translated by Peter Connor, Lisa Garbus, Michael Holland, and Simona Sawhney. Minneapolis: University of Minnesota Press, 1991.

———. *The Sense of the World.* Translated by Jeffrey S. Librett. Minneapolis: University of Minnesota Press, 1997.

Nilsen, Thomas R. "Criticism and Social Consequences." *Quarterly Journal of Speech* 42 (1956): 173–78.

———. "Free Speech, Persuasion, and the Democratic Process." *Quarterly Journal of Speech* 44 (1958): 235–44.

Norton, Janice. "Rhetorical Criticism as Ethical Action: Cherchez la Femme." *Southern Communication Journal* 61 (1995): 29–45.

Nuttal, John R., Jr. "The Re-evaluation of the Place of Speech in the Educational Process." *Proceedings of the 1934 Western Association of Teachers of Speech Convention.* Western Speech Communication Association Records, ms. 620, box 1. J. Willard Marriott Library, University of Utah, Salt Lake City.

Oliver, Robert T. "Communication—Community—Communion." *Today's Speech* 15, no. 4 (1967): 7–9.

———. "Conversational Rules—Their Use and Abuse." *Today's Speech* 9, no. 2 (1961): 19–22.

———. "Ethics and Efficiency in Persuasion." *Southern Speech Journal* 26 (1960): 10–15.

———. "Takers All: Our Human Destiny." *Today's Speech* 5, no. 4 (1957): 31–33.

———. "The Varied Rhetorics of International Relations." *Western Speech* 25 (1961): 213–21.

O'Neill, J. M. "Aims and Standards in Speech Education." *Quarterly Journal of Speech Education* 4 (1918): 345–65.

Ono, Kent A., and John M. Sloop. "Commitment to *Telos*—A Sustained Critical Rhetoric." *Communication Monographs* 59 (1992): 48–60.

———. "The Critique of Vernacular Discourse." *Communication Monographs* 62 (1995): 19–46.

Pellegrini, Angelo M. "Public Speaking and Social Obligations." *Quarterly Journal of Speech* 20 (1934): 345–51.

Perelman, Chaim. "Rhetoric and Politics." *Philosophy and Rhetoric* 17 (1984): 129–34.

Phifer, Gregg. "The New Breed and Our Old Tradition." *Southern Speech Communication Journal* 37 (1971): 1–10.

Phillips, Gerald, and Julia T. Wood, eds. *Speech Communication: Essays to Commemorate the 75th Anniversary of the Speech Communication Association.* Carbondale: Southern Illinois University Press, 1990.

Phillips, Kendall R. "The Spaces of Public Dissension: Reconsidering the Public Sphere." *Communication Monographs* 63 (1996): 231–48.

Platz, Mabel. *The History of Public Speaking: A Comparative Study of World Oratory.* New York: Noble and Noble, 1935.

Pollock, Della, and J. Robert Cox. "Historicizing 'Reason': Critical Theory, Practice, and Postmodernity." *Communication Monographs* 58 (1991): 170–78.

Poulakos, John. "The Components of Dialogue." *Western Speech* 38 (1974): 199–212.

Powers, John H. "On the Intellectual Structure of the Human Communication Discipline." *Communication Education* 44 (1995): 191–222.

Program of the 1930 Conference of the Western Association of Teachers of Speech. Western Speech Communication Association Records, ms. 620, box 1, folder 2. J. Willard Marriott Library, University of Utah, Salt Lake City.

Program of the 1935 Conference of the Western Association of Teachers of Speech. Western Speech Communication Association Records, ms. 620, box 1, folder 7. J. Willard Marriott Library, University of Utah, Salt Lake City.

Program of the 1940 Conference of the Western Association of Teachers of Speech. Western Speech Communication Association Records, ms. 620, box 1, folder 5. J. Willard Marriott Library, University of Utah, Salt Lake City.

Program of the 1953 Conference of the Western Speech Association. Western Speech Communication Association Records, ms. 620, box 4, folder 4. J. Willard Marriott Library, University of Utah, Salt Lake City.

Railsback, Celeste Condit. "Beyond Rhetorical Relativism: A Structural-Material Model of Truth and Objective Reality." *Quarterly Journal of Speech* 69 (1983): 351–63.

Redfield, Robert. "The Difficult Duty of Speech." *Quarterly Journal of Speech* 39 (1953): 6–14.

Rieke, Richard D., and David H. Smith. "The Dilemma of Ethics and Advocacy in the Use of Evidence." *Western Speech* 32 (1968): 223–33.

Robinson, Karl F. "Speech—The Heart of the Core Curriculum." *Quarterly Journal of Speech* 26 (1940): 367–80.

Rogge, Edward. "Evaluating the Ethics of a Speaker in a Democracy." *Quarterly Journal of Speech* 45 (1959): 419–25.

Rowland, Robert C. "Why Rational Argument Needs Defending." *Philosophy and Rhetoric* 30 (1997): 82–88.

Schiappa, Edward. "Interdisciplinarity and Social Practice: Reflections on Dow, Condit, and Swartz." *Communication Studies* 46 (1995): 140–47.

Schrag, Calvin O. "Rhetoric Resituated at the End of Philosophy." *Quarterly Journal of Speech* 71 (1985): 164–74.

Schweinsberg-Reichart, Ilse. "Speech Education—Ways and Means of Political Education in Germany." *Today's Speech* 11, no. 4 (1968): 35–39.

Scott, Robert L. "Communication as an Intentional, Social System." *Human Communication Research* 3 (1977): 258–68.

———. "Epistemic Rhetoric and Criticism: Where Barry Brummett Goes Wrong." *Quarterly Journal of Speech* 76 (1990): 300–303.

———. "A Fresh Attitude toward Rationalism." *Speech Teacher* 17 (1968): 134–39.

———. "The Necessary Pluralism of Any Future History of Rhetoric." *Pre/Text* 12 (1991): 195–209.

———. "On *Not* Defining 'Rhetoric.'" *Philosophy and Rhetoric* 6 (1973): 81–96.

———. "On Viewing Rhetoric as Epistemic." *Central States Speech Journal* 18 (1967): 9–17.

———. "On Viewing Rhetoric as Epistemic: Ten Years Later." *Central States Speech Journal* 27 (1976): 258–66.

———. "A Philosophy of Discussion: 1954." *Southern Speech Journal* 19 (1954): 241–49.

———. "Some Implications of Existentialism for Rhetoric." *Central States Speech Journal* 15 (1964): 267–75.

———. "A Synoptic View of Systems of Western Rhetoric." *Quarterly Journal of Speech* 61 (1975): 439–47.

Scott, Robert L., and Donald K. Smith. "The Rhetoric of Confrontation." *Quarterly Journal of Speech* 55 (1969): 1–8.

Sillars, Malcolm O. "Rhetoric as Act." *Quarterly Journal of Speech* 50 (1964): 277–84.

Simons, Herbert W. "Patterns of Persuasion in the Civil Rights Struggle." *Today's Speech* 15, no. 1 (1967): 25–27.

Slagle, R. Anthony. "In Defense of Queer Nation: From *Identity Politics* to a *Politics of Difference*." *Western Journal of Communication* 59 (1995): 85–102.

Smith, Craig R., and Howard Streifford. "An Axiological Adjunct to Rhetorical Criticism." *Central States Speech Journal* 27 (1976): 22–30.

Smith, Joseph F., D. Mack Easton, and Elwood Murray. "The Integrated Speech Program." *Proceedings of the 1935 Western Association of Teachers of Speech Convention.* Western Speech Communication Association Records, ms. 620, box 1, book. J. Willard Marriott Library, University of Utah, Salt Lake City.

Smith, William S. "Toward a Philosophy of Speech." *Southern Speech Journal* 28 (1962): 1–5.

Southern States Communication Association Records. J. Willard Marriott Library, University of Utah, Salt Lake City.

Stewart, John. "Foundations of Dialogic Communication." *Quarterly Journal of Speech* 64 (1978): 183–201.

———. "A Postmodern Look at Traditional Communication Postulates." *Western Journal of Speech Communication* 55 (1991): 354–79.

———. "Speech and Human Being: A Complement to Semiotics." *Quarterly Journal of Speech* 72 (1986): 55–73.

Stinchfield-Hawk, Sara. "Speech Community Service in Time of War." *Western Speech* 6, no. 2 (1942): 8–13.

Strine, Mary S. "Critical Theory and 'Organic' Intellectuals: Reframing the Work of Cultural Critique." *Communication Monographs* 58 (1991): 195–201.

Swartz, Omar. *Conducting Socially Responsible Research: Critical Theory, Neopragmatism, and Rhetorical Inquiry.* Thousand Oaks, Calif: SAGE, 1997.

———. "Interdisciplinary and Pedagogical Implications of Rhetorical Theory." *Communication Studies* 46 (1995): 130–39.

Tallmon, James M. "Casuistry and the Role of Rhetorical Reason in Ethical Inquiry." *Philosophy and Rhetoric* 28 (1995): 377–87.

Thomas, Douglas E. "Deconstructive Rationality: A Response to Rowland, or Postmodernism 101." *Philosophy and Rhetoric* 30 (1997): 70–81.

Trillingham, C. C. "Speech Education in Democracy." *Western Speech* 3, no. 2. (1939): 7–9.

Turner, W. Homer. "In the Beginning Was the Word: The Responsibility for Good Communication." *Central States Speech Journal* 12 (1961): 197–206.

Utterback, William E. "The Appeal to Force in Public Discussion." *Quarterly Journal of Speech* 26 (1940): 1–6.

Van de Vate, Dwight. "Reasoning and Threatening: A Reply to Yoos." *Philosophy and Rhetoric* 8 (1975): 177–79.

Van Wye, B. C. "Speech Training for Patriotic Service." *Quarterly Journal of Speech Education* 4 (1918): 366–71.

Wales, Beulah Kite, and Chloe Zimmerman. "Activity Unit Analysis with Curriculum Emphasis Outline Relative to Speech Education." Internal report produced for the Western Association of Teachers of Speech and the California Department of Higher Education, 1937. Western Speech Communication Association Records, ms. 620, box 2, folder 2. J. Willard Marriott Library, University of Utah, Salt Lake City.

Wallace, Karl R. "An Ethical Basis of Communication." *Speech Teacher* 4 (1953): 1–9.

———. "The Substance of Rhetoric: Good Reasons." *Quarterly Journal of Speech* 49 (1963): 239–49.

Walter, Otis M. "On Views of Rhetoric Whether Conservative or Progressive." *Quarterly Journal of Speech* 49 (1963): 367–82.

Wander, Philip. "The Ideological Turn in Modern Criticism." *Central States Speech Journal* 34 (1983): 1–18.

———. "The Third Persona: An Ideological Turn in Rhetorical Theory." *Central States Speech Journal* 35 (1984): 197–216.

Warnick, Barbara. "Leff in Context: What Is the Critic's Role?" *Quarterly Journal of Speech* 78 (1992): 232–37.

Washburn, Wilcomb E. "Speech Communication and Politics." *Today's Speech* 16, no. 4 (1968): 3–16.

Wells, Earl W. "Ethical Problems in the Teaching of Public Speaking: Are We Teaching Students to Use High-Pressure Salesmanship Methods?" *Proceedings of the 1933 Western Association of Teachers of Speech Convention.* Western Speech Communication Association Records, ms. 620, box 1. J. Willard Marriott Library, University of Utah, Salt Lake City.

Wendt, Ronald F. "Answers to the Gaze: A Genealogical Poaching of Resistance." *Quarterly Journal of Speech* 82 (1996): 251–73.

Western Speech Communication Association Records. J. Willard Marriott Library, University of Utah, Salt Lake City.

Westfall, Alfred. "What Speech Teachers May Do to Help Win the War." *Quarterly Journal of Speech* 29 (1943): 5–9.

Whittenberger-Keith, Kari. "The Good Person Behaving Well: Rethinking the Rhetoric of Virtue." *Southern Communication Journal* 58 (1992): 33–43.

Wichelns, H. A. "Tendencies in Speech Education Today." *Southern Speech Bulletin* 2, no. 2 (1937): 1–3.

Wieman, Henry Nelson. "The Philosophical Significance of Speech." *Central States Speech Journal* 12 (1961): 170–75.

Wieman, Henry Nelson, and Otis M. Walter. "Toward an Analysis of Ethics for Rhetoric." *Quarterly Journal of Speech* 43 (1957): 266–70.

Wiley, Earl W. "The Rhetoric of American Democracy." *Quarterly Journal of Speech* 29 (1943): 157–63.

Williamson, A. B. "Democracy or Aristocracy in our Association." *Quarterly Journal of Speech* 17 (1931): 354–62.

Winans, James A. *Speech Making.* New York: D. Appleton-Century, 1938.

Windt, Theodore Otto. "Everett Lee Hunt and the Humanistic Spirit of Rhetoric." In *Twentieth-Century Roots of Rhetorical Studies*, edited by Jim A. Kuypers and Andrew King, 1–30. Westport, Conn.: Praeger, 2001.

Winter, Irvah Lester. "The Teacher of Public Speaking." *Public Speaking Review* 4 (1914): 21–28.

Winterowd, W. Ross. "The Rhetoric of Beneficence, Authority, Ethical Commitment, and the Negative." *Philosophy and Rhetoric* 9 (1976): 65–83.

Wood, Julia T. "Diversity and Commonality: Sustaining Their Tension in Communication Courses." *Western Journal of Communication* 57 (1993): 367–80.

Woolbert, Charles H. "The Ethics of Public Address." *Public Speaking Review* 4 (1914): 65–72.

———. "A Problem in Pragmatism." *Quarterly Journal of Public Speaking* 2 (1916): 264–74.

Zelko, Harold P. "Franklin D. Roosevelt's Rhythm in Rhetorical Style." *Quarterly Journal of Speech* 28 (1942): 138–41.

Index

coercion/force vs. persuasion, 34, 41,
51–52, 77–81, 144–45, 160
Cohen, Herman, 5–8, 18, 36, 172 n17
communication. *See* rhetoric as epistemic; speech
communication studies, histories of, 3–7,
10, 14, 19, 55, 165–67
community, 6, 36, 49, 103–4, 133–34,
141–44, 153–67
Condit, Celeste Michelle, 116, 121–22,
139
Cooper, Martha, 130, 136–37
Cox, J. Robert, 119–20
Crable, Richard, 135
Crenshaw, Kimberle, 164
crisis, ethics in 45–46, 61–66, 114–15
critical rhetoric, 128–30, 143, 163
critical theory, 118–20, 149
Croasman, Earl, 120–23

Darwin, Thomas J., 122
Day, Dennis G., 76, 106
deconstruction, 143–44
definition, the problem of, 89, 96–101,
111–14, 151–52, 165–67
democracy, 3, 5, 32–35, 37–38, 41–54,
57–59, 74–75, 80, 91–93
demagoguery, 39, 42, 55, 65–67, 76, 106,
115
Dewey, John, 20, 37–38, 40, 70, 83–84
dialectic, 12, 40, 43, 68, 123, 125, 137–39,
141, 165–66
dialogue, 36, 38–39, 42–43, 91, 98, 101–7,
114, 145, 150, 157, 160; rhetoric and,
101–5
Dickens, Milton, 41–43, 46
Diggs, B. J., 109
difference. *See* alterity/otherness; Other,
the
discussion theory, 5, 31–45, 51–53, 56, 102,
157, 160
Dow, Clyde W., 51

Easton, D. Mack, 35, 36, 39
Ehninger, Douglas, 64, 73, 94, 96, 153
Eisenstadt, Arthur A., 70
Ellis, Carroll Brooks, 57

Ellis, Donald G., 135
Enholm, Donald K., 64, 94, 96
epistemology, 111–12, 117–18, 120–26,
129, 132, 162–63
Esenwein, J. Berg, 15–17, 19, 24, 26, 28,
30, 55, 148
Eubanks, Ralph T., 63, 86, 89–90, 92–94,
99–101, 114, 118, 122–24, 157
existentialism, 2, 12–13, 61–62, 72, 81–
83, 85–90, 94, 112, 118, 120, 147, 149,
152–53

Falzer, Paul R., 117
Farma, William, 23
feminism, 164
Fisher, Walter R., 114, 184n13
Flynn, Lawrence J., 74, 90–91
Flynt, Wayne, 67, 75
Foss, Sonja K., 125–26
Foucault, Michel, 125–26, 128–30, 134,
136, 161, 166, 184n13
Four-Minute Men, 49–50
Freeman, Patricia Lynn, 78

Gaonkar, Dilip Parameshwar, 134–36
Gill, Ann, 125–26
Gislason, H. B., 7, 15–16, 19
Gorgias, 162
Gray, Giles Wilkeson, 18–19, 29, 35–37,
39
Greaves, Halbert, 37
Grey, Lennox, 36, 39, 50
Gronbeck, Bruce E., 86
Gullan, Marjorie, 36–37
Gulley, Halbert E., 62, 66

Haiman, Franklin S., 74–76, 78, 80, 83,
93
Hale, Lester L., 48, 57
Halloran, S. M., 62, 70, 72–73, 96–97,
100
Hance, Kenneth G., 46
Hansen, John D., 44, 50, 51
Hardwig, John, 101–2
Harvey, Irene, 2
Held, McDonald W., 61–62
Hesseltine, William B., 98, 149

Pat J. Gehrke is an associate professor of communication and rhetoric in the Department of English at the University of South Carolina, where he teaches communication ethics and rhetorical theory with an emphasis on civic engagement and contemporary continental thinkers. His work has been published in *Philosophy and Rhetoric, Critical Studies in Media Communication, Argumentation and Advocacy*, and a handful of other journals. In recent years, he has served as vice-chair and then chair of the communication ethics division of the National Communication Association. He is currently working with a multi-institutional, grant-funded project on communication's role in the emergence of a practicable democracy.